THE CARDINAL'S HAT

THE CARDINAL'S HAT

Money, Ambition, and Everyday Life
in the Court of a Borgia Prince

MARY HOLLINGSWORTH

THE OVERLOOK PRESS
Woodstock & New York

First published in the United States in 2005 by
The Overlook Press, Peter Mayer Publishers, Inc.
Woodstock & New York

WOODSTOCK:
One Overlook Drive
Woodstock, NY 12498
www.overlookpress.com
[for individual orders, bulk and special sales, contact our Woodstock office]

NEW YORK:
141 Wooster Street
New York, NY 10012

Cataloging-in-Publication Data is available from the Library of Congress

Printed in the United States of America
ISBN 1-58567-680-2
1 3 5 7 9 8 6 4 2

In Memory of My Father and Rosie

Contents

Maps

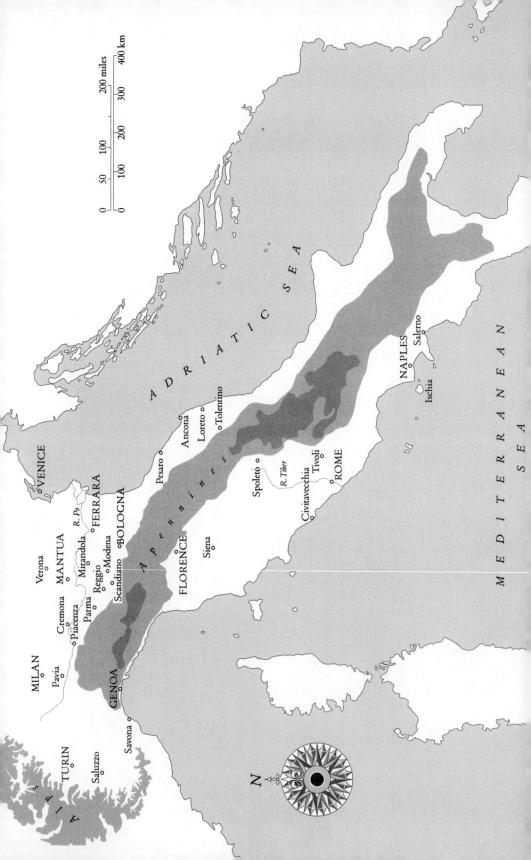

200 miles
400 km

200
300

100
200

50
100

0
0

A D R I A T I C   S E A

M E D I T E R R A N E A N   S E A

VENICE

FERRARA

BOLOGNA

MANTUA

Verona

Cremona
Piacenza
Parma
Reggio
Modena
Scandiano
Mirandola
R. Po

MILAN

Pavia

TURIN

Saluzzo

A l p s

Savona

GENOA

FLORENCE

Siena

A p e n n i n e s

Pesaro

Ancona
Loreto
Tolentino

Spoleto
R. Tiber

Civitavecchia
Tivoli
ROME

NAPLES

Salerno

Ischia

N

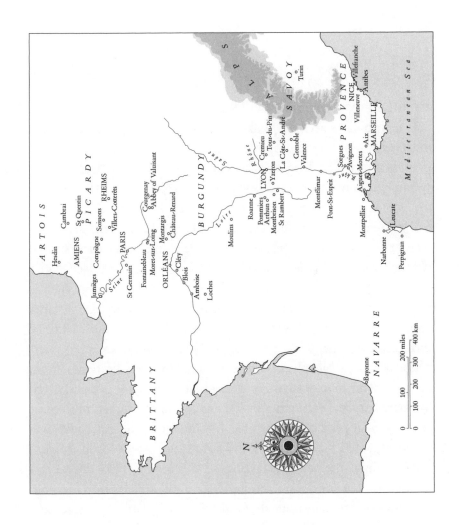

ARTOIS

Hesdin

Cambrai

AMIENS   St Quentin

PICARDY

Compiègne Soissons   RHEIMS

Villers-Cotterêts

PARIS

St Germain

Jumièges

Seine

Fontainebleau   Moret-sur-Loing   Gourgnay

Abbey of Valuisant

ORLÉANS   Montargis   Château-Renard

Cléry

Blois   BURGUNDY

Amboise

Loches   Loire

Moulins

Saône

Roanne

Pommiers   Arthun

Montbrison

St Rambert

Montélimar

Pont-St-Esprit

Sorgues

Avignon   Aigues-Mortes   Aix

Montpellier

Narbonne

Perpignan   Leucate

Rhône

LYON   Cremieu   Tour-du-Pin

Yzeron   La Côte-St-André

Grenoble

Valence

SAVOY

Turin

ALPS

PROVENCE

NICE   Villefranche

Villeneuve   La Turbie

MARSEILLE   Antibes

Mediterranean Sea

BRITTANY

Bayonne

NAVARRE

0   100   200 miles

0   100   200   300   400 km

N

A Note on Money

THE RELATIONSHIP BETWEEN the various currencies that appear in Ippolito's account books is enormously complex. Most states in sixteenth-century Europe had their own silver-based coinage. France, which had long been a centralized monarchy, had a single system based on the *livre* (1 *livre* = 20 *sous* = 240 *deniers*). In Italy, where the peninsula was fragmented into numerous different states, each city had its own local currency: Ferrara, for example, used the *lira march-esana* (1 *lira* = 20 *soldi* = 240 *denari*), while Rome preferred a decimal system based on the *scudo di moneta* (1 *scudo di moneta* = 10 *giulii* = 100 *baiocchi*). There were also internationally recognized gold coins, such as the Venetian ducat, the Florentine florin and the gold *scudo*. The latter appears frequently in Ippolito's account books and could clearly be used across Europe. Wealth was assessed in gold, the currency of international trade, while silver coinage was used for everyday transactions, such as buying food or paying wages. These currencies, gold and silver, fluctuated against each other in response to market forces: during the years 1534–40, the period covered by this book, the gold *scudo* was worth 45 *sous* in France, 70 *soldi* in Ferrara and 105 *baiocchi* in Rome.

To simplify the bewildering number of currencies that appear as a result of Ippolito's extensive travels, I have translated all prices into gold *scudi*, only occasionally using the local currency to clarify exchange rates.

What was the gold *scudo* worth in today's terms? There is no single answer to this question. In 1536–40 a *scudo* would buy 28 chickens or 50 kg of flour and represented one week's wages for a master builder. Nowadays a builder can easily earn £500 a week, but 50 kg of flour costs only £30.

Introduction
The Archives at Modena

IPPOLITO D'ESTE WAS the second son of Alfonso d'Este and Lucretia Borgia. His grandparents on his father's side were Ercole d'Este, the Duke of Ferrara, and Eleonora of Aragon, daughter of the King of Naples. Lucretia's parents were Rodrigo Borgia, better known as Pope Alexander VI, and his beautiful Roman mistress, Vanozza de' Cataneis. Ippolito's lineage was impressive, and so was his career. One of the leading cardinals of the sixteenth century, and a serious contender for papal election on several occasions, he was also one of the most important patrons of the arts in Rome, the builder of the magnificent Villa d'Este at Tivoli and the benefactor of the musician Palestrina. His artistic achievements have been thoroughly researched by scholars but his life and career have so far largely been ignored. This is surprising considering the astonishing quantity of his papers that have survived. The state archives at Modena contain over 2,000 of his letters, as well as many written to him, and over 200 of his account books. As one particular friend, Julian Kliemann, pointed out to me, Ippolito would be a fascinating subject for research.

Even so, I kept putting off my visit to the archives in Modena until I was finally forced there by accident. One freezing morning in January 1999 I was negotiating the fog-bound autostrada north of Turin, on my way back to Florence where I was living at the time, when my landlady rang to say that my central heating had broken down. The weather was far too cold to consider going home and the Modena exit was only two hours away. The next day I went to the archives. They are housed in what had been a very grand palace. There was a car parked between the columns of the entrance hall, and what had once been an elegant courtyard was now a kitchen garden.

Once the staff realized that I wanted to look at *all* Ippolito's papers, they could not have been more helpful. The Director sent me down into the stores, the cavernous reception rooms of the old palace, now musty and cold, and lined with shelves filled with leather-bound volumes, acres and acres of the Este family's past, dating back to the fourteenth century. For a historian, this was heaven. I found Ippolito's account books stacked high up in a corner under one of the ceilings, accessible only by a narrow metal ladder. For the following three months I sat in the little reading room upstairs and immersed myself in the minutiae of Ippolito's life as I read through the volumes of accounts and box upon box of papers.

Floodwater had damaged many of the letters – some crumbled in my hands, while others were legible only under the ultra-violet light of the lamp by the photocopying room. But a surprising quantity were as clear as the day on which they had been written, 450 years ago. Neither the language nor the handwriting were as hard to decipher as I had feared. Unlike English, Italian has changed little since the sixteenth century, though it took some time to get used to the local dialect, and to the bewildering variety of currencies Ippolito encountered as he travelled across Italy and France. Some hands were impossibly cramped, but others wrote in a perfectly formed italic script. Much harder were the coded letters, several of which I have still not managed to decipher.

As the days progressed I gradually discovered Ippolito himself, his habits, his tastes and his personality, embodied in the large, open and exuberant signature which he penned at the bottom of each of his letters. However, it was not just Ippolito who began to emerge across the centuries, but also the bookkeepers who meticulously filled in his ledgers, the men who belonged to his household and were listed year after year in the registers of salaried employees, the shopkeepers who supplied the velvets, silks and taffetas for his clothes, the painters who decorated his palaces, the butchers who provided the meat for his kitchens, and the blacksmiths who supplied his horses with shoes.

What I had stumbled upon was a unique account of life in sixteenth-century Europe, a detailed record of how a Renaissance prince lived. Here were not only the gold and silver, the silks and velvets, the fripperies and baubles that we associate with pomp and prestige, but also the soap, the candles, the shoelaces, the cooking pots and the drains, the stuff of everyday life. Above all, these ledgers bore witness to one of the major preoccupations of the period, and something much loved by Ippolito – money.

1

A Family Man

LUCRETIA BORGIA MADE her official entry into Ferrara late one
clear, cold afternoon in February 1502 through streets lined
with crowds of citizens eager to see the woman who had married
Alfonso d'Este, the heir to the duchy. Her reputation was electrify-
ingly scandalous: she was widely believed to be guilty of adultery,
murder and incest. Much to the surprise of those who caught a
glimpse of her, she was pretty, slender and blonde, with neat white
teeth and unblemished white skin. She was also magnificently
dressed in cloth-of-gold striped with dark purple satin, her gold
cloak thrown back over one shoulder to display its ermine lining and
her diamond and ruby necklace, a present from Duke Ercole I, her
new father-in-law. There was more than a hint of affection in the
crowds who witnessed her laughter after she fell off her horse, which
had reared in fright at the roar of the cannon celebrating her arrival.
They were also impressed with the size of the dowry that Duke
Ercole had extracted from Lucretia's father, Pope Alexander VI.
Seventy-two mules, covered in the Borgia colours of black and
yellow, followed her train laden with 100,000 ducats in cash and
75,000 ducats' worth of jewels, silver plate and other valuables.

The choice of Lucretia as a wife for Alfonso had been forced on
Duke Ercole by political necessity. Faced with the alternative of
losing his state to the armies of Cesare Borgia, Lucretia's eldest
brother, Ercole had capitulated to the Pope's offer of an alliance.
Lucretia was far from ideal. The Este belonged to Italy's old nobility.

The Borgias were Spanish and foreign, and although they boasted of royal descent from the ancient Kings of Aragon, most Italians laughed contemptuously at this claim. Moreover, Lucretia, who was only 21, had already been married twice. She had divorced her first husband, the Lord of Pesaro, on the unlikely grounds that the marriage had never been consummated. There were, conveniently, no children, but Alexander VI had forced his unfortunate son-in-law to sign a statement declaring that he was impotent, even though, as he would tell anyone who would listen, the marriage had been consummated a thousand times. Her second husband, a Neapolitan noble, thankfully did not insist on a gynaecological examination to ensure she was still a virgin, something he had a right to do, but he was not to enjoy his new wife for long. Two years after the marriage, he was strangled by one of Cesare's minders while lying in bed in the Vatican recovering from a failed assassination attempt that had taken place very publicly on the steps of St Peter's.

Lucretia's reputation had been further tarnished by rumours of several lovers and of incest, not only with her four brothers but also with her father, the Pope. These accusations had all been circulated by her first husband who was infuriated by the suggestion that he had been unable to do his duty in the marriage bed. The rumours spread. The King of France gave Alfonso a shield decorated with the figure of Mary Magdalen as a wedding present, to show, as the French ambassador explained, that his wife was a woman of virtue; but, as everyone would also have known, Mary Magdalen's past was far from virtuous. There was, however, one significant point in Lucretia's favour, and one Duke Ercole must have acknowledged: she had proved herself capable of bearing sons, one by her second husband and another by one of her lovers.

The Este rulers of Ferrara were a colourful and eccentric family. Duke Ercole's father Niccolò III had been married three times and had had countless extra-marital liaisons that had produced sixteen children (twelve of them illegitimate) and earned him the nickname 'Cock of Ferrara'. He had been succeeded by two of these illegitimate

Lucretia Borgia

sons, Leonello and Borso. They were named after Sir Lionel and Sir Bors, knights of Arthurian legend, but there the similarities ended. Leonello was austere and ascetic, his tastes intellectual rather than military, and he made Ferrara a major centre of fifteenth-century humanism. Plump little Borso was probably gay and certainly a bon viveur, and he spent much of his time hunting, dressed in cloth-of-gold and accompanied by his pet leopards. When Borso died in 1471

Alfonso I d'Este

he was succeeded by Ercole, Niccolò's eldest legitimate son, who was named after the classical hero Hercules. Ercole exploited this connection by using the Deeds of Hercules to decorate his tapestries and door hangings, and even as subjects for the sugar sculptures that ornamented his banqueting tables. Although he lacked the swashbuckling audacity of his namesake, he was a soldier and had been badly wounded in battle. Earnest, serious and cautious, both in war and as

Duke, he limped around Ferrara dressed for preference in sober black. He was also an outstanding patron of the arts, favouring poetry and the theatre, and he loved his cats, for whom he installed flaps in the heavy wooden doors of the ducal castle.

Lucretia's husband, Alfonso, was Ercole's eldest son, and he inherited the family's tendency towards the eccentric. With a swarthy skin and long, aquiline nose, he was not particularly good-looking. He was also notoriously uncouth – he used to stroll around Ferrara on hot summer afternoons stark naked. But he did have taste. He was a skilled musician and a connoisseur of the arts. Inspired by literary descriptions of the works of art of antiquity, he commissioned Titian to paint a series of Bacchanalian pictures (including *Bacchus & Ariadne*, now in the National Gallery in London) to decorate his private study. He was also obsessed with artillery. Louis XII of France sent him a recipe for gunpowder as a wedding present along with the shield of Mary Magdalen, and Alfonso even learned how to cast his own cannon: he famously had Michelangelo's statue of Pope Julius II melted down so that he could use the bronze to make a cannon which he wittily named La Giulia (he acquired the statue after it had been torn down during anti-papal riots in Bologna). His relationship with Julius II's successor, Leo X, was not much better. He celebrated that Pope's death with a medal inscribed *de manu Leonis* (out of the Lion's paw).

The Este family were members of the old imperial nobility and had risen to power during the eleventh century, gradually extending their authority across the eastern part of the fertile Po valley. By the sixteenth century their territory included three major cities: the imperial fiefs of Modena and Reggio, and the papal fief of Ferrara, capital of the duchy. They were the powerful rulers of a prosperous state that stretched 160 kilometres from the mineral-rich uplands of the Apennines, where they mined precious metals, through the lush farmlands of the Padana and down to the Adriatic coast and the marshes of the Po delta. Their neighbours to the north were the huge state of Milan, the modest duchy of Mantua and the fiercely

Late fifteenth-century woodcut of the city of Ferrara showing the ducal palace, the main square and the wharves along the banks of the Po

independent republic of Venice; to the south lay the Papal States and, beyond the Apennines, Florence.

Ferrara was a prosperous city, built on the banks of the Po, 90 kilometres south of Venice. With a population of 40,000 (about the same size as the modern cities of Durham or Winchester), it was large by sixteenth-century standards, though smaller than the great metropolises of the day, Venice (150,000) and Paris (200,000). To the visitor approaching the city across the Po plain, Ferrara had a distinctively defensive air. The imposing towers of the ducal castle and the massive circuit of brick walls built by Duke Ercole dominated the surrounding fields. Inside the atmosphere was quite different. The new walls had doubled the size of Ferrara, enclosing not only the cramped medieval quarters of the old town but also an enormous new extension, laid out by Duke Ercole with spacious streets, orchards, villas and, a particularly impressive feature, a hunting park with its own purpose-built racecourse. The streets were paved and the city was bright with colour. All who could afford the expense painted the brick façades of their palaces, as well as their chimneys and their garden walls, with geometric patterns or stripes of contrasting colours ornamented with coats-of-arms and swags of fruit. The Este colours of red, white and green were particularly visible.

Duke Ercole's efforts to tempt traders into his new town had not been entirely successful. Most shopkeepers and artisans preferred to remain crowded in the old centre, in the narrow streets between the ducal palace and the wharves along the Po. The streets were busy and noisy, and thronged with people: porters jostling and shouting as they delivered their parcels, itinerant knife-grinders and fishmongers hawking their wares, and carters delivering wood, grain, building materials and crates, which they had picked up from the bargemen docking at the wharves on the Po.

Ferrara was cosmopolitan and prosperous. Many of her inhabitants had come from towns across northern Italy, and there was a sizeable Jewish community, most of whom had emigrated from Venice. Those merchants who could afford the rents ran their businesses under the arcades of the grand square in front of the palace, much as they do today, and many catered for the tastes of an affluent bourgeoisie: dealers in silks and velvets, haberdashers and tailors, booksellers and printers, swordmakers and armourers, silversmiths and saddlers. Apothecaries' shops, lined with blue and white *albarello* jars, sold nutmeg, cinnamon, saffron and other spices imported from the East as well as pigments for painters and medicines to treat the sick. Grocers stocked everything from sausages to soap and string. Many traders specialized in a particular product or skill. Artisans working in the building industry earned their livings as bricklayers, plumbers, glaziers, carpenters or painters, and even as specialists in clearing blocked drains. There were dealers in cheap woollen cloth and second-hand clothes-sellers, butchers whose shops were hung with the carcases of cows, sheep and goats, and poulterers with their cages of squawking chickens, capons and geese. The habit of specialization had its disadvantages for the customer: you bought copper pots and pans for the kitchen from the coppersmith, but you had to get their iron handles made by the blacksmith.

The citizens of Ferrara ate well. The weather was damp and cold in winter, but hot summers and the fertile soil of the Po plain made for ideal agricultural conditions. Much space within the city walls was given over to vegetable gardens. The sixteenth-century diet, at all levels of society, included a lot of bread. The rich could afford white loaves made from wheat flour but the poorer sections of society had to bulk out the expensive cereals with cheaper crops such as millet: the worst bread, dark brown in colour, was made with bran. Pork was the staple meat of the area. The wealthy rented smallholdings in the countryside where they grew fresh food and fattened their pigs, but even ordinary artisans kept a pig in their backyards in the city. The profits made by the city's butchers were high enough to attract tax, and the duchy charged a levy on all live animals entering the city. Cattle and sheep provided expensive veal and lamb for the rich, tougher beef and mutton for the less well-to-do. They also produced milk for cheeses, from the hard nutty salted cheeses similar to parmesan (which came from Parma) to the soft bland sheep's milk cheeses such as ricotta, which was either eaten fresh or wrapped in reeds to mature. An Italian writing in the 1540s praised Ferrara for her wonderful salamis, candied herbs and fruits, her sturgeon and her eels. There were two fish markets selling freshwater varieties such as pike, tench, carp and crayfish from the lakes, ponds and rivers near Ferrara, and sea fish from the Adriatic, only 50 kilometres away. The Este duchy included Comacchio, a town in the marshes of the Po delta which was famous for its eels, sold fresh, marinated or smoked.

The preoccupations of this provincial population surface clearly in their diaries. There is endless talk of the price of food (and of wheat in particular), of the weather and of the marriages and deaths of fellow citizens. More sensational news included outbreaks of the plague, dysentery and syphilis, or the occasional public hangings of thieves and murderers which made compelling viewing. A particularly dramatic execution took place in 1506 after Alfonso had uncovered a plot for his own assassination, led by two of his brothers. The other conspirators were beheaded in the piazza in front of the cathedral, but Alfonso spared the lives of his brothers, sentencing them instead to life imprisonment in the castle dungeons. Renaissance society was violent, but in fact Ferrara seems to have been much quieter than other places, notably the notoriously ungovernable city of Rome. Above all, the Ferrarese diarists were obsessed with the comings and goings of members of the Este family: Alfonso and several of his brothers catching syphilis, their titled guests arriving by river in elegant boats, or the Duke fishing for sturgeon in the lagoons at the mouth of the Po.

Life in Ferrara was dominated by the court. At Epiphany (6 January) the Duke and his courtiers rode into the great piazza in front of the castle to give presents to his people, in imitation of the Three Kings. The gifts were mostly provisions he could spare from his own larder, and the list of them gives an idea of the food available in Ferrara: the meat included salted ox tongues, rabbits, ducks, hares, turtle doves, pheasant and partridge, quails, peacocks and even a crane; there were also boxes of oysters, salted pike, barrels of olives, oranges and lemons, dried figs, sugar, marzipan, boxes of sugared fruits and wine. Easter too was celebrated by prominent almsgiving ceremonies at all the major churches. On Maundy Thursday the Duke and his family gave a dinner at the palace for 150 poor men, serving their food and washing their feet just as Christ had done for his Apostles. There was also a performance of the Passion play staged in the cathedral on Good Friday. During her first Easter in Ferrara, Lucretia watched a five-hour spectacular in which angels descended from the roof to hover over Christ as he prayed in the garden of Gethsemene, followed by his Crucifixion, staged on a hill specially built in front of the high altar, and his descent into Hell through an enormous serpent's head.

Religion played an immensely important role in the lives of the people of sixteenth-century Europe. Like all European cities of the period, Ferrara was full of convents and monasteries housing the wide variety of religious orders that existed before the Counter-Reformation. There were over fifty churches, many built by earlier Este rulers: the old Duke Ercole had built fourteen as part of his modernization of the city, and he had contributed funds to the rebuilding or repair of another twelve. One of the family's thirteenth-century ancestors, Beatrice d'Este, had been beatified, and her ornate tomb in San Antonio in Polesine wept tears every year on the anniversary of her death.

Over 2,000 men and women, say 10 per cent of the adult population of Ferrara, worked inside the castle, either for the ducal administration or for one of the smaller households belonging to the Duchess and other members of the Este family. Here there were opportunities for all but the lowest social classes. The ducal courtiers and the gentlemen who ran the household departments all belonged to the Ferrarese nobility and many had started their careers as pages, entering ducal service as young boys to learn the rules of courtly behaviour. Men from more modest backgrounds worked as assistants to these courtiers or were in charge of departmental sections, such as the larder, the wine cellars and the kitchens. The educated middle class took posts as lawyers, accountants and bookkeepers in the bureaucracy that administered the ducal estates and industries, which included the manufacture of soap, bricks, textiles and gun-powder, the production of salt in the Po delta and the mining of gold, silver, iron ore and copper in the Apennines. There were also hundreds of jobs for cleaners, maids, laundresses and other menial servants. The castle employed fifty soldiers as guards and there were four gaolers in charge of the prisons who were assisted by a cook and three servants; they were also responsible for Alfonso's brothers who were locked up in windowless dungeons in the tower. In the stables there were blacksmiths and saddlers as well as coachmen and over a hundred stable boys who looked after the horses – mounts for riding, hunting, jousting and battle, as well as draught animals – while more men and boys cared for the dogs and falcons.

The Este court aspired to grandeur, in the way that provincial centres often do, and tried hard to emulate the magnificence of the royal courts of Burgundy and France. They hunted, jousted, banqueted and danced as splendidly as they could. Imported leopards, cheetahs and panthers added an exotic air to the hunting in Duke Ercole's park. The Este racehorses were famous and the city celebrated St George's Day (23 April), the feast of Ferrara's patron saint, with a race meeting. The winning owner, usually a member of the family, received the customary prize of a bolt of gold brocade, a sow and a cock. The ducal palace might have been small but it was sumptuously decorated and provided a fitting setting for theatrical performances and other courtly entertainments. Alfonso employed over thirty musicians, many of them French, and there were dwarves and buffoons to amuse as well as masters to teach dancing, fencing and real tennis.

Tennis was a sport much favoured by the King of France, Francis I, but it was still a novelty in Italy. Not surprisingly, given their aspirations, the Este were one of the first Italian dynasties to add a purpose-built tennis court to their palace complex. The game had developed in France out of the anarchic ball-games played in city streets and monastic cloisters across medieval Europe. By the sixteenth century it had become a formal game, with formal rules, played exclusively by the nobility. The ancestor of the much simpler game of lawn tennis, real tennis was played with rackets and balls in an indoor court divided in two by a cord (the net was only introduced in the seventeenth century). The ball, made of leather and stuffed with horsehair, was always served from the same end. Serving was not done by the players but by a servant who 'served' the ball up on to the sloping roof of the gallery on his left and then exited the court through a special door to allow the game to proceed. Unlike modern tennis, this was a three-dimensional contest where the walls as well as the floor were used to provide players opportunities to outwit their opponents. This was a game of guile not of strength. The successful player had to read his opponent's game (and disguise his own strategy) by anticipating the direction and speed of the ball as it glanced off the multitude of angles formed by the slopes and buttresses of the court.

Lucretia brought elegance and gaiety to Ferrara. She persuaded her father-in-law to let her keep her Spanish buffoons, but she adapted happily to local traditions and soon became a major patron of Italian singers, a taste she shared with her sister-in-law Isabella d'Este (Alfonso's sister, married to Francesco Gonzaga, the Marquis of Mantua). Lucretia enjoyed music, dancing and banquets, the staples of court entertainment. She also enjoyed that other staple, flirtation, and had several affairs. One of her lovers was the poet Pietro Bembo. Many of their letters and poems to each other have survived, and the lock of her blonde hair that Lucretia gave Bembo is now on display at the Biblioteca Ambrosiana in Milan. Nevertheless, she did her duty to her husband and produced heirs, something for which she gained much credit in Ferrara (it was widely believed then that the mother determined the sex of a child). Over the following seventeen years she bore Alfonso eight children. Her first child, a daughter, conceived immediately after her marriage, arrived prematurely in September 1502 and was still-born. (Lucretia had been ill with malaria for two months that summer and nearly died of puerperal fever after the birth.) Her next child, born in September 1505, was male, but he only lived for a few days. Bembo sent her a horoscope he had had prepared for the baby, 'so you may find consolation knowing how much we are ruled by the stars'.

The pressures to produce a male heir were real enough. Duke Ercole I had died in January 1505 and it was vital that Lucretia produce an heir for her husband who had now succeeded his father to the dukedom. Finally, in April 1508, she had a healthy boy, who was named Ercole after his grandfather. Sixteen months later, on 25 August 1509, she gave birth to Ippolito. Two more sons and a daughter followed: Alessandro, named in honour of his papal grandfather, died aged 2, but Eleonora and Francesco both survived childhood. In June 1519, just before Ippolito's tenth birthday, Lucretia gave birth to another daughter and died herself, of puerperal fever, with her husband at her bedside. She was only 39. Alfonso was devastated, and fainted at her funeral. Despite her salacious reputation, Lucretia had proved an excellent Duchess by sixteenth-century standards, leaving Alfonso with a substantial family – the heir and the spare, and more besides: Ercole (11), Ippolito (9), Eleonora (4), Francesco (2) and the baby Isabella, who died the following year.

Ippolito, as the second son, was destined for a career in the Church. He was named after his father's brother, a spectacularly wealthy cardinal with a string of benefices that included Zagreb as well as Capua, Ferrara, Modena and Milan. In May 1519, a month before Lucretia died, Duke Alfonso persuaded his brother to resign the archbishopric of Milan in favour of his young nephew. Pope Leo X confirmed the appointment and the young Ippolito gave him a expensive golden vase worth 600 scudi in return (a skilled craftsman did well to earn 60 scudi a year). Aged only 9, he was now one of the premier archbishops of Europe (though his uncle retained all the income from the see). When the Cardinal died in 1520, at the early age of 41, Alfonso also gave Modena to Ippolito, but this time the Pope refused to ratify the appointment and Ippolito had to be satisfied with a pension on the bishopric as compensation when the dispute was finally settled in 1534. Ippolito also inherited the Cardinal's income from Milan and the benefice of Bondeno, together with its rich agricultural estates near Ferrara. Luckily he did not inherit his uncle's vicious character: the elder Ippolito had once ordered a servant to stab his brother Giulio in the eye simply because he was jealous of Giulio's success with a lady whom he also favoured.

We know little about Ippolito's childhood but his education was conventional for a prince of the period. He was taught Latin and Greek, literature, history and philosophy by the humanists attached to the Este court; he studied musical theory and learned to play several instruments; and he spent a lot of time honing the skills essential for a young aristocrat – jousting, hunting, falconry, tennis and card-playing. He lived in his own apartments in the ducal castle, looked after by his own staff of personal servants, including a chaplain and two musicians. Duke Alfonso also gave him the use of Belfiore, one of the Este villas on the northern edge of the city, where Ippolito kept his falcons, dogs and horses, and entertained his guests. One ledger survives from his youth, covering the years 1526–9, and it shows that his father gave him an allowance of 25 scudi a month to supplement his income from Milan and Bondeno. Much of the money was used to pay his household's salaries and expenses, but the ledger also reveals the young Ippolito's love of pleasure. There are payments for armour and lances for jousting, velvet to make caparisons for his horses and to line the scabbards of his swords, red velvet collars for his hunting dogs, leather hoods for his falcons, balls for tennis, elab-orate outfits for Carnival and tournaments, and the expenses involved in hosting lavish banquets.

Ippolito spent his childhood surrounded by family. After the death of Lucretia, Duke Alfonso took another wife. Unusually for a ruling prince, he married his mistress, Laura, a beautiful girl of low birth. She was probably only ten years older than Ippolito and pro-duced two further sons for Alfonso (confusingly called Alfonso and Alfonsino). In 1534 Ippolito had at least fourteen close relations living in Ferrara, and hordes of more distant cousins who were the offspring of Niccolò III's illegitimate brood, many of them employed in the ducal households (one of these was Ippolito's chief valet, Scipio Assassino, who was descended from the mother of Duke Borso). Ippolito's aunt, Isabella d'Este, was a frequent visitor to Ferrara. His two uncles, Ferrante and Giulio, remained prisoners in the castle, and another aunt, Violante, reigned as Abbess of the convent of San Antonio in Polesine, where she had charge of the weeping tomb of Beatrice d'Este. Monastic life was a respectable alternative to marriage, for legitimate and illegitimate daughters alike. Eleonora, Ippolito's sister, entered the convent of Corpus Domini at the age of 8 and was Abbess by her nineteenth birthday.

The d'Este family of Ferrara

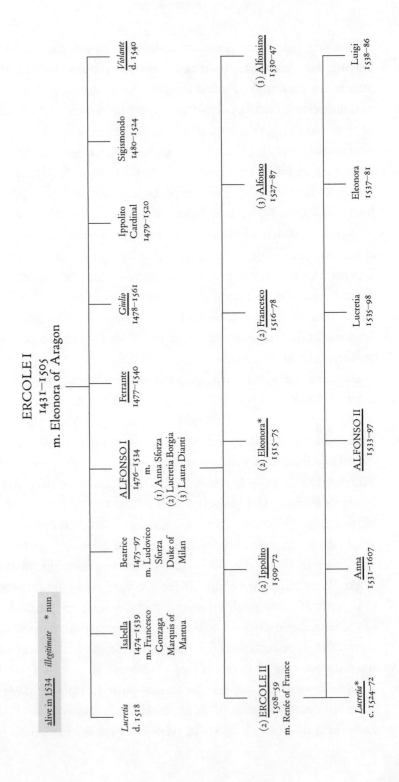

alive in 1534   *illegitimate*   * nun

ERCOLE I
1431–1505
m. Eleonora of Aragon

Lucretia
d. 1518

Isabella
1474–1539
m. Francesco
Gonzaga
Marquis of
Mantua

Beatrice
1475–97
m. Ludovico
Sforza
Duke of
Milan

ALFONSO I
1476–1534
m.
(1) Anna Sforza
(2) Lucretia Borgia
(3) Laura Dianti

Ferrante
1477–1540

Giulio
1478–1561

Ippolito
Cardinal
1479–1520

Sigismondo
1480–1524

Violante
d. 1540

(2) ERCOLE II
1508–59
m. Renée of France

(2) Ippolito
1509–72

(2) Eleonora*
1515–75

(2) Francesco
1516–78

(3) Alfonso
1527–87

(3) Alfonsino
1530–47

Lucretia
c. 1524–72

Anna
1531–1607

ALFONSO II
1533–97

Lucretia
1535–98

Eleonora
1537–81

Luigi
1538–86

The Abbess of San Bernardino, where Ippolito's mother was buried, was Camilla, the illegitimate 32-year-old daughter of his uncle, Cesare Borgia — she had been brought up by Lucretia and was sufficiently fond of Ippolito's mother to chose the name Lucretia when she entered San Bernardino at the age of 7. There were a lot of Lucretias in the family tree. Ercole's affection for his mother was so great that he gave the name Lucretia not only to an illegitimate child (who also entered Corpus Domini at a young age), but also to his second legitimate daughter.

Ippolito and his brother Ercole were very close, in age and in affection. They had been educated together and no doubt competed fiercely as they jousted and hunted, or played tennis and cards. But their future careers meant different choices as they grew up. In 1528 Ercole married Renée of France, daughter of King Louis XII and sister-in-law of his successor, Francis I. On 20 May 1529 Ippolito held a banquet at Belfiore in honour of the bridal couple. His sister-in-law was very French. Her insistence on an all-French household — she even had her account books kept in French — grated on Ercole, as did her sympathies with the Protestant reform movement, but she got on exceptionally well with Ippolito. The banquet gave him a chance to show her that Ferrara could provide entertainment and food just as sophisticated as that she had left behind in France.

Renaissance banquets involved far more than just eating and drinking. They were designed to appeal as much to the eyes and ears as to the palate. Originality was crucial. The artistry of the table decorations and the subtle skill with which the cook ornamented his dishes mattered just as much as the food. A banquet also involved entertainments, chosen, like the wines, to suit each part of the menu. The musician in charge carefully orchestrated contrasts in mood and style: light popular madrigals, classical plays, elegant dancers, martial trumpets and pipes, comic dwarves and buffoons.

There were also several features peculiar to Italy which would have been new to Renée. One of these was the appearance of vegetables and salads as an integral part of the meal, a fashion which had

BANCHETTI

COMPOSITIONI DI
VIVANDE, ET AP-
PARECCHIO GE-
NERALE, DI
CHRISTOFORO
DI MESSI
SBVGO,

ALLO ILLVSTRISSIMO
ET REVERENDISSIMO
SIGNOR IL SIGNOR
DON HIPPOLITO
DA ESTE,
CARDINALE DI-
FERRARA.

Con gratia Et Priuilegio.

IN FERRARA PER GIOVANNI
De Buglhat Et Antonio Hucher Compagni.
Nell'Anno. M. D. XLIX.

Frontispiece to Messisbugo's treatise on banquets with its dedication to Ippolito

emerged during the early years of the sixteenth century. Traditionally these foods were peasant fare – the poor were commonly mocked as eaters of beans, garlic and onions – but the notion of the urban rich imitating the agricultural poor to create high fashion sounds all too familiar. The fashion also added another level of subtlety to the art of dining in sixteenth-century Italy. These cold dishes were not served from the kitchen but from the *credenza*, an elaborate serving table set up in the dining-room and lavishly decorated with silver plates and candlesticks.

Ippolito's banquet for Ercole and Renée is particularly well documented. One of the ducal household involved in its organization was Cristoforo Messisbugo, who later wrote a treatise on dining which he dedicated to Ippolito (it was published in Ferrara in 1549). He described this particular evening hosted by the 19-year-old Ippolito in minute detail.

The banquet was a spectacularly grand affair. The day was a fast day, the feast of St Bernardino, so the menu consisted of fish rather than meat. The guests spent the afternoon watching a display of jousting before going into the palace for a short concert. Then they went out into the garden for dinner. In the cool of the early evening, swags of flowers decorated with Este devices hung from the trees. Musicians played under a canopy decorated with festoons of greenery as the fifty-four guests were led out by eight youths who danced their way across the torchlit garden. The *credenza* glittered with silverware under the loggia, and beside it was a table laden with fine wines. The dining table was covered with three layers of white linen tablecloths, one on top of the other, and beside each place there was a napkin, artfully folded into one of several shapes, a knife and a bread roll. Decorating the table were flowers and salt cellars, and fifteen great gilded and painted sugar sculptures – five figures each of Venus, Bacchus and Cupid, which set the tone for the meal that followed.

Once the guests were seated they were handed bowls of scented water to wash their hands before starting on the hors-d'oeuvres (*antipasti*): salads of asparagus, anchovies and herbs, marzipan biscuits and pasta. There were eighteen courses to follow, none of them very large but all exquisitely presented and each accompanied by a different entertainment. The meal lasted seven hours.

The first course was served ceremonially with loud dramatic music played by three trombones and three horns. Its centrepiece was an enormous boiled sturgeon, decorated with Ippolito's own coat-of-arms picked out in garlic and red sauce. The second course, eaten to the sound of lighter music played on the flute and oboe, included pike (strewn with little blue borage flowers) and tench dressed, in honour of Renée, *alla francese*. Each course consisted of seven or eight different dishes, which meant a lot of work for the men serving the banquet and an awesome undertaking for the cooks sweating away in the kitchens. Instrumental music continued until the fifth course, when clowns and tumblers capered round the tables, followed by singers and dancers. During the ninth course, which consisted simply of 1,000 oysters served with plates of oranges and pears, the pipers started to play. Everyone thought the meal was over, but now the squires removed the first layer of tablecloths, napkins and sugar sculptures, and relaid the tables. This time the centrepieces were fifteen nudes (eight male, seven female) made of black biscuit flavoured with honey and sesame, their gilded heads garlanded with bay leaves, and 'the parts that are normally hidden' covered with flowers.

Following the theme of a 'new' meal, the diners started again with salads, this time served with caviare, to the sound of a solo bassoonist. And so it went on, and on. Sturgeon and cuttlefish arrived to the accompaniment of a lutist who sang madrigals 'divinely'; fried squid, crayfish in a French sauce and macaroni *alla napolitana* were accompanied by singers dressed as peasants who pretended to cut the grass in the garden. The fish finally stopped with the seventeenth course – fresh broad beans and parmesan (a combination still eaten in Tuscany every spring), cherries, raw artichokes and junket. After this course the second layer of tablecloths was removed, and the tables relaid with clean napkins. The squires then brought perfumed toothpicks and more bowls of scented water for the guests to wash their hands. The final course – candied fruits, candied lettuce and cucumber, sweets and cakes – was accompanied by a small chamber orchestra and six singers singing motets and madrigals, conducted by Duke

Alfonso's composer, Alfonso dalla Viola. To end the meal Ippolito gave his guests presents – necklaces, bracelets, earrings, rings and perfumed gloves – which he distributed from a vast silver bowl.

∾

As with his own marriage, Duke Alfonso's choice of bride for his son had strong political overtones. His reign, and Ippolito's childhood, had been dominated by the wars between two rulers – Francis I, King of France, and Charles V, Holy Roman Emperor and King of Spain – for the control of Italy. Alfonso had had to make several difficult political decisions. Early in 1527, as Charles V's army marched unhindered through northern Italy towards Rome, he abandoned Ferrara's traditional pro-French policy to back the Emperor. This was an astute move, as it turned out: not only did Alfonso retain his state, unlike several of his contemporaries, but he also managed to enlarge it. Charles V's troops sacked Rome with a viciousness that shocked the Christian world. Every house and church was looted, priceless relics destroyed, women raped and the rich ransomed – Isabella d'Este was only saved by the intervention of her son, Ferrante Gonzaga, who was an imperial commander. The Sistine Chapel was used as a stable and Pope Clement VII, who had hidden in the fortress of Castel Sant'Angelo, was forced to surrender. Duke Alfonso took advantage of the ensuing power vacuum to repossess the cities of Modena and Reggio, which were traditionally part of his duchy but which had been captured by Julius II in 1512 and incorporated into the Papal States. Clement VII was furious but impotent. Charles V, in gratitude for Alfonso's support, confirmed his rights to the two cities and also gave him the imperial fief of Carpi, whose ruler had unwisely insisted on adhering to France.

An uneasy peace followed the violent upheaval initiated by the Sack of Rome. Duke Alfonso made a deliberate move to shore up his strained relations with Francis I by agreeing to the marriage of Ercole and Renée of France. However, there was little he could do to improve his relationship with Clement VII, whose antagonism towards the Este family only deepened with time. While this Pope remained on the throne of St Peter, Alfonso had no hope of acquiring a cardinal's hat for Ippolito and thereby providing his second son with a route to riches and power. There must have been considerable relief in the palace in Ferrara when Clement VII died, aged only 55, in September 1534, and anticipation for the future when the 66-year-old Cardinal Alessandro Farnese was elected as Pope Paul III on 13 October. But excitement was soon overtaken by grief. Just two weeks later, Alfonso himself also died. Ippolito's chances of acquiring a cardinal's hat now depended on the relationship between two new rulers – one, his brother, young and untested; the other, the Pope, an old man but a consummate politician.

2

The Palazzo San Francesco

'... and the said Duke leaves to his second son Ippolito the palace of San Francesco together with its orchards and gardens and all other appurtenances. He endows the aforementioned Don Ippolito with 13,000 scudi which he commands and desires to be granted and paid forthwith to the said Don Ippolito to the effect that the said Don Ippolito may and should furnish the said palace with all the goods and furniture necessary and appropriate to the rank of the said Duke and of the said Ippolito.'

Last will and testament of Duke Alfonso d'Este, 1533

THE PEDANTIC LANGUAGE of Duke Alfonso's will is that of lawyers down the centuries – why use one word when two will do? But the emphasis the Duke placed on the direct relationship between rank and display is significant. Ippolito was his son; he was also Archbishop of Milan and hoped one day to become a cardinal. In his will the Duke stressed the importance of conspicuous expenditure 'necessary and appropriate' for his son's position. It was to that end that he left Ippolito 13,000 scudi. This was an awful lot of money, and even the extravagant Ippolito was unable to spend it all on refurbishment.

Duke Alfonso died on 31 October 1534, aged 58, leaving his duchy to his eldest son, Ercole, and his favourite leopard to a cousin. To Ippolito he left both money and property, providing the income necessary for Ippolito to pursue a career in the Church and his goal of a cardinal's hat. In addition to the palace, Ippolito's rights to Belfiore were confirmed and he was given a valuable set of silver plates to ornament his *credenza*. He was assigned a monthly allowance, which Ercole was obliged to pay out of ducal revenues, as well as the income from the town of Brescello, the taxes raised on butchers in Reggio and on all live animals entering Ferrara (he had to share this last item with his stepmother), and agricultural estates in Fóssoli, Pomposa and the Romagna. By the end of November Ippolito's newly painted coats-of-arms adorned the walls in each centre, announcing the change of ownership. Duke Alfonso's death marked an important rite of passage for the 25-year-old Ippolito: financial and domestic independence. It also marks the point at which Ippolito himself begins to emerge from the accounts' ledgers and letters preserved in the Modena archives.

The Palazzo San Francesco was a grand house, close to the old city centre. It had been built in 1485 by Ippolito's grandfather, Ercole I, and had been home not only to his father but also to his uncles, Giulio and Ferrante, who were still imprisoned in the ducal castle. The palace was a rectangular two-storey block built around two courtyards, which opened directly on to the street (now Via Savonarola). At the back was nearly a hectare of garden. Visitors entered the larger of the two courtyards through a grand portal, flanked with fluted piers and crowned by an elegantly carved arch. A smaller arch, the tradesman's entrance, led into the second court-yard where the stables and kitchen were located. As was the custom in Italian palaces, the main reception rooms and private apartments were all on the first floor (*piano nobile*), which was reached by a stair-case leading up from the far side of the main courtyard. The largest room was the Great Hall. Extending the full length of the street façade, it measured 30 metres by 10 metres and was used mainly for banquets and grand entertainments. There was also a slightly small-er hall at the back of the palace, overlooking the courtyard, which was used for more intimate gatherings. Behind this hall were the pri-vate apartments, all facing the garden. The building was serviceable

Ferrara, Palazzo San Francesco, garden loggia

but the decor was old-fashioned and, given the terms of his father's will, Ippolito decided to modernize it completely. He lost little time: just over two weeks after his father died, the builders arrived.

The work took a year to complete and Ippolito did not move in until November 1535. As is the way with builders, the palace soon became uninhabitable. The courtyards were littered with heaps of sand and lime, piles of bricks, stone for the window frames, planks of wood and tiles for roofs and floors. The wells and drains were dismantled and repaired, and so was the staircase. All the rooms were redecorated, and their tiled floors relaid. New fireplaces, doors and doorframes were installed in all the important rooms. A roofer and his boy spent all summer replacing broken tiles and mending the guttering. There was scaffolding in all the main reception rooms where the painters were decorating the ceilings and Ippolito's own rooms had gaping holes where the builders were installing new windows. The garden was also redesigned. Ippolito took on two new gardeners, one full-time employee (with a salary of 17 scudi a year, and a new pair of shoes every month) and a part-time assistant

	Scudi
Building materials and transport	707
Istrian stone doors	151
Wages to builders and carpenters	711
Wages to painters	184
Pigments and materials	171
Garden plants and work	49
Total	1,973

The cost of modernizing the Palazzo San Francesco

to help prepare the ground for planting – they planted 130 fruit trees that October.

Most of the money Ippolito spent on the palace went on building work. Architecture was considerably more expensive than painting and accounted for 80 per cent of the total. The Istrian stone doorways he installed in his own apartments were a particularly extravagant detail. Specially made for him in Venice, they arrived by barge in July and were installed by the men who had carved them. Ippolito was delighted with the result and presented each of the stone cutters with a pair of stockings. The biggest single project for the builders was the garden walls. These were repointed and embellished with new brick merlons, a traditional Ferrarese feature which had been revived and popularized by Duke Ercole. The walls were then decorated with frescoed landscapes, painted by a local artist, Jacomo Panizato, and two others brought in from Bologna. The total cost of this lavish garden wall came to 380 scudi, enough to pay the annual wages of ten master builders.

The teams of builders, labourers, carpenters and painters employed on the palace normally worked Monday to Saturday, dawn to dusk. There was no conventional two-week holiday, though the men were given the day off for all major Church feasts and local festivals, making a working year of about 250 days. They were hired and paid by the day – no work, no pay – and they could be laid off if there was insufficient work or, for those working outside, if the weather was bad. Pay day was Saturday, a busy afternoon for Ippolito's bookkeeper, Jacomo Filippo Fiorini, who had to record the sum given to each of the workers, the number of days they had worked that week, what they had been working on and the rates at which they were paid.

Fiorini's entries are somewhat impersonal but they do provide an insight into the lives of ordinary artisans in sixteenth-century Ferrara. The head of the team of painters employed to decorate the ceilings of the reception halls and those in Ippolito's apartments was Andrea – in the accounts he was known simply as Andrea the painter (*Andrea depintore*). These were no ordinary ceilings but elaborate wooden affairs, studded with rosettes and inlaid with panels surrounded by several bands of moulding. Andrea and his team spent most of the year painting them with intricate floral patterns in red and gold against a dark background, and gilding the carved details of the mouldings and the rosettes. Andrea was taken on in late November 1534 and got work every week for the following twelve months. Initially it was sporadic – he and one other painter worked only eleven days before the end of the year – but it picked up in January. By February there were six men at work on the ceilings and Andrea was given a pay rise in recognition of his role as team leader. They continued to work steadily through the spring and summer, with a short break in August when they helped the painters decorating the garden walls. The garden team had been working under a large canopy to protect the frescos as they dried and to shield the artists from the fierce summer sun, but it blew down in an unexpectedly violent storm which lashed Ferrara on 12 August and ruined all the unfinished painting. Andrea might have been ill one week in early September when he only worked for a day and a half, while the rest of the team managed six days each. There were two other thin weeks in late July and early October, which affected them all. As mid-November, the date for Ippolito's move, drew closer, work became more frenetic. During the last four weeks Andrea only had three days off and worked solidly for over two weeks, including two Sundays and the feast of All Saints (1 November).

Over the year Andrea worked a total of 224½ days and earned just over 28¼ scudi, a sum augmented by another ½ scudo which his wife received for sewing sheets for Ippolito. Compared to the cost of Ippolito's extravagant garden walls their income was minimal, but it was enough to be able to live comfortably in Ferrara. The rent on a modest family home was about 5 scudi a year, and the standard food allowances paid to the courtiers of the ducal household, which pro-vided half a kilo of meat and one kilo of bread per person per day, added up to less than 11 scudi a year.

During the summer, while the builders and decorators were busy on the Palazzo San Francesco, Ippolito and his brother assembled Ippolito's new household. Like the palace, it was designed as a delib-erate statement of Ippolito's rank and prestige, and, though smaller than Duke Ercole's entourage, it was identical in composition. It also established Ippolito at the head of his own power structure and cre-ated a new network to weave into the complex web that formed the framework of European political patronage. Ippolito's own success would reflect directly on the members of his household: a cardinal's cook might not earn more than that of an archbishop but he had appreciably more status. At all levels of Renaissance society the right connections mattered, and the opportunity to join the household of this ambitious young man was not one to be missed.

The sixteenth-century term for a household was a 'family' (*famiglia*), a word that meant much more then than it does now. When speaking about his 'family', Ippolito included all his domestic staff – the men who dressed him, prepared and served his food, made his clothes, looked after his wine and horses, ran his errands and cleaned his palace. Despite the fact that its members came from all walks of life, the household was a close-knit unit. Loyalty was expected, and in return Ippolito was generous towards his men. Apart from their wages and living expenses, he gave practical help when needed, settling debts with a pawnbroker for one, paying for the funeral of another whose widow was too poor to afford it herself. When his valet died in 1534, Ippolito gave his family regular presents of flour and clothes for the children and put up the money for one of the daughters to enter a convent. He also gave food and money to a retired member of the dining staff, 'because he has been a faithful servant, and is poor and burdened with children'. It was not surprising that Ippolito paid a doctor's bill after one of his stable boys had been badly kicked by a stallion, but it is a reminder of how attitudes to staff have changed to see that he also paid for a doctor to treat a monk who had been knifed by his gardener's son.

At the beginning of 1535 Ippolito employed a staff of just twenty-two; by the end of the year he had eighty-two men on his books (there were no full-time women). This was a dramatic increase and a reminder, in case he needed it, of his new independence. The number of men employed to run his estates increased from three to ten. His household proper quadrupled in size. In addition to the valets and staff who had looked after him in his apartments in the ducal castle, and his animals at Belfiore, he now had his own courtiers, dining-room staff, cooks, footmen and squires, and even his own pages, young sons of noble families attached to his household to learn the art of court etiquette.

The most important members of Ippolito's household were his courtiers: five gentlemen, a secretary and another five men who held the posts at the head of the various household departments. The gentlemen were all young, much the same age as him, and handpicked to be his closest companions, those with whom he hunted and jousted, played cards and tennis, gossiped and dined. All came from aristocratic families with close links to the ducal court. Antonio Romei, the son of a ducal courtier, had become Ippolito's secretary in 1534.

Tomaso Mosto, Master of the Wardrobe

Scipio Assassino, a cousin, albeit on the wrong side of the blanket, had been Ippolito's valet since 1527 and was now promoted to Master of the Chamber (*maestro di camera*). Alfonso Cestarello took the job of major-domo (*maestro di casa*), Girolamo Guarniero became the Steward (*sescalco*) and Ippolito Zuliolo was appointed as the Master of the Stables (*maestro di stalla*). The post of Master of the Wardrobe (*guardarobiero*), however, posed a problem. In Ferrara this job was traditionally combined with that of treasurer and, since 1530, the two roles had been undertaken by Ippolito's bookkeeper, Jacomo Filippo Fiorini. He was good at his job but his father was an artisan, and he himself had trained as a painter before starting to work for Ippolito. Class mattered at the courts of sixteenth-century Europe, and Fiorini did not have the right social background. Ippo-

Post	Salary in scudi	No.	Name
Gentlemen	100	3	Niccolò Tassone, Scipio d'Este, Ippolito Machiavelli
Gentlemen	0	2	Provosto Trotti, Tomaso del Vecchio
Secretary	0	1	Antonio Romei
Major-domo	0	1	Alfonso Cestarello
Master of the Wardrobe	0	1	Tomaso Mosto
Steward	62	1	Girolamo Guarniero
Master of the Chamber	41	1	Scipio Assassino
Master of the Stables	41	1	Ippolito Zuliolo

Courtiers' salaries

lito therefore appointed Fiorini as his chief factor in Ferrara, to take charge of the overall management of his estates, and gave the job of Master of the Wardrobe to Tomaso Mosto, the brother of one of Ercole II's valets.

All the courtiers received expenses for their servants as well as hay and straw for their horses, but their remuneration varied considerably. Five of them were not in the salary lists at all. They had opted for careers in the Church and had joined Ippolito's household in the expectation of benefiting as their patron advanced up the clerical ladder. Cestarello already had a canonicate at Bondeno, one of Ippolito's benefices near Ferrara. Mosto and Trotti both held benefices attached to the cathedral of Ferrara: Trotti was Provost there and was known in the accounts ledgers as Provosto Trotti.

Below these courtiers came the rest of the household, their status more precisely graded by salaries and perks (see table overleaf). Neither of the two chaplains received salaries, but they did receive expenses and shared a house rented for them by Ippolito.

It was not just salaries and perks that identified rank in the household but also the standard of accommodation provided in the

Salary No. in scudi	Stables	Wardrobe	Chamber	Palace	Dining	Misc.
0 11		Master	Pages	Major-domo		Chaplains
						Secretary
						Gentlemen
51–100 4					Steward	Gentlemen
41–50 3	Master	Master				Musician
31–40 11	Trainer	Assistant	Valets	Factor	Purveyor	
	Assistant		Doctor		Squires	
21–30 6	Saddler				Carver	
	Farrier				Head cook	
	Under trainers					
11–20 24			Barber	Larderer	*Credenzieri*	Kennelmen
			Footmen	Cellarmen	Cooks	Falconers
			Servants	Head gardener	Sommelier	
				Bookkeeper		
1–10 13	Muleteeers	Servant		Under-gardener	Kitchen boys	Falcon boys
	Stable boys			Servants	Servants	

Ippolito's household in 1536

Palazzo San Francesco. The size and location of each man's room (or rooms), whether his windows had glass in them or were just covered with waxed cloth, and the type of bedding he was given, all had a real impact on their lives. The courtiers lived in considerable comfort. They were housed on the first floor, each with their own rooms opening off the spacious balconies that flanked the upper storey of the main courtyard. The rooms had been redecorated for their new occupants and all had glass windows. There were fireplaces for warmth in winter, and the air that circulated through the shaded loggias lessened the stifling heat of summer. Assassino's salary may not have been very high but his room was smart enough to be allocated to the French ambassador when he visited Ferrara in April

1537. The other two valets shared a large room in the same part of the palace, as did the three squires.

Further down the ranks life was less comfortable. The kitchen staff lived in the side wing of the palace, sharing rooms which looked out on to the smaller courtyard that served the kitchen and the stables. Their cloth windows could not have provided much protection from the weather, nor from the smells rising from below. The five footmen had to share a windowless room in the attic, or, as Fiorini vividly recorded in his ledger, 'under the tiles', which must have been unpleasant in both winter and summer. Perhaps the most telling nuance in distinguishing status was the quality of the mattresses and sheets Ippolito supplied for all the men living in the palace. His own sheets, made of the finest linen, cost three times as much as the rough cloth bought for the household beds. Fiorini took charge of organizing mattresses for the entire household. He bought three different kinds of wool and ticking, and he commissioned a mattressmaker to make up the mattresses in various different combinations of wool and weights. The bill for fortytwo mattresses, which Fiorini paid in June, listed the following:

No.	Quality of wool	Weight (in kg)
5	Cheap	10
15	Medium	14
3	Medium	15½
1	Medium	16
14	Medium	17
2	Expensive	19
2	Expensive	22

Mattresses

The best pair were for Ippolito himself, made of fine lambswool. Fiorini did not allocate any of the others in his ledger, though it is likely that the five cheap mattresses were for the five footmen in the attics. The stable boys had to make do with shared straw palliasses in the stables.

The stables were in a two-storey building immediately on the right after the arched entrance into the second courtyard, with stalls for the horses, tack rooms, storerooms for Ippolito's elaborate caparisons and harnesses, and workshops for the saddler and farrier. They were large, perhaps 20 metres by 10, and had been substantially renovated during the summer of 1535 with new brick floors, a tiled roof and six cloth windows. They had their own well and drains, and they were lit with candles and with glass lanterns fuelled by oil supplied by the palace larder. During the summer of 1535 they had also been newly furnished with quantities of sieves, forks and heavy metal buckets, as well as wooden feed chests secured with heavy padlocks.

The stables employed about twenty men, though the total varied, depending on the number of stable boys. In January 1536 there were eleven on the books, as well as skilled technicians such as the saddler, the farrier and four trainers. This was also the department with the widest cross-section of social backgrounds, from the aristocratic Zuliolo down to the lads. A stable boy's life was hard manual labour and involved mucking out stalls, measuring feed, harnessing the horses when they were needed and washing them down when they were returned after a long day's hunting. The lads earned pitifully low salaries, hardly a living wage – 5 scudi a year, which would have bought them just two capons a week, or two small pigs a year – though at least they had somewhere to sleep. Nor did they eat in the palace like the rest of the stables' staff. Instead they received a daily allowance of a hundredth of a scudo, which would buy them half a kilo of cheap beef or 800 grammes of bread each day. Unsurprising-ly, given their physical and social isolation, they did not have the same sense of loyalty as other members of the household. Theft was a problem – hence the heavy padlocks on the feed chests. Most were casual labourers who just wanted to earn a few lire before moving on, and as a result the turnover of stable boys was markedly higher than that in any other department. Few of them stayed as long as a year, and one left after only six days.

The basic diet fed to the horses and mules consisted of hay, millet and bran, though barley was also given to weak foals and to the stallions when they were covering the mares. Foaling and covering were annual events which required a lot of extra work for the stable boys who, in addition to their normal day's labour, had to stay up most of the night as well: larger than usual quantities of tallow candles were taken from the larder so that they could keep an eye on the mares and stallions, and they were rewarded with salamis, also from Ippolito's larder. Organizing fodder for these animals, stabled in the centre of town, was a major undertaking. The gardener at the Palazzo San Francesco was paid each year for cutting the grass to make hay, but this provided only a tiny proportion of the quantity needed. Most of the hay, straw and grain came from Ippolito's estates at Bondeno and Codigoro, transported by barge along the Po to the wharves below the Via Grande from where hired carters delivered it, either to the barns built in the gardens at Belfiore or to Ippolito's granary. In preparation for the move to the palace 160 cartloads of hay were delivered during the first two weeks of June, and 246 cartloads of straw arrived in October.

Zuliolo, Ippolito's Master of the Stables, had little professional expertise to offer and his post was largely a sinecure. It was his assistant, Jacomo Panizato, who took charge of the funds. Fiorini gave him regular advances of cash every week, 50 scudi or so at a time, to cover the stables' expenses, and Panizato had to account for every penny, recording each item in his own ledger. This job required someone both literate and trustworthy, though not necessarily skilled in looking after animals. Nevertheless, Panizato's appointment was unusual. He was a painter by training and had spent the summer of 1535 working at the palace, producing ornamental panels for ceilings in several rooms and painting landscapes on the garden walls. Perhaps there was not enough work for him in Ferrara, or perhaps he was bored of painting, but the career move certainly improved his social status. By 1538 he was no longer referred to in the account books as an artisan (*maestro*) but was described as *Messer*, the title given to men of standing, though below the rank of noble (*Magnifico*).

The horses themselves were the responsibility of Pierantonio, the chief trainer, who had been with the household since 1530. He earned a salary of 34 scudi a year, with expenses for himself, a servant and a horse, and Ippolito rented a house for his wife Catelina and their family. Pierantonio also had a room above the stables which had glass windows, a mark of the importance of his job. It was Pierantonio who bought all Ippolito's horses and mules, a task which frequently took him away from Ferrara, to nearby cities such as Mantua and Bologna, and also to places further afield such as Aquileia, north of Venice, or across the Apennines to Florence and even Naples. Horses and mules were the only forms of transport in sixteenth-century Europe. Ippolito had an impressive number of horses and mules, all named. The mounts he himself used for travelling, hunting, jousting and ceremonial occasions were all thoroughbreds, but he also owned ordinary hacks for the use of his household, as well as carthorses and pack mules. Pierantonio could buy an ordinary hack for as little as 5 or 6 scudi, but a good mount could cost up to 40 scudi. Surprisingly, mules were far more expensive. A cheap pack mule cost over 30 scudi, and a good one as much as 80 scudi.

Pierantonio was responsible for buying and mending all the equipment needed for his charges – bits, stirrups, whips and harnesses – and these he ordered from tradesmen across Ferrara. His job also involved veterinary skills. He took candles from the larder to treat cracked hooves and bought various compounds from the apothecary's shop which he mixed to make medicines, salves and poultices for more serious conditions. The apothecary also sold a special oil to treat scorpion bites. Among the compounds Pierantonio used regularly to make his salves were vinegar, turpentine, pig fat, incense, mastic and even mercury, as well as verdigris, Armenian bole (a reddish clay) and a bright red resin known as dragon's blood. These last three items were also used by the painters to gild the ceilings inside the palace and were bought in large quantities to be stored in the wardrobe.

Inside the palace the man with the greatest responsibility was probably Tomaso Mosto, the new Master of the Wardrobe. With the help of his two assistants and a bookkeeper, he was in charge of the purchase, manufacture, laundering, storage and repair of Ippolito's clothes. This was no small task. Ippolito's collection of clothes was huge: in 1535 Mosto had charge of over 350 items. Depending on what Ippolito was doing each day, Mosto might have to prepare as many as five outfits to suit the diary. All the laundry was done by hand, and many items also needed starching with sugar. Mosto bought all the materials for new outfits and commissioned tailors to make up the garments. The embroidery on Ippolito's shirts was done by nuns in various convents in Ferrara. Mosto particularly favoured a Sister Serafina at San Gabriele: she might have been Middle Eastern in origin (she was once described as *persiana* in the ledgers) and she was paid 1½ to 3 scudi for each shirt (the money, of course, went to the convent).

The responsibilities of the wardrobe, however, extended far beyond the care of Ippolito's clothes. Mosto had to organize the special outfits worn by the valets, footmen and pages when they escorted Ippolito in public. He looked after Ippolito's armour and weapons, his perfumes, jewels, silver, books and other valuables, as well as the palace furnishings, notably the tapestries, paintings and bedhangings, and the huge quantities of table and bed linen used by the household.

Stocking the wardrobe at the Palazzo San Francesco was an enormous undertaking and it was shared by Mosto and Fiorini. During January and February 1535, Mosto spent over 240 scudi on huge quantities of sheets, tablecloths and napkins for the palace. He bought most ready-made in shops in Ferrara, especially from two Jewish second-hand clothes dealers: Jacob, who specialized in cheap sheets and tablecloths, both new and used, and Isaac, who stocked better-quality linen. It was Isaac who supplied Ippolito's new goose-feather bed for 22 scudi (he threw in ten pillows for free). The range in quality was considerable. Ten fine linen napkins for Ippolito cost

Mosto 3 scudi, the same sum as he paid for twenty-five plain household ones. He also had to commission people to sew and hem. Much of this work went to women connected with the household. Malgarita, the wife of one of Ippolito's falconers, sewed four dozen napkins and eight household sheets for ½ scudo (just under two weeks' wages for her husband), and the task of sewing Ippolito's own sheets was given to Catelina, the wife of Andrea the painter.

Meanwhile, Fiorini was sent off to Venice in February (leaving Mosto to keep the books) with an enormous shopping list – mainly equipment for the kitchen and dining-rooms, but also candlesticks, fire-irons, colours for the painters at work on the palace ceilings, sugar for the wardrobe, glass window panes and the loads of wool that he needed to make mattresses for the household. This was quite a task and he was away from Ferrara for almost a month. Everything had to be bought from specialist suppliers. He commissioned various coppersmiths, tinsmiths and pewterers to make each individual item of kitchen and dining equipment according to his specifications, and paid blacksmiths to add iron handles. He had to hire a boat to go out to Murano to order the window panes and glasses. The bill for this shopping expedition came to over 400 scudi, and it cost another 6 scudi to get the goods shipped back to Ferrara. Why travel all the way to Venice, a two-day journey, when Ferrara was amply supplied with shops? There were two reasons: quality and price. The city – aptly described by one historian recently as the Bloomingdales of Renaissance Italy – was famous then, as now, for its glass, and for the high quality of the goods imported by Venetian merchants from overseas. In Venice Ippolito could buy the best glass in Europe, the best pigments from the Middle East and the best sugar from Madeira. The sheer size of the Venetian market also meant competitive prices on cheaper goods. The metalware that Fiorini commissioned was 30 per cent cheaper than it would have been in Ferrara.

Mosto and Fiorini also shared the onerous task of drawing up an inventory of all Ippolito's possessions prior to the move into the Palazzo San Francesco. It took most of October and it cannot have

A page from the inventory compiled by Fiorini and Mosto in October 1535.
Listed on it are Ippolito's paintings, mirrors, clocks and clavichords

been easy for Fiorini. As he recorded in his ledger at the start of each day's work, it marked the point at which he handed over responsibil-ity to the new Master of the Wardrobe. Ippolito had accumulated an astonishing number of possessions in his twenty-six years. The clothes alone took the best part of four days to itemize, the armour and weapons another day. The inventory listed the entire furnishings of the palace and ran to nearly a thousand entries. Some of these were individual items but many were multiple. It must have been tedious work. One wonders how many times the two men had to count 468 shoelaces (Ippolito owned 611 in all), 215 antique coins, 199 rosary beads, 102 handkerchiefs or 70 curtain rings. Each of the 116 bolts of cloth had to be unrolled, measured with a wooden rod and then care-fully rolled up again, while Fiorini recorded the details in his ledger. Averaging five minutes a roll, this would have taken them the best part of ten hours. The velvets, damasks, silks and satins for Ippolito's clothes, and the lengths of cheap cotton and canvas for household use – a total length of 1,500 metres and ranging from a 30-centimetre strip of red velvet to 400 metres of the blue cotton cloth that was used to line Ippolito's tapestries – all were treated with the same care and measured with the same precision. For Fiorini and the assistants, there must have been some sensual pleasure in seeing and handling these luxury fabrics, but the same could not have been true for the table linen and sheets. There were no standard sizes for these items. Each of the 112 sheets and 298 napkins and tablecloths also had to be meas-ured, length and width, before being refolded and replaced, while Fiorini entered the size and material of each item in his ledger. And, although Mosto could go home at the end of the day, Fiorini still had to do his new job as Ippolito's factor. Saturday, 2 October, must have been particularly gruelling. After spending the morning at the ducal castle itemizing the candelabra and fire-irons, and recording the details of 99 tablecloths and napkins, Fiorini returned to his office at the Palazzo San Francesco to pay the week's bills and wages, filling in another two pages in his ledger.

The move took several weeks. All Ippolito's possessions had to be transported from the ducal castle, a ten-minute walk away from the palace. Fiorini hired a carter in early October to move the heavy furniture (the first items he and Mosto had inventoried) and a porter was taken on to help move the lighter stuff. The palace needed extensive cleaning before the textiles arrived.

The builders had done a magnificent job. The grand reception halls and the rooms of Ippolito's apartments looked splendid. There was glass in all the windows, new stone fireplaces with carved and gilded mantelpieces, and polished walnut doors set in carved Istrian marble door frames. The heavy wooden ceilings were now brightly painted, their mouldings and rosettes glittering with gold. On the ceiling of the Great Hall were the gilded arms of the Duke and Duchess, and carved eagles, Ippolito's personal device. His own coat-of-arms, picked out in gold and silver, sparkled over the fireplace in the smaller hall at the back of the palace. The walls were freshly white-washed and hung with tapestries, many of which had been bought specially in Venice by Duke Ercole's agent (Fiorini had not been trusted with this task). Mosto and Fiorini counted seventy-two individual pieces of tapestry of varying shapes and sizes. Fiorini recorded their precise measurements in the inventory but not the stories they represented, referring to them generically as scenes of hunting, animals, figures, woods or landscapes. Ippolito's kennel master, whose talents also extended to needle and thread, had spent much of the summer (fifty-five days in total) lining the tapestries with blue cloth and sewing on pieces of leather to hold the rings used to hang them.

Ippolito's apartments were at the back of the palace, away from the noisy clatter of the street. The rooms looked out over the garden and faced north, cool in summer and furnished with elegant fireplaces for winter. The suite consisted of five rooms and there were no corridors. Each room opened directly into the next and, though they were smaller than the reception halls, they were just as lavishly decorated. Like the halls, they were hung with tapestries.

It is difficult to be certain of the exact size of the rooms in Ippolito's apartments since this part of the building has been considerably altered since he lived there, but the quantity of new glass windows he installed gives us a rough guide. The first room, and the most public, was his private drawing-room, which had four windows overlooking the garden. The next room was the antechamber, which had only two windows. It was also the only room without an elaborate paint-ed ceiling and contained instead nine painted panels (sadly Fiorini did not record their subjects), four of which had been done by Jacomo Panizato before he took up employment in the stables. The third room, Ippolito's bedroom, had three windows, and off it lay the *camerino*, a small room with only one window (and a windowless bathroom beyond). Finally there was his study, or *studiolo*, a room with two windows where Ippolito stored and displayed his collection of valuables.

Rooms of the period were sparsely furnished by our standards. Ippolito's inventory lists just two armchairs, one of which was cov-ered in white leather. Most of the seating furniture was light and portable. There were plain wooden benches, which were covered with tapestry cushions decorated with greenery and animals. Many of the rooms had tables, some covered with valuable Eastern carpets and rugs, and all the fireplaces were furnished with fire irons and wooden bellows, though only one fire screen was listed in the inventory. The principal ornaments in each of the rooms were large carved wooden chests which were used for storing clothes, linen and other goods. Ippolito owned twenty-nine in all, most of them made of walnut and many equipped with heavy locks. Fiorini had bought several of these in Venice, and others had been ordered from cabinet-makers in Milan 'in the French style'. One particularly grand walnut chest, which had drawers for displaying his collection of medals, had been a present from his father. A small cypress wood box in which he kept his handkerchiefs and nightcaps had been a present from his sister Eleonora, Abbess of the convent of Corpus Domini. There were also two painted cupboards, one of which was in the *camerino* and contained his library, a rather grand description for the ninety-nine books he owned.

In striking contrast to his scanty collection of furniture, Ippolito had amassed a princely collection of precious *objets*. He owned carved crystal reliefs, carved crystal cups, two astrological globes, pieces of coral, an ivory sundial, two mirrors of polished steel, fifteen antique bronze statues including one of a satyr which had been made into a lamp, and over 300 medals and coins. One of the medals, in gold and enamel, had been made in 1531 by the goldsmith Giovanni da Castel Bolognese and was inscribed with a bear. The bear was the symbol of the early Christian martyr St Euphemia and of Callisto, the nymph seduced by Jupiter and turned into a bear by Diana for abandoning her vow of chastity. It was also widely used as a symbol of gluttony.

Even the objects Ippolito used every day were expensively made. His inkwell was of gilded alabaster, the sandbox he used to dry the ink on his letters was made of silver, his chamber pots were crystal and his air-fresheners were perforated balls of copper and silver filled with musk. The pestle and mortar used to grind the perfumes that filled the balls and that scented his gloves were made of alabaster. Rather surprisingly, for a man whose father had been a patron of Titian and who himself would become one of the greatest patrons of art twenty years later in Rome, Ippolito's collection of paintings, at this point, was not particularly impressive. He owned just ten. Eight were religious: a *St John the Baptist*, a *St John the Evangelist*, five scenes from the life of Christ, including a *Circumcision* and a *Massacre of the Innocents*, and a devotional image of the Virgin, a common feature in bourgeois and noble homes across Europe. Ippolito's Virgin was, inevitably, particularly lavishly set in a carved wood frame decorated with expensive ultramarine which, as Fiorini recorded in October, was in the process of being being touched up by Jacomo Panizato. The other two paintings were secular: large oil portraits of women by the Venetian artist Palma Vecchio. One would like to think that Ippolito followed contemporary fashion and hung these two paintings of women on the walls of his bedroom. (His cousin Guidobaldo della Rovere commissioned Titian's *Venus of Urbino* for his own bedroom. This was not a Venus, as modern art historians

Post	Salary in scudi	No.	Names
Chief valet	41	1	Scipio Assassino
Valet	31	2	Alessandro Rossetto, Girolamo Bonazolo
Doctor	n/a	1	Maurelio Santi
Barber	14	1	Moiza
Servant	14	2	Ercole Zudio, Jacomo da Parma
Footman	12	5	Ippolito d'Argenta, Cavreto and 3 others
Page	0	3	Diomede Tridapalle and two others

The Chamber staff

coyly describe her, but a sensuous and seductive female nude, a sixteenth-century version of the Pirelli calendar.)

Ippolito's bedroom was the grandest room in his apartments. He slept in an enomous four-poster bed, supported on gilded classical columns complete with bases and pedestals. His fine linen sheets were embroidered with silk and the bed-hangings were made of red and white silk. The painted ceiling of the room, with its 110 gilded rosettes, had taken Andrea and his team 320 man-days to complete.

The staff in charge of Ippolito's apartments were the officials of his Chamber. Head of this department was Scipio Assassino, Ippolito's valet for the last eight years, who was now in charge of fourteen men and boys. The men of the Chamber were Ippolito's public face. The valets, footmen and pages were an essential part of his escort on official occasions. Dressed in outfits made by the Wardrobe, in various combinations of his personal colours (orange, white and red), they accompanied him to mass in Ferrara cathedral on major feast days, to the gates of the city to greet important visitors or to dine in state at the ducal castle. The footmen were in control of access to Ippolito's private rooms, escorting visitors to their master's presence (and making expedient excuses to those he did not wish to see). It was Ippolito d'Argenta's job to hand out alms, while more personal presents were delivered by the valet, Alessandro Rossetto.

These men were also in charge of Ippolito's private and personal life. Ippolito had to trust them with his most intimate habits, in the bedroom and in the bathroom – though any interesting secret or scandal would doubtless have been a topic of gossip throughout the palace. It is not surprising to find that Assassino, Moiza and Zudio had all been with him since he was 16. Their names are interesting. Despite its connotations Assassino was an aristocratic surname, but Moiza and Zudio were both nicknames. Moiza was local dialect for Moses – perhaps the barber was elderly – and Zudio translated as Jew, though it is not clear whether this was a reference to his race, his personality or his facial features.

Assassino and the valets dressed and undressed Ippolito, woke him up in the morning and put him to bed at night, and ran his errands about town. Moiza the barber trimmed Ippolito's beard and perfumed it with citrus and jasmine oils. Zudio took charge of Ippolito's linen and washed his underwear and nightcaps. Most of the menial work was done by the footmen who cleaned the floors, tidied tables, lit the fires, filled the copper warming-pans with hot charcoal, replaced the burnt-out candles in the silver candlesticks, heated his bath water in a huge copper, changed his bedding and emptied his bedpans. Two of the three pages attached to the household were Ferrarese, but the third was a Mantuan noble, Diomede Tridapalle, who remained with Ippolito for the rest of his life, ending up as Master of the Wardrobe. It was the job of one of the servants, Jacomo da Parma, to look after the pages. He did their washing, bought soap, shoelaces and other necessary supplies, and ensured their heads were washed every fortnight to keep the nits at bay.

~

Ippolito led an incredibly busy life in Ferrara, though not, at this stage, a particularly productive one. He was exactly the kind of rich secular cleric who goaded reformers to condemn decadence and idleness in the Church. Ippolito had not been to Milan since his appointment as the city's archbishop, though there were political reasons for this. Nor is there any evidence to suggest that his religious duties went beyond the conventional behaviour expected of a layman of his background. The fact that he had three chaplains tells us more about his position in society than his piety. Indeed reading the account books and letters, it is often difficult to remember that he was an archbishop. Once his official duties were done, and they were minimal, he devoted himself wholeheartedly to the pursuit of pleasure.

In February 1535 he went off to Bologna for the Carnival celebrations as the guest of a friend, Ridolfo Campeggio. Ridolfo was the son of Cardinal Lorenzo Campeggio, a devout lawyer and a reformist who had taken religious vows after the death of his wife and who owed his red hat mainly to his legal talents. One has to wonder what he made of Ippolito. Ippolito was initially rather scornful about the quality of entertainment on offer in Bologna, complaining to Ercole that there were no grand jousting tournaments or masked balls. He had a decided view of his own standing in society and Bologna was not an aristocratic court (it was ruled by a papal governor). But his mood improved as the celebrations reached their crescendo. There were parties every night and, though they may have lacked the courtly flair to which he was accustomed, they did not lack female charm. The last night of Carnival culminated in an all-night party hosted by Ridolfo, where, as he happily anticipated in a letter to his brother earlier in the day, 'there will be a great quantity of the ladies of the city'.

~

By May Ippolito felt jaded and went to Reggio, an area still famous for its mineral springs, to take the waters. Even there, pleasure came first. It took him a week to start the cure. First he complained it was raining too heavily and then that he was unable to refuse an invitation from Ercole's governor in Reggio to attend his wedding. He finally

started the health regime two days later but had to stop almost immediately because of the moon (it is not clear from his letter which particular phase of that heavenly body was interfering with the cure).
Two weeks later he was well enough to go hunting and set off with
his courtiers up into the Apennines outside Reggio to stay with
another friend, Count Giulio Boiardo, whose estate at Scandiano
was part of the Este duchy. The first evening they went out with their
sparrowhawks and caught several pheasant. The next day, while they
were messing around after lunch, Tomaso del Vecchio, one of
Ippolito's gentlemen, managed to fall off his horse and break his leg
so badly that the shin bone protruded through the flesh.

Ippolito indulged in all the sports, physical and sedentary, available to a young aristocrat in sixteenth-century Europe. Amongst the
furniture in his apartments was a chess set, a *zarabotana* board (a game
of chance, played with dice) and a bag for his gambling money,
which, as Fiorini noted in the inventory in October 1535, contained
75 scudi. Like the rest of his family he was a keen musician. He
owned two clavichords and there were eighteen song books in his
library. His household included a musician, Francesco dalla Viola,
who was the brother of Alfonso, the master of Ercole's music. The
importance the Este attached to music was reflected in Francesco's
handsome salary of 46 scudi a year, more than Ippolito's valets or
even the Master of the Stables. Ippolito was also a keen card-player
and a successful gambler, but his preference seems to have been for
more physical sports. He played a lot of real tennis, wagering bets on
the outcome of the matches. Above all, he hunted and jousted. The
list of his weapons and armour covers more than three pages of the
inventory. He owned over fifty assorted spears, lances, swords, axes
and daggers. Many of the swords had Spanish blades imported from
Toledo and were topped with elaborate silver hilts made in Ferrara.
There were also more exotic weapons such as a catapult, a crossbow
and a scimitar, but no gun (a weapon of war not sport). Then there
were caparisons for his horses, as well as iron neck-pieces, shin-pads,
spurs, elaborately gilded and decorated shields and several complete

sets of armour, one of which was specified as battle armour, complete with steel gauntlets.

Hunting and hawking were perhaps Ippolito's greatest passions. Many of the weapons listed in the inventory were spears for hunting boar and deer. This sport required special clothes and equipment. Ippolito owned leather jerkins and coats split up the back for riding, six hunting horns, one of which was described as English, several game bags, silver and gilded brass collars for his dogs, and sets of jesses, leashes, bewits, bells and hoods which he bought in Milan for his falcons. Both the dogs and the falcons were kept at Belfiore, where he employed two kennelmen and five falconers, all of whom were given thick black fustian jackets, rough white shirts, stockings and leather boots as part of their salaries. Ippolito owned boarhounds, pointers and greyhounds, dogs that were highly prized. Since most of them were acquired as presents, it is difficult to guess how much they cost, but they were comparatively cheap to feed: they ate sheep's heads on occasion but mainly slops thickened with the sweepings of husks collected in the granaries.

Hawking was a more expensive hobby. Ippolito owned sparrow-hawks, goshawks, lannarets, sakers and especially peregrines. They were expensive both to buy and to keep. Sparrowhawks cost 1 to 2 scudi each, but a peregrine falcon could cost as much as 10 scudi, the price of two ordinary horses. Fiorini's ledgers contain payments for herons and bitterns, used to train the birds, and medicines to treat their numerous ailments, especially powdered orpiment (arsenic trisulphide) to get rid of lice. They were fed on raw meat, at 25 *soldi* (0.36 scudi) each a month, exactly the same rate as Ippolito paid members of his household for their food expenses – the men were not undernourished, it was the hawks who were expensively fed.

~

The principal pleasures of the rich in sixteenth-century Europe were taken at the table. Dining and its associated entertainments were an

Post	Salary	No.	Names
Major-domo	0	1	Alfonso Cestarello
Chief steward	62	1	Girolamo Guarniero
Purveyor	34	1	Zoane da Cremona
Squire	31	3	Vicino, Ascanio Peri, and 1 other
Carver	27	1	Alfonso Compagno
Larderer	17	1	Carlo del Pavone
Cellarer	17	1	Marcantonio Testino
Official for wood	n/a	1	Alfonso da Reggio
Official for flour	n/a	1	Francesco Salineo
Table-decker	14	1	Arcangelo
Credenziero	14	2	Zebelino, Gasparino
Sommelier	14	1	Priete
General servant	14	1	Antonio da Como
Assistant to credenza	8	1	Iseppo
Chief cook	24	1	Andrea
Under-cook	14	1	Turco
Under-cook	9	1	Piero
Servant	4	2	Francesco Guberti and 1 other

The Officials of the Mouth

essential part of the culture of the Renaissance. Nearly half of Ippolito's staff were directly concerned with food and drink, and were known, in the quaint terminology of Ferrara, as the Officials of the Mouth (*Offitii della Bocca*).

The basic running of the Palazzo San Francesco was in the hands of Alfonso Cestarello, the major-domo, who did not receive a salary but who was rewarded with benefices. It was his job to ensure that the palace was adequately stocked with essentials such as wine, firewood, candles and brooms as well as non-perishable foodstuffs. The firewood was kept in a storehouse which Cestarello had rented in April

1535 (for 6 scudi a year) in the narrow alley between the palace and the church of San Francesco, and it had been stocked during the summer with large quantities of wood from Ippolito's estates. It was Cestarello's job to draw up contracts with butchers, poulterers and fishmongers for regular supplies of meat and fish. He was also responsible for the stocks of live poultry, which were fattened in coops near the kitchen. He had a new chicken coop built, which must have been quite a substantial construction because during October and early November it was stocked with 149 birds (63 capons and 86 pullets). Most of the pullets came from Cestarello's own estates, and he charged Ippolito the market price for them.

Cestarello also supervised the stocking of the wine cellar, which was furnished with new tubs for pressing grapes, barrels for wine and vinegar, handcarts for moving the heavy containers, trestles for stacking the barrels, locks for the cellar door and, of course, wine. Ippolito himself drank fine wine, much of which was imported. He was particularly fond of *malvasia* (malmsey), a strong sweet wine which he bought in Venice. Cheaper wine for the household came from Ippolito's estates, and once again Cestarello took the opportunity to sell Ippolito several barrels of his own. Wine had a variety of uses. Not only was it the basic drink at all levels of the household (there was no tea or coffee, and the water was dangerously full of germs), but it was also used in the stables to wash down the horses and mules.

Easily the most expensive item on Cestarello's shopping list for the palace was oil. He commissioned two huge new stone vats (at 2 scudi each) for the larder – six porters were needed to carry them from the stone-cutter's workshop to the palace. These vats were filled with high-quality oil from the Marche and Puglia, bought by Cestarello from local apothecaries: a total of 4,800 kilos, surprisingly measured by weight, at a cost of 182 scudi.

The larder (*dispensa*) and its stock of non-perishable goods were under the care of Carlo del Pavone, the new larderer (*dispensiero*). These goods were regularly inventoried to avoid theft. Carlo counted or weighed goods as they came in and went out, using a set of scales which was checked annually, and then entered the details in his ledger. Cestarello inspected the ledger weekly. The larder must have been a haven for the hoarder, and it was filled with pungent odours. Most of the spices were bought in Venice, where saffron, ginger, nutmeg, mace, pepper, cinnamon and cloves were all easily available, at a price. The loaves of Madeira sugar and white beeswax candles also came from Venice, but the rancid tallow candles and torches, made from rendered animal fat, were supplied by local tradesmen, as were the blocks of lard, jars of almonds, raisins and other dried fruit, and pasta. The bulk of the stores came from Ippolito's estates: honey, lentils, beans and other pulses from his farms, and cheese sent as part of his dues from Milan. The hams and salamis that hung from hooks in the ceiling were all made from his own pigs. It was normally Cestarello's job to supervise the making of these but he must have been busy elsewhere in January 1535, because Tomaso Mosto was put in charge of this annual event. Mosto organized the killing of over fifty pigs and bought the other necessary materials: salt to treat the meat, intestines to case the salamis, string to bind them and pepper and powdered cloves to spice them. The meat and the materials were all transported to the house of Laura Dianti, Ippolito's stepmother, who supervised the work: she sent 82 hams to the larder in February and 209 salamis in April.

The man responsible for dining in the palace was Girolamo Guarniero, the chief steward. He was in charge of the preparation and presentation of all Ippolito's meals. He had to organize the menus for lunch and dinner each day, and the banquets if there were guests. He planned the cooked dishes with Andrea and Turco in the kitchen, the salads with the *credenzieri*, Gasparino and Zebelino, and the wines with Priete (these last two were nicknames: did Zebelino resemble a little marten or Priete a priest?). Guarniero then ordered the necessary staples from the palace stores, Cestarello's department, and gave a shopping list of fresh ingredients to Zoane da Cremona, the *spenditore*, or purveyor. (Zoane was Ferrarese dialect for Giovanni.)

Neither Guarniero nor Cestarello did any shopping themselves, but Zoane went out most days, including Sundays and holidays, to buy the stores needed by Cestarello. In addition he purchased all the perishable goods for Guarniero to give to the cooks and *credenzieri* for that day's meals, inspecting the greengrocers' shops for salad, fruit and vegetables, and combing the market stalls for seasonal produce, such as pheasant, partridge and the other little game birds of which Ippolito was particularly fond. He also bought extra items of meat and fish, especially delicacies such as oysters and eels which were not supplied on contract. His job was a responsible one. Like Panizato at the stables, he was regularly given large sums of cash – 50 to 100 scudi, two or three times a week – and he had to account for every penny, recording each item he bought in his ledger, which was regularly checked by Guarniero.

Guarniero had been busy throughout 1535 stocking the various sections of his department, in particular the kitchen. The room had been completely refurbished by the builders, who had rebuilt the well, retiled the floor and installed two new windows, their panes covered with cloth. Ippolito's chief cook was Andrea. Like Andrea the painter, he was simply described as Andrea the cook (*Andrea cuogo*) in the ledgers. He had trained in the ducal kitchens, working as an under-cook for Duke Alfonso, and he received a modest golden hello of 4½ scudi in February 1535 from Ippolito. He seems to have lived at home with his wife Catelina and their children because the family received allowances of firewood, candles and wheat in addition to his salary of 24 scudi – it is a mark of the importance Ippolito attached to his food that he paid his chief cook nearly the same salary as the much more public post of carver. The same month Guarniero sanctioned Andrea's order for forty-two items of kitchen equipment from a merchant who sold copperware on the Via Grande in Ferrara. The goods, which came to 21 scudi, were mostly copper and iron saucepans, but they also included three steel frying-pans. Either the price or the quality, or both, must have shocked Guarniero, because a week later Fiorini was sent to Venice to buy the

Kitchen interior

rest of the equipment needed. He returned with glasses and wine jugs for Priete, two large candlesticks for the *credenza* and another ninety-eight items for the kitchen (which only cost 30 scudi) – more saucepans, large copper cauldrons for boiling water, copper mixing

Sixteenth-century cooking pots

bowls and others for skimming cream from the top of the milk, copper baking tins, iron ladles for soups, iron graters to grate sugar from the loaf and glazed terracotta pots for stewing, as well as iron pot chains, trivets and meat spits. One of the chaplains, who had business in Verona, returned with fire bricks for the palace fireplaces and two pestles and mortars, made of the red marble for which Verona was famous (the same red marble that decorates the façade of the Doge's Palace in Venice). A surprising gap in the shopping list was kitchen knives: one of Andrea's jobs, for which Ippolito reimbursed him, was sharpening these knives, but it is likely that the cook provided them himself as the tools of his trade.

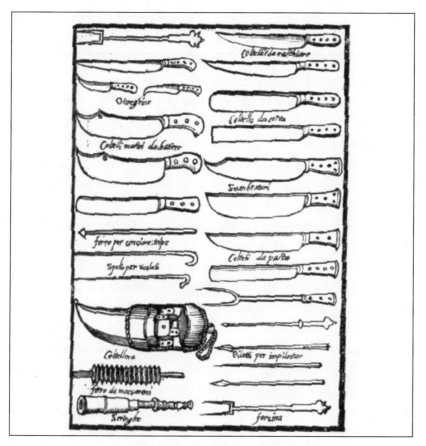

Sixteenth-century kitchen knives

Ippolito and his household ate three times a day. Breakfast was little more than a snack. The footmen just had bread and wine, though Ippolito himself ate something slightly more substantial when he got up in the morning. The two main meals of the day were lunch, eaten at midday, and dinner, eaten in the late afternoon or early evening. The basic diet of the entire household was good, and those from the lower levels of society almost certainly ate better than they would have done at home. There were large quantities of meat and fish, as well as fruit and vegetables. The daily food allowance Ippolito paid to the top members of his household was based on 460 grammes of meat or fish a day. The courtiers had veal, while their servants and less important members of the household ate only cheap beef, but they all had fish on fast days. The number of lean days varied from eight to twelve days a month, and of course the whole of Lent was lean. Above all there was bread. One academic has estimated that an average of 1 kilo of bread per person per day was eaten in the palaces of the rich. Ippolito supplied some of his household with monthly allowances of wheat, enough to make an 800-gramme loaf of bread every day – the same weight as a modern sliced loaf. These quantities of bread must have helped to mop up the 2 litres of wine they each drank every day.

With the exception of Ippolito, who dined at his own table, and the stable boys, who made their own eating arrangements, the house-hold all ate together in the staff dining-room (*tinello*). This was a big room near the kitchen with three large cloth windows and a fireplace. At the ducal palace the gentlemen and senior valets ate in their own dining-room, but there is no mention at this stage of a separate room for them in Ippolito's ledgers. However, the *tinello* was divided into two by a brick screen, and it seems likely that the grander staff did have an element of privacy from the rest of the household. The fur-nishings were serviceable. On his trip to Venice Fiorini had bought eighteen brass candlesticks for the room, cheap plain glasses and pewter plates, bowls and wine jugs. Another feature of the room, specially commissioned by Fiorini, was a purpose-built urinal set, which consisted of an iron stand holding a copper basin for hand-washing and a copper pail below. It was the job of Arcangelo, the table-decker, to lay the tables in the staff dining-room, using plain white tablecloths and napkins which he got from the wardrobe, all of which were duly detailed in the wardrobe ledgers. He was also responsible for clearing the tables, tidying the room afterwards and, presumably, for emptying the basin and urinal.

Ippolito's table was, inevitably, far more grandly furnished. He dined with his guests, male and or female, using crystal glasses, which cost as much as four times those in the staff dining-room (Fiorini had bought these glasses in Murano, and many were gilded).

His candlesticks were silver, and so were his plates. His tablecloths and napkins, also supplied by the wardrobe, were made of fine linen. His pages brought round bowls of scented water for him and his guests to wash their hands – no urinal set for them – his meals were served by Vicino and the other squires, and his meat was carved by Alfonso, his professional carver. Guarniero worked hard to create an atmosphere of gracious living. It was his responsibility to ensure that the tables were laid to perfection, that Priete was serving the correct wines and that he had washed the glasses properly. Guarniero also had to ensure that the *credenza* looked suitably impressive. In addition to preparing the salads and other cold dishes, Zebelino and Gasparino had to decorate the *credenza*, using the silver left to Ippolito by his father and freshly laundered tablecloths and napkins, which they collected from Mosto, and signed for in the wardrobe ledgers.

It is difficult to tell exactly what Ippolito and his guests ate in the Palazzo San Francesco during the winter of 1535/6 because Zoane da Cremona's ledgers are missing. However, Messisbugo's treatise on banquets includes a lot of recipes which give some idea of Ippolito's diet. Lunch and dinner usually consisted of four courses: a first course of fashionable salads, followed by two courses of meat or fish (depending on whether the day was fat or lean) and a dessert of sweet dishes, jellies, fruit and cheese. Meat and fish could be boiled, roasted, fried or grilled, and either served plain or with an accompaniment. Messisbugo gives recipes for grilled bream with parsley and chives, fried sardines with oranges and sugar, and roast veal with morello cherry sauce. Many of the recipes are surprisingly familiar – though more highly spiced and richer than we might choose – such as one for an apple and onion sauce, flavoured with ginger and nutmeg, another for fresh egg pasta stuffed with meat or, more exotically, with pine nuts, raisins and spices, and a dessert recipe for a ricotta cheese tart filled with pears, apples, quinces or medlars. In keeping with the fashionable interest in peasant fare, some recipes were austerely plain. A 'thin English soup' was made with scraped parsley roots and ginger, thickened with egg yolks beaten with a little vinegar, and poured over toast.

Another soup was actually called a peasant dish (though it is difficult to imagine a peasant being able to afford it). It was made of chopped roasted hazelnuts boiled in meat stock with a piece of beef fat, flavoured with sugar, cinnamon, pepper, cloves and saffron, and served cold (a Lenten version was boiled in stock made from pike).

The international ambitions of the Ferrarese court were evident in recipes for French and English sauces. The French sauce (which Messisbugo particularly recommended for boiled or roast capon) was made simply by adding orange juice to the pan juices and flavouring the sauce with sugar and cinnamon. The sauce he called English, which he thought would suit boiled sturgeon or veal, was the same as the French version, but with the addition of pepper, a few cloves and a little mashed ginger root, with fresh fennel seeds sprinkled over the finished dish. He also described an Italian sauce which was made by mashing a cooked calf's kidney with two or three egg yolks, flavoured with spices and salt. The presentation of food and the importance of appealing to the eyes as well as the stomach were constant themes. Messisbugo's recipe for boiled eels – a much-prized speciality of Ferrara – served with a spiced sauce included the advice that it should be poured over the eels in a window-pane pattern.

Ippolito's first major banquet at the Palazzo San Francesco was held on Saturday, 5 February 1536, in honour of his aunt, the 61-year-old Isabella d'Este, who was on a visit to Ferrara. The guests included Ercole and Renée, and his other brother, Francesco. During the afternoon there was jousting in the street in front of the palace, which was covered with twelve carts of sand (at a cost of 10 scudi). Inside the palace the Great Hall was lavishly decorated for the feast. Three carpenters spent a whole day hanging the chandeliers – Ippolito borrowed fourteen from one of Ercole's courtiers, as well as 350 wicks (bundles of greased rags) to light them. They also erected a wooden frame which was hung with greenery. Two painters spent four days painting and gilding the paper decorations which hung from the chandeliers together with the coats-of-arms of all the principal guests – Ercole, Renée, Francesco and Isabella. Even the candles were painted in dark red and orange, Ippolito's own colours. Without the details of Zoane da Cremona's account book, it is difficult to work out exactly what food the purveyor bought for the banquet but it was certainly expensive. His advances, recorded by Fiorini, doubled from an average of 37 scudi a week to 69 scudi during the week of the banquet. Fiorini also entered a payment of 5 scudi for sugared almonds and another of 34 scudi to cover the cost of pheasant, partridge and truffles supplied for the party.

~

Ippolito and his household were destined to spend only another month enjoying the luxury of the Palazzo San Francesco. In the summer of 1535 Ippolito had received a formal invitation from Francis I inviting him to join the French court, and the King had given him a lucrative benefice as a sign of his favour. However, there seemed to be no urgent need to fix a date for his departure. Besides, Ercole wanted his brother in Ferrara that autumn while he was absent in Rome and Naples, trying to resolve various political issues with Pope Paul III and Emperor Charles V.

On 1 November the situation changed dramatically when the Duke of Milan died without an heir. Charles V adroitly moved his armies into the duchy and claimed the title. Francis I responded immediately by provocatively invading Savoy. The uneasy peace that had existed in Italy for the last six years was now threatened. Duke Ercole, keeping his options open, decided to send Ippolito to France, and their younger brother Francesco to the imperial court. Despite the season Ippolito must leave immediately.

Shortly before his departure, Ippolito held another, more intimate, dinner party. Once again, we know nothing about the menu, though the shopping list included a whole calf, ten chickens, sixteen pigeons, six ducks, spices, cheese, oranges, lemons, pears, raisins and white bread. However, the guest list was intriguing. The guest of honour was a lady named Violante Lampugnano. She was probably

the daughter of Pietro Lampugnano, a Milanese noble who had
been Lucretia Borgia's steward, and she may well have been a friend
of Ippolito's since childhood. She was certainly a regular guest at his
banquets and she was probably also his mistress, a rumour widely
reported by the diarists of Ferrara. Even more intriguingly, the
scandalmongers suggested that Violante bore Ippolito a daughter.

The child certainly existed. She was named Renea after Ippolito's
sister-in-law, brought up in Ferrara and educated in Bologna under
the guidance of the wife of Ridolfo Campeggio. In 1553 she was
married to Ludovico della Mirandola, with a trousseau of clothes
and jewels worth over 3,000 scudi supplied by Ippolito. In 1554
Renea gave birth to a daughter named Ippolita, an unmistakable
token of her affection for her father. She died the following year of
quinsy. But when was Renea conceived? Assuming Violante was
indeed the mother, the options are limited. After his departure for
France Ippolito did not return to Ferrara until the summer of 1539
and then only stayed for two months. If Renea was conceived during
that brief period, she would have been only 13 when she married,
young by the standards of Este princesses who did not usually marry
until they were 16 or 17. It seems more likely that Renea was conceived some time in 1535 or early 1536 and that when Ippolito set off
for France a week or so after the dinner, he left behind either a baby
daughter or a pregnant mistress.

3

On the Road

IPPOLITO LEFT FERRARA for France on the morning of Monday, 13 March 1536, saying a formal farewell to his brother in the main square in front of the ducal palace. Ahead of him lay the long journey to Lyon, from where Francis I was masterminding the invasion of Savoy. Neither Ippolito nor his entourage of 116 men knew how long it would be before they would return. As their horses clattered down the narrow streets, through the city gates and out into the countryside, one wonders how they viewed the journey ahead. The younger members of the party might have looked forward to a month in the saddle but the older men must have viewed the prospect of stiff and aching joints with understandable apprehension. The stable boys and muleteers were about to make the entire journey on foot. Few of the men had been beyond the borders of the duchy. Even Ippolito had never travelled out of northern Italy, and none of them had ever crossed the Alps. They would also have to pass through the duchy of Milan, currently in imperial hands. They were unsure of what sort of reception they would receive, particularly in light of the recent news that Francis I's armies had invaded Savoy and were poised to take Turin, an action deliberately designed to provoke Charles V into war.

Ippolito was taking most of his household proper with him to France: fifty-two out of a total of seventy-two. All the gentlemen were leaving, as well as his secretary Antonio Romei, his musician Francesco della Viola, and his Master of the Wardrobe Tomaso

Mosto, together with his two assistants. Scipio Assassino and all the Chamber staff were in the party, including the three young pages. One of the footmen, Cavreto, was leaving his wife behind with their baby daughter, who had been born a few days earlier – Ippolito gave her a present of 3 scudi. Most of the stables' staff were travelling: Pierantonio, the chief trainer, Jacomo Panizato, who looked after the stables' expenses, the saddler, the farrier and twenty-three stable boys and muleteers (two assistants were left behind to look after Ippolito's carthorses and brood mares). There were also three of the falconers with their cages of falcons, though Ippolito decided to leave his dogs behind, perhaps unsure of how they would look in France, though they joined him later that year. Girolamo Guarniero was taking all the dining staff: Alfonso the carver, Priete the sommelier, Andrea and the other cooks, the two *credenzieri*, Zebelino and Gasparino, and their assistants. Alfonso Cestarello was coming too, but his staff were staying behind to look after the stores at the Palazzo San Francesco, under the watchful eye of Jacomo Filippo Fiorini, Ippolito's factor. Zoane da Cremona was also travelling, with his ledger carefully stowed away in his pocket. It is this ledger, a thin notebook the size of a green Michelin guide, which reveals so much about the process of travelling in sixteenth-century Europe.

Nearly half the men waiting outside the ducal castle were not members of Ippolito's household but their servants. His gentlemen were travelling with three servants each, Romei and Assassino had two, and Guarniero had four, while the two chaplains shared one. The other ten belonged to Zoane da Cremona, Francesco dalla Viola, Pierantonio, the two valets, the doctor, the three squires and the carver. It was a sign of Ippolito's rank in society that even his valets and squires were grand enough to have their own servants.

Most of the men were young and single, and some of the older ones had opted for Church careers rather than marriage. There were no women in the party, though there must have been plenty of broken hearts left behind in Ferrara that day. Ippolito made no special arrangements with Fiorini for the care of girlfriends or mistresses of his staff while he was away (nor for Violante), but he did do so for the few of his men who had wives. Catelina, the wife of Andrea the cook, was to receive half her husband's salary every month (12 scudi a year), as well as an allowance for food, enough to buy 460 grammes of meat a day (worth over 4 scudi a year), and regular handouts of candles, wheat and firewood. The arrangements made for Pierant-onio's wife, also called Catelina, were more generous. In addition to half of her husband's salary (17 scudi), she was also to get a month-ly allowance of wheat, and Ippolito paid the rent on a house for the family (5 scudi). Onesta, the wife of Besian the falconer, received none of her husband's income, but Ippolito rented a house for her (7 scudi a year) and arranged for Fiorini to give her regular supplies of wheat. He also bought a house costing 20 scudi for the family of Zudio, his faithful personal servant. Much the saddest tale is that of Bagnolo, the head stable boy, who had been with Ippolito since 1531. He seems to have lost his wife in childbirth, and their baby son, judi-ciously named Ippolito, was left in Ferrara with Bagnolo's brother-in-law. Fiorini paid him 3 scudi a year, a sum not deducted from Bagnolo's wages, to cover the extra costs of caring for the child, as well as supplying him with flour and wheat.

~

The start of the journey must have been a welcome relief for the household. Ippolito had no concept of travelling light (though it should be said in his defence that he was effectively emigrating, not just going on holiday), and they had spent two exhausting months preparing for the trip. Twenty-three pack mules and three horses laden with luggage followed the horsemen out through the city gates.

The first piece of evidence in Fiorini's ledgers to indicate that the date of Ippolito's departure had been set came on 21 January when Pierantonio started to buy mules. A week later he sent Vicino to Pesaro, who returned with two more (costing 109 scudi) and a mule-teer. Other mules and muleteers were generously lent by Ercole II from the ducal stables, and Pierantonio had to negotiate the choice of these with his counterpart at the castle. He also had to find mounts for all the household. In late February he spent 188 scudi on thirty-seven horses. At an average price of 5 scudi per horse, these were not thoroughbreds but ordinary hacks, and Ercole the saddler spent much of January and February making saddles and harnesses for them.

There was also the luggage itself. There was no question of simply buying a number of identical tea chests or ready-made suitcases: everything had to be custom-made. The basic boxes were constructed in wood by local carpenters and delivered to the stables, where Ercole the saddler covered them in leather. Fiorini bought eight cowskins, dyed red, black or green, for this purpose, as well as 4 kilos of fat to grease them. Many of the boxes had to be reinforced with iron bands and secured with heavy locks. Ippolito already had his own gilded vanity cases, which Zudio filled with soap, powder and perfumes, but most of the luggage was new. There were small cases for Moiza the barber to pack his oils and shaving equipment, boxes for Jacomo to pack clothes for the pages, two large crates for Zebelino to fill with the *credenza* silver and another pair in which Priete packed Ippolito's gilded crystal glasses. Andrea the cook was allocated one mule for all the kitchen equipment. Most of the crates were made to transport the linen, furnishings and clothes in Ippolito's wardrobe. Ercole covered special flat cases to hold the tapestries, and quantities of crates for all the furnishings, table linen, bed linen and jewels Ippolito wanted to take to France. Mosto ordered black velvet bags for Ippolito's prayer books and four more small boxes to hold Ippolito's communion set (the cross, two candlesticks and the calyx). These were too delicate for Ercole the saddler to cover, so they were given to a scabbard-maker in Ferrara who also lined them. Finally, Mosto commissioned a large strong box, heavily reinforced with iron bands and secured with padlocks, to carry all the money and valuables. Ippolito took a credit note for 2,000 scudi from Renée, which he could cash with his sister-in-law's bankers in Lyon, and over 3,000 scudi in cash for the journey.

The prospect of life at the French royal court provoked a veritable orgy of shopping. Ippolito bought twelve jewelled rosaries as presents for the ladies at court, a suit of armour and an expensive sword with a gilded black hilt. He spent 21 scudi on two Flemish tapestries and bought several new chairs, rather grandly upholstered in black velvet ornamented with gold studs. He also ordered a lot of silver to enhance the glamour of his dinner parties: three gilded salt cellars and three silver candelabra with ten branches each, for the table, and twelve spoons and twenty-four plates to add to his father's silver on the *credenza*. Mosto commissioned these items on Ippolito's behalf from two silversmiths in Ferrara, giving them 4,636 silver coins, worth 441 scudi, to melt down to make the items, together with 3 gold coins to use for gilding the salts. The contracts he drew up with the silversmiths were very precise, specifying the exact amount of silver to be used for each item, and the fee that the silversmiths would be paid for manufacturing the goods. The spoons were the most expensive item per weight, suggesting that they were highly decorated.

There were also more practical purchases. Mosto ordered three fine linen shirts for Ippolito, two of which were embroidered by Sister Serafina at San Gabriele. He paid hatters for several new hats, four of which were made in black English cloth, and bought 170 kilos of good-quality white soap from Venice (7 scudi). Dielai, Ippolito's shoemaker, put in a bill for 6 scudi for boots and shoes, including two new pairs of tennis shoes, which he would certainly need in France. Ippolito's superb four-poster bed was too large to transport, so he bought a smaller one, made of walnut, with two new mattresses and a lot of bed linen, while Mosto found a rather ornate set of hangings, costing 5 scudi, for the new bed, made of dark red satin with cords and fringes of gold and silver thread. Ippolito also took a large quantity of materials to France. Mosto ordered black velvet from Venice and silks from Florence, and also bought a large quantity of red silk thread in Ferrara. They must have been busy in the wardrobe that day as this was collected from the haberdasher's not by Mosto's assistant but by one of the stable boys. Finally, the day

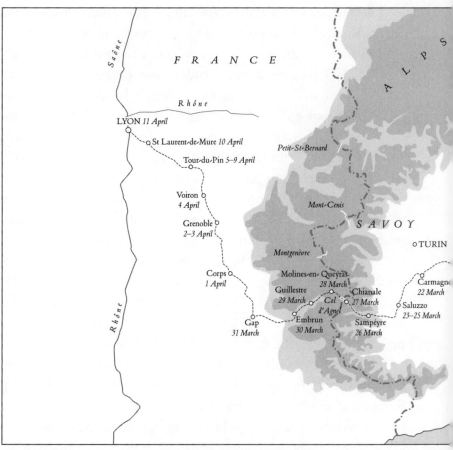

Ippolito's journey from Ferrara to Lyon in March 1536

before they left, Mosto paid all the bills he had run up with Ippolito's regular suppliers since the beginning of the year, a total of 226 scudi.

~

The journey to France was not particularly long by the standards of the time. Ferrara to Lyon was 720 kilometres, whereas Rome to Paris was twice the distance. By our standards, however, it was a journey of epic proportions. Now one can do the journey in under an hour by aeroplane, or in six hours by car. Ippolito and his men did the whole trip on horseback, while the stable boys walked the distance, and it

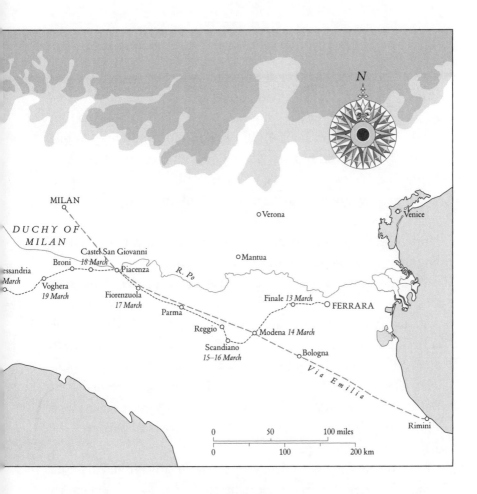

took them a month. It was possible to travel more quickly in sixteenth-century Europe. Those on important missions did the journey in as little as six days, averaging 110 to 120 kilometres a day, though travelling at this speed required frequent changes of horses, and a lot of money to pay for them. Really important letters were sent along a chain of couriers and could take as little as two or three days. Ippolito's business was less urgent, and he was travelling with mules, which only walked at 5 or 6 kilometres an hour.

In fact the first week was astonishingly relaxed. One gets the feeling that Ippolito, understandably, was suddenly reluctant to leave familiar surroundings and embark on a journey that would mark the start of a new phase in his life. The party took two days to cover the 75 kilometres to Modena and spent Tuesday night with Ercole's governor in the city. That evening Ippolito wrote to his brother complaining that he had had a splitting headache – the 'hammer', as he called it – ever since leaving Ferrara. However, it did not stop him accepting an invitation from Giulio Boiardo to go hunting. While the rest of the household travelled the short distance to Reggio, Ippolito and his courtiers rode off into the hills for two nights at Scandiano – luckily there were no mishaps like the year before when Tomaso del Vecchio had broken his leg.

Ippolito left Scandiano on the morning of Friday, 17 March, riding the 11 kilometres down to Reggio, where he joined the Via Emilia. Some time that morning he crossed the border of the Este duchy into the more lawless world of the Papal States, and the journey started in earnest. The party rode 64 kilometres that day up the Via Emilia, avoiding Parma, where riots had made the city unsafe, to Fiorenzuola, where they joined the rest of the household. The following day they left the Via Emilia at Piacenza and headed west towards Turin, 280 kilometres away. There they planned to rest for a couple of days before tackling what would be the hardest part of the journey, crossing the Alps.

The daily routine on the road is easy to reconstruct from Zoane da Cremona's ledger. The party normally covered 30 to 40 kilometres a day, riding in three different groups. Pierantonio left soon after dawn with the stable boys and muleteers leading the baggage horses, the mules and the spare horses. Walking along the road at 4 to 6 kilometres an hour, with stops for lunch and other necessities, it took them eight hours or so to complete each leg of the journey. The men on horseback could cover the same distance in half the time, providing the road was good. Vicino also left early, with one of the other squires and their two servants, to ride ahead to the next town to announce the party's arrival. Their principal task was to arrange accommodation for the men, horses and mules for the coming night. Ippolito had a leisurely breakfast (while his staff bought last-minute necessities in the local shops and packed his possessions) and then rode with the rest of the household for two hours or so before stop-ping for lunch at an inn. For most of the party the ride was the relax-ing part of the day. None of them had any work to do, a marked change from life in the Palazzo San Francesco. They could bask in the prestige of travelling in the party of an important man, chat with their friends, marvel at the changing landscape or look at the people they passed on the road: parties of rich merchants, bands of itinerant jugglers, musicians and other entertainers, couriers galloping south with urgent letters for Rome and soldiers travelling north to the war.

Late in the afternoon Ippolito's party met up with Vicino, Pierantonio and the stable boys in order to make their entry into the town where they were to spend the night. These were not grand occasions like the formal entries staged for the arrival of spouses or important guests, but Ippolito was officially received, with decorum by civic functionaries and with loud ceremony by the town's trum-peters, pipers and drummers. There were formalities to observe. Ippolito had to tip the gate-keepers, armed guards and musicians, who often received as much as 1 scudo each (the equivalent of a month's salary for the footmen, over two months' pay for a stable boy). Enterprising townspeople seized the opportunity to make a quick scudo. Ippolito would tip itinerant musicians, boys and girls who danced for him, buffoons who amused him, and even those who gave him presents of wine and food. The poor begging on the street also benefited. Generosity was expected of a man in Ippolito's position, and he gave orders to his footman to dispense coins to the crippled, the poor, the old and the infirm. In Italy Ippolito was par-ticularly fond of destitute French soldiers, though in France he favoured Italians. The tradesmen also stood to profit from the arrival of the party. Zoane da Cremona bought large quantities of food most evenings from the butchers and greengrocers in the town. Far-riers would have horses to shoe, saddlers would be given harnesses to mend, and laundresses often had unexpected loads of linen to wash and starch that night. Women must also have been in demand for other reasons – it is difficult to imagine that all 117 men stayed celibate for the entire month, and there are several tips in Zoane's ledger to unspecified females.

Above all, it was the innkeepers in the town who stood to make the most substantial profits from 117 hungry men and their animals. The party was too large to be accommodated in any single inn and might be lodged in as many as six different establishments, divided up according to rank, with Ippolito and his gentlemen in the best hotel. Negotiating prices with innkeepers in an unfamiliar town must have been a logistical nightmare for Vicino and his fellow squire. The inns had reassuringly familiar names – The Three Kings, The Angel, The Crown – and equally reassuringly familiar ways of extracting cash from their customers. They charged a flat rate for dinner for each man (the price included their beds) and a separate rate for stabling each horse. The rates for the men varied according to the quality of the inn but the price of stabling was usually standard across town, whether for a thoroughbred horse, a hack or a mule. Innkeepers made their profits by charging extra for essential items. The cost of stabling did not include fodder, the cost of dinner included neither wine nor bread, and the cost of the beds did not cover firewood, candles or breakfast. Ippolito also had to pay to have his luggage guarded overnight, another essential service that varied widely in its cost.

The sleeping arrangements were considerably more cramped than at home for all levels of the household. Ippolito had to make do with only a bedroom and a private drawing-room, while his gentlemen had one room each. They had all brought their own mattresses and sheets from Ferrara, and their beds were made up by their own servants. The accommodation may have been uncomfortable by their usual standards but it was much worse for the rest of the household. Many were obliged to share rooms and often beds, probably flea-ridden and certainly dirty. Assassino had to share a room with the other two valets, Zoane da Cremona shared a bed with Gasparino, and other servants slept three to a bed.

The arrival in a town was the start of the evening's work for most of the household. In particular the stable boys and muleteers had a lot to do. Bagnolo bought cheap wine (usually from the innkeeper) which the stable boys used to wash down the animals to remove the grease and grime which had accumulated after a day on dusty or wet roads. They rubbed fat into sprained muscles and into the places where the leather harness straps had chafed. Bad sores might need one of Pierantonio's salves, and he would have to buy honey, turpentine and dragon's blood from the local apothecary. Pierantonio also had to check all the animals each evening, prescribing barley for overtired animals, and give orders to Panizato, who organized their fodder. He went out most days to get broken harnesses repaired or to buy new parts for the pack saddles, which were continually breaking under the weight of Ippolito's crates. It was a credit to the stables' staff, and particularly to Pierantonio, that they did not need to replace any of the horses or mules on the journey.

There was also a lot of work to do in the hotel where Ippolito was staying. Assassino and the Chamber staff had to look after their master, unpack their equipment, arrange his rooms and make his bed (and then repack everything the next morning). Zudio often had dirty washing to take to the local laundress. Even on the road Ippolito wore a clean white shirt every day and his sheets were changed regularly. The pages also changed their shirts (though not so frequently) and Jacomo da Parma had to ensure that their heads were regularly deloused.

For some members of staff the work load was markedly lighter than usual. With the wardrobe packed away in its chests, there was not much for Mosto and his assistants to do, which must have made a pleasant contrast to the weeks of hard work before they left. Nor, without a house to run, was there much for Cestarello to do. Ippolito himself had few official duties. He had letters to read and replies to write, or rather to dictate to Romei, his secretary. He was not a great letter-writer and could blame his laziness on the discomfort of travelling.

Ippolito's large and exuberant signature, a marked contrast to Romei's more businesslike script

Guarniero's job was also slightly easier than it had been at the Palazzo San Francesco, for he no longer had the household dining-room to consider. As in Ferrara, the stable boys and muleteers ate separately and were given a daily allowance for their food. Most of the rest of the staff ate in the communal dining-rooms of the taverns alongside other travellers. Innkeepers offered at least two set menus, a cheap one for the less well-off and a better one for merchants and other prosperous travellers, as well as an *à la carte* selection of dishes. The parties that ensued must have been lively because Ippolito was frequently charged for broken crockery and glasses. Ippolito himself ate upstairs in his rooms, together with some of his men. This meal was specially prepared by his own cooks and *credenza* staff under the supervision of Guarniero. Zoane was sent out to buy the necessary ingredients, while others were supplied (at a premium, of course) by the innkeeper. The dishes were then cooked in the hotel kitchens by Andrea the cook, and most innkeepers charged Ippolito extra for the wood Andrea used.

It is worth looking at the night they spent in Voghera, Sunday, 19 March, in detail. That afternoon Vicino had organized accommodation for 90 men, 23 mules and 96 horses. The stable boys and muleteers would sleep, as usual, with their charges in the stables. There were slightly fewer men in the inns that particular evening, because Alfonso Cestarello (with his three servants and their four horses) spent the night as a guest of Paolo Albertino, one of his close friends. Albertino was Ippolito's agent for the diocese of Milan and had escorted an unnamed ambassador and his entourage to Voghera, where they joined Ippolito's party for two days on the road, probably *en route* for Turin. Ippolito later reimbursed Albertino for the cost of their accommodation in Voghera.

The cost of stabling was uniform, but the price of dinners and beds varied. When Zoane settled the bills the next morning there were charges for morning feeds for all the animals, though only the landlords of The Hat and The Mountain billed him for extra candles and firewood. The innkeeper of The Hat was given a tip, but the landlord of The Cock, where Ippolito was lodged, was not. It is clear from Zoane's ledger (see overleaf) that Vicino and the two squires were staying at The Cock as well, and, although we do not know the identities of the other men, it is likely that they included Ippolito's senior courtiers. Guarniero organized dinner for the men at The Cock, which was prepared by Andrea and Zebelino in the hotel kitchens – the innkeeper charged the enormous sum of 60 *soldi* (just over ½ scudo) for the firewood used in the kitchen and bedrooms that night. The food cost an average of 27 *soldi* (¼ scudo) a head, substantially more than the set menus eaten by the other staff and servants. Zoane went out shopping soon after the party arrived in Voghera to buy the necessary meat, eggs and salad, while the rest of the ingredients were provided by the innkeeper.

What stands out from Zoane's shopping list and the innkeeper's

Hotel	Stabling	Price	Dinners	Price
The Crown	25 animals	@ 5 *soldi*	16	@ 10 *soldi*
The Cross	7 animals	@ 5s	7	@ 8s
The Sun	7 animals	@ 5s	7	@ 8s
The Hat	33 animals	@ 5s	7	@ 8s
The Moon	4 animals	@ 5s	15	4 @ 8s; 11 @ 10s
The Mountain	8 animals	@ 5s	13	@ 8s
The Cock	35 animals	@ 5s	(dinner for 25 cooked in hotel)	

currency: 110 *soldi* = 1 scudo

Voghera, 19 March

bill are the quantities of bread, wine and meat consumed. One won-ders just how big the jugs of wine were, because they drank almost four each. Meat was the largest item of expenditure and, although there was some poultry and a tiny amount of fish, veal was the main dish on the menu. This is surprising because it was still Lent. Ippo-lito certainly did not observe the fast as strictly on the road as at home. In fact a calf formed the basis of most of the meals Ippolito ate on the Italian leg of the journey. The animals were bought almost every day from local butchers by Zoane. The calf he purchased in Ferrara just before their departure on Monday, 13 March, had to be left behind because of a dispute over the price, and Ippolito had to make do with fish and lamb that first night. On Tuesday evening in Modena, Zoane bought two more calves, one of which was taken to Reggio in a specially hired cart, and he bought a third in Reggio on Wednes-day. The normal Friday fast was observed that week at Fiorenzuola where they ate fish, but Zoane was out shopping for the usual calf again on Sunday in Voghera, on Monday in Alessandria and on Tuesday in Asti. The calf Zoane bought in Alessandria was quite small and had to be augmented with some veal supplied by the innkeeper.

Ippolito, and others who liked it, ate salad every day, usually

---

Zoane's shopping list

1 calf, 1 liver and 2 tripe	210s	
20 eggs and salad leaves	5s 9d	
Total	215s 9d	1.96 scudi

Bill from the innkeeper of The Cock

96 jugs of wine	@ 2s each	192s	
144 bread rolls	@ 4s a dozen	48s	
4 capons	@ 15s each	60s	
4 hens	@ 10s each	40s	
10 pigeons	@ 5s each	50s	
2kg of pork fat	@ 6s a kg	12s	
3kg of tallow candles	@ 8s a kg	24s	
1kg of small fish	@ 20s a kg	20s	
2kg of oil	@ 6s a kg	12s	
Total		458s	4.16 scudi

currency: 12 *denari* = 1 *soldo*; 110 *soldi* = 1 scudo

Dinner at The Cock in Voghera

bought by Zebelino or Gasparino, though sometimes it was supplied by the innkeeper. At Alessandria and Asti they bought leeks, onions and herbs to make soup. Eggs also featured very prominently. Ippolito and the men eating with him consumed over 200 eggs in the six days it took them to travel from Fiorenzuola to Saluzzo. Most days Zoane also bought delicacies. In Fiorenzuola he found twenty-four freshwater crayfish, which were carted all day in a sack to be eaten that night at Castel San Giovanni, and he bought oranges in Castel San Giovanni and Alessandria. In Asti he found raisins and four eels – probably not as good as those back home in Ferrara. Zoane was also responsible for maintaining stocks of the non-perishable goods which they carried on the journey – staples such as sugar, flour, rice, lard and various other sorts of cooking fats, candles, cheese and oil.

A page from Zoane da Cremona's ledger,
signed at the bottom by Guarniero the steward

Town	Value of 1 scudo
Ferrara	£3 10s
Modena	£3 16s
Reggio	£5 13s
Fiorenzuola	£3 15s
Castel San Giovanni	£5 12s
Voghera	£5 10s
Alessandria	£5 10s
Asti	£5 12s
Carmagnola	85 grossi

Exchange rates

By the time they reached Voghera he had accumulated so much that Pierantonio had to buy a horse (an old hack which cost 8 scudi, plus a small sum to pay the agent who negotiated the deal), as well as baskets to carry it all.

Zoane da Cremona's evenings were particularly onerous. In addition to shopping, he also had his accounts to complete. His first task was to establish the exchange rate between the gold scudo and the local currency. If funds were running low, he had to find Tomaso Mosto who would advance him another 50 or 100 scudi (and then record this advance in his own ledger). Each town had its own currency, methodically entered by Zoane at the top of every page of his ledger, and also its own system of weights and measures, which he did not enter. Most of these currencies were based on the same system of pounds, shillings and pence – £.s.d or *lire*, *soldi* and *denari* – which Britain only abandoned in 1971 (one *lira* was worth 20 *soldi*, or 240 *denari*). In Carmagnola and Saluzzo the currency was decimal, with 100 *grossi* to a local ducat.

Zoane detailed all his purchases of food for the evening meals and the stores he bought for the journey in his ledger. He also recorded the sums he paid to the falconers for the pigeons and hens they needed to feed their birds, as well as the money he handed out to Pierantonio and Bagnolo to cover what they needed for the stables (Panizato got his funds directly from Tomaso Mosto). Each morning Zoane had to visit the inns where the household had stayed, check the bills and pay the host for dinners, accommodation and stabling. He also noted the tips to women, in the plural the night they stayed in Asti, just the one in Carmagnola. All the prices were recorded in the local currency. At the bottom of each page Zoane totalled his expenditure and then converted it back into scudi, listing the extra sums, in their original currencies, on a separate page. He was meticulous and neat, and astonishingly good at arithmetic – Ippolito had been very fortunate in his choice of purveyor.

Travelling at this leisurely pace, with an entourage the size of Ippolito's, was inevitably extremely expensive. The payments listed by Zoane come to over 560 scudi, a sum which would have covered half the annual salary bill for the men travelling to France with Ippolito. Moreover, Zoane's ledger only tells us part of the story. The expenses incurred by other household departments were recorded by Tomaso Mosto, though his ledger for 1536 has not survived. In addition to the sums he advanced to Zoane, Mosto gave money to Assassino and Zudio to pay for Ippolito's laundry, to Jacomo da Parma for the pages and to various members of the household for their incidental expenses. He also recorded the substantial sums Ippolito gave out in alms to the poor and tips to dancing girls, gate-keepers and ferrymen. On a similar journey in 1540, Mosto's expenditure added another 300 scudi to the cost of travel.

However, Zoane da Cremona's book is very informative about the cost of inns, stabling and food. Ippolito spent an average of 38 scudi a day over the six days he took to travel from Fiorenzuola to Saluzzo, each night in hotels. This was more than the annual salary he paid either Vicino (31 scudi) or Zoane da Cremona (34 scudi). Take the night in Voghera again.

The total cost of housing and feeding the party for the night at Voghera came to 37 scudi, close to the average, but this does not

Accommodation and food bills (in scudi)

27 dinners and beds @ 10*s* each	2.5
38 dinners and beds @ 8*s* each	3
Food for Ippolito's dinner party	4
Cestarello and the ambassador's party	1
Extras	1.5
Food bought in shops	2
Breakfast for 50 mouths	2.5
Food expenses to 23 stable boys and muleteers	2.5
Stable bills	
Stabling 23 mules and 96 horses @ 5*s* each	5.5
Fodder	10.5
Cestarello and the ambassador's party	1.5
Other expenses	0.5
Total	37

currency: 110 *soldi* = 1 scudo

The cost of staying in Voghera

include the 8 scudi which Pierantonio had to spend on the horse that was needed to carry the household stores. Horses were a major expense. Not only did they have to be stabled, they also had to be fed, which added almost twice the sum to the bill. The cost of each animal per night was more than a week's wages for a stable boy and, significantly, only slightly less than the average Ippolito spent on food and accommodation for each of his men. Even so, by our standards, the cost of a night's accommodation was cheap: there are few hotels in Italy that charge as little as the equivalent of 2 kilos of ordinary stewing steak for dinner, bed and breakfast.

Ippolito and his courtiers may have been uncomfortable, but for many of the household this was an experience few of them would have been able to afford themselves. For the footmen, dinner, bed and

breakfast in Voghera represented four days' wages; for Iseppo, Zebelino's assistant in the *credenza*, who earned 7 scudi a year, it was nearly
a week's pay. The expense of travel was evident in the daily allowance
Ippolito paid the stable boys, who were given almost ten times more
than they received in Ferrara. For Ippolito himself there were financial drawbacks to a conspicuous display of wealth and prestige.
There is plenty of evidence to show that innkeepers and others took
advantage of the party. Innkeepers made a hefty profit from feeding
travellers, and the host of The Cock in Voghera was no exception.
The prices for the poultry he supplied for Ippolito's dinner were considerably higher than they would have been in the market in Ferrara:
50 per cent more for a capon, 300 per cent more for a pigeon. Pierantonio was so incensed at being given short measures of fodder for the
horses that he bought a new wooden basket in Alessandria the following night so that he could be sure of getting the correct amount.

∿

The day the party arrived at Voghera had been an eventful one. Early
that morning they had crossed into the duchy of Milan and, just outside Broni, they had been met by a company of imperial soldiers.
The leader of the company was Ferrante Gonzaga, second-in-
command of the imperial armies currently occupying Milan and a
rising star in Charles V's entourage. However, although he was on
the opposite side of the political divide, Ferrante was also the son of
Isabella d'Este and therefore Ippolito's first cousin. Ippolito must
have been relieved to recognize him. Their meeting was 'most amic-
able', as Ippolito reported that night in a letter to Ercole, but Ferrante's news was not good. Francis I's armies had now taken Turin,
and Ferrante warned him that he had been ordered to lead his own
troops to the border with Savoy. War might be only days away. Ferrante told Ippolito that he would need an official safe-conduct to get
through the duchy, and he offered to escort one of his courtiers to
Charles V's Captain-General, Anton de Leyva. Count Niccolò

Tassone went off to Leyva's camp and returned to Voghera that evening with the safe-conduct. Leyva, he said, had been most polite and helpful, signing a pass that required the imperial armies to give Ippolito and his party any assistance they needed. It certainly helped to have the right connections.

Ferrante also advised Ippolito to change his travel plans. Turin was no longer safe and, as the usual passes across the Alps were now full of soldiers, he had to find an alternative. There were three routes that most travellers used to cross the Alps in the sixteenth century: up the Val d'Aosta to the Petit-St-Bernard Pass (2,146 metres) or through the Susa valley from Turin to either the Mont-Cenis (2,083 metres) or the Montgenèvre passes (1,850 metres). The safest option available to Ippolito was to travel south-west to Saluzzo and take the Col d'Agnel, one of the smaller, less-frequented routes over the Alps. Vicino was sent on ahead to announce Ippolito's arrival to the Marquis of Saluzzo. The change of route was bad news for a number of reasons. It was perhaps 90 kilometres further, which would add another three or four days to the journey. Worse, at 2,748 metres, the Col d'Agnel was considerably higher than the other passes, and in March it would still be covered with snow. It was difficult to see the Alps from Broni but, if the weather was good, the line of elegant white peaks stretching across the horizon would have been clearly visible the next day once they got to Alessandria. The mountains were not frightening at that distance, but as the party moved closer they must have become an awesome sight for men who had spent most of their lives on the lush Po plain.

They spent the night of Tuesday, 21 March, in Asti and the next day left the Turin road to travel south to Carmagnola. Once off the main road they needed guides – there were no signposts in sixteenth-century Europe, nor were there any road maps. On 23 March they reached Saluzzo, a city perched high on a hill overlooking the Lombard plain. By now the Alps were clearly visible, and they were dominated by the peak of Mont Viso (3,841 metres) which overlooked the Col d'Agnel. Entering the ornamental stone gateway, the party climbed up through the narrow cobbled streets of the town to the castle. Ippolito was warmly greeted by the Marquis, a distant relation and a captain in the French army – he was to be appointed Francis I's lieutenant-general in Piedmont a few weeks later.

Staying as a guest in the castle may have been considerably more comfortable than the hotels Ippolito had just experienced, but it was not much cheaper. It was standard good manners to tip the staff who had looked after you during your stay. This involved tips of 1 scudo each to all the cooks, the *credenzieri*, the sommelier and the other dining staff, and the same amount to the each of the musicians and buffoons taking part in the entertainments. The tips Ippolito gave out at Saluzzo were recorded in Mosto's missing ledger, so we do not know how much he actually spent, but it was unlikely to have been much less than the average of 38 scudi he spent at an inn.

The court at Saluzzo was much smaller than that at Ferrara, but it had a reputation for excellent musicians, and Ippolito and his courtiers looked forward to several pleasant evenings. There were also other guests staying who had been forced by the impending war to take the Col d'Agnel. One was Guillaume de Dinteville, a courtier of Francis I, who was on a diplomatic mission to Venice (his brother Jean was one of the French ambassadors painted by Holbein, a picture now in the National Gallery in London). Another was Galeazzo Ariosto, one of Ercole II's courtiers, who was travelling to France with messages for Francis I and who joined Ippolito's party. Reassured by Dinteville that the pass was open, Ippolito wrote a short letter to Ercole on 24 March, which he gave to Dinteville to take to Ferrara, to say he would be leaving the next day. But once again he delayed his departure. Perhaps the old reluctance had returned, or he might have been having fun, but the most likely reason must have been the weather. He would certainly have been advised to avoid the Col d'Agnel in a blizzard.

Ippolito finally left Saluzzo on Sunday, 26 March, intending to spend that night at Sampéyre, and Monday at Chianale, before crossing into France. Early on Sunday morning, a small advance

View of the towering peak of Mont Viso from the road between Carmagnola and Saluzzo. The Col d'Agnel crosses the Alps just to the south of the mountain

party set out, consisting of Galeazzo Ariosto, Vicino and another squire, Ascanio, together with their three servants, three spare horses and a guide provided by the Marquis. Ascanio was to organize accommodation for the party at Sampéyre and Chianale, but Vicino and Ariosto were to carry on across the Col'Agnel, taking the spare horses in case of accident. Vicino would then wait for the main party in the village on the other side of the pass and arrange lodgings there, while Ariosto continued on to Lyon to find Francis I and to announce Ippolito's impending arrival. Ippolito and the rest of the party left Saluzzo later that morning, accompanied by a guide and by two wagons, one for the hay Pierantonio had bought in Saluzzo, the other to carry the flasks of wine thoughtfully provided by the Marquis. Pierantonio had spent nearly 60 scudi in Saluzzo, mending harnesses and stocking up for the journey across the Alps. Apart from the hay, he had also bought wine, fat, fodder and 140 horseshoes. One of the muleteers also needed new shoes.

Zoane advanced him the money, deducting the sum from the mule-teer's wages.

The route from Saluzzo up the valley to the Col d'Agnel is a deceptively gentle climb. The party rode through wooded hills, the mountains looming ever higher in the distance. The horses were much slower now they had left the well-worn roads of the plain, while the sturdy mules plodded on at their usual 5 kilometres an hour. The hamlets through which they passed were more prosperous than most Alpine villages. Sampéyre and Chianale were small but their inhabitants were able to augment an otherwise meagre existence in an inhospitable region with income from travellers to and from France. But these villages were a far cry from the bourgeois affluence of Ferrara, or even Asti. When he finally found time to describe this part of the journey to his brother, Ippolito recalled with horror the appalling lodgings and the miserable skinny animals. In late March, with their stocks of winter food and fodder running low, it is difficult to imagine that the locals greeted this huge party with quite the same enthusiasm as had the innkeepers on the Po plain. The taverns – Sampéyre had only two – were small and the food basic. On the menu were goat, bread, cheese and wine. There were no fashionable vegetables, fruit or salad.

On the morning of Tuesday, 28 March, they crossed into France, the stable party travelling separately from the others, each group with their own guide. The journey was a nightmare. In his letter to Ercole, Ippolito listed the horrors of the pass: the inaccessible road, the banks of snow and the appallingly rocky terrain. The Col d'Agnel is awe-some, even in a car in midsummer. The modern single-track tarmac road is used mainly by hikers, or cyclists keen to test their muscles and their nerves – buses and lorries are forbidden, and the road is only open from June to September. It snakes up from Chianale through a series of viciously steep hairpin bends, taking the traveller from 1,797 metres to 2,748 metres in under 10 kilometres. Perched at the top of the pass is a very narrow platform with stupendous views down into the valleys that fall sharply away on either side. Whatever the weather conditions when Ippolito crossed the pass, he would immediately have been aware that he had reached the summit when suddenly the exhausting climb was transformed into a treacherously steep descent and the horses began to slither their way down an icy road plunging through another series of sharp bends into France.

It was 16 long kilometres from the summit of the Col d'Agnel to the village of Molines-en-Queyras, where Vicino waited anxiously. Surprisingly, only one muleteer and his three mules got into difficulty crossing the pass and failed to arrive before nightfall. There do not seem to have been any inns in Molines. Vicino organized lodgings in thirteen different houses, with the animals in seventeen separate stables, some so small they could take only one horse. As on the Italian side of the mountains, the food was basic. Dinner consisted of bread, wine, eggs and two small calves. It was also expensive – the price of stabling the horses and mules was 10 per cent more than elsewhere in France, while wine cost twice as much.

∾

The return to civilization is eloquently charted in Zoane da Cremona's ledger. Rather than face another mountain pass, Ippolito decided not to take the quickest route but instead to head south to Gap, adding at least a day to the journey. There the party joined the main road from Nice to Grenoble. After the tiny hamlets of the Alps, the bustling town of Gap must have been a considerable relief. It was a Friday, a lean day. There had been no fish in the mountains, but that evening Zebelino managed to find two types of salted eels in the market, as well as herrings and anchovies, onions, almonds and cheese. He bought so much that it took a porter three trips to get all the food to the inn. From Gap onwards their diet consisted almost entirely of fish. It is difficult to tell whether this was because Lent was observed more strictly in France than in Italy, or because Ippolito himself was conscious of needing to adhere to convention now that he was abroad.

At Corps the following night, 1 April, they had a real feast. There were just three inns in the small town with rooms for the party – The Falcon, The Lion and The Three Kings. More than half the men were put up in private houses. Cestarello's servants had to lodge at the blacksmith's. Ippolito stayed at the Three Kings, where his dinner, which he must have shared with others, was organized by Guarniero. The ingredients supplied by the innkeeper included tuna, salmon, trout and 308 eggs. Zoane had also bought apples and salad, the first they had eaten since Saluzzo, a week before. For the first time too since Saluzzo, there were shops where one could stock up on essentials. Pierantonio bought 1,000 nails, a quantity that suggests there had been plenty of mishaps in the mountains. He also bought ingredients for a poultice for one of the mules and had two pack saddles mended. Jacomo took the pages' shirts and other linen to the laundry and bought them some treats – sugar to make posset, almonds, candied plums and other sweets.

Ippolito reached Grenoble on Sunday, 2 April. Ariosto, who had been waiting for two days, had welcome news. The French court was hunting outside Tour-du-Pin, and the King was looking forward to Ippolito's arrival. The party stayed in Grenoble for two nights, recovering from the ordeal of their journey across the Alps. Grenoble was swarming with soldiers but the goods on sale in the shops showed that they were once again in a prosperous city. Zoane bought raisins, oranges, spices such as saffron and cinnamon, parsley and other herbs, as well as salad ingredients and two hares (game was allowed during Lent). Many of the household were ill, including Cestarello and Mosto. Ippolito too may have been unwell because Assassino, the Master of the Chamber and not normally one to do the shopping, was reimbursed by Zoane for a Savoy cabbage and other ingredients to make an *acquacotta,* a light soup made from vegetables and water, and ideal for a delicate appetite.

France must have seemed strange to the household. For Zoane the clearest indication that he had left the mosaic of small states that made up Italy and was now in a large centralized monarchy, was the fact that the currency did not change every day, nor did the weights and measures. It must have made totalling up his accounts at the end of the day considerably easier – it certainly makes the ledger easier to read. One wonders what the party made of the language. Ippolito himself spoke good French, one of the languages current at the Ferrarese court, but Zoane had more difficulties. He italianized many French names, writing Georges as Giorgio, and Jean as Gian (though not as Zan or Zoane, as it would have been in the Ferrarese dialect). Similarily he Italianized local terminology – *concierge* became *consergio*, *marons* (the Alpine term for guides) became *maroni*. He must have read the inn names from their signs, because he described several hotels simply as 'inns without signs'. Another surprising feature of life in France was the quantity of women trading as bakers, haberdashers and even innkeepers. The only females who had featured in Zoane's books while they were in Italy had been laundresses and women tipped for their favours. France was also considerably cheaper than Italy. The average bill for the party for a night dropped from 38 scudi to 31 scudi. French innkeepers had a different system of pricing, charging separately for dinner, bed and breakfast, and the rates for stabling varied. However, they still charged extra for essentials such as firewood, candles and fodder, and they made a profit on the ingredients they supplied for Ippolito's dinner – pigeons were twice the price they had been in Ferrara.

On leaving Grenoble on Tuesday, 4 April, the household divided. One party stopped at Voiron for the night while the other rode all the way to Tour-du-Pin 60 kilometres away. Ippolito himself took the easier option and stayed at Voiron with Romei, Provosto Trotti, Scipio d'Este and Cestarello, who was so ill that he had to be carried from Grenoble in a litter. Besian and Bresan the falconers also stopped at Voiron where they managed to lose one of Ippolito's falcons. Mosto had recovered and was well enough to go to Tour-du-Pin, along with the rest of Ippolito's courtiers, Guarniero, Vicino and the squires, Andrea and the cooks, Assassino, the valets, Moiza and Zudio. The Tour-du-Pin party stayed at The Angel and all ate together that night in the communal dining-room of the inn. There was a lot of work to do, preparing for Ippolito's arrival at court, which had been fixed for the next day. Mosto had to unpack an outfit of suitably splendid clothes from the wardrobe chests, and make sure it was fit to wear. Assassino, Moiza and Zudio needed to perfume Ippolito's gloves, wash his linen and make sure everything was ready to shave and dress Ippolito when he arrived in the morning. Guarniero and the cooks had an important meal to organize at The Angel, a lunch party for Jean d'Humières, the envoy of Francis I who was to escort Ippolito to the King. Ippolito must have left Voiron early on Wednesday morning and ridden the 34 kilometres to Tour-du-Pin in time to wash and change before Humières arrived. Lunch was impressive. Guarniero, or rather one of the cooks, had spent over 3 scudi on crayfish, oranges, almonds, figs, pullets and eighteen carp, which had cost nearly 2 scudi and were the centrepiece of the meal.

Ippolito and Humières left after lunch to ride out into the countryside where Francis I was hunting. Ippolito was escorted by twenty-six of his household, the minimum number needed to ensure that his entourage was appropriately impressive and to look after his personal needs. Most of the men were noble. He took ten of his eleven courtiers (Cestarello was too ill) and Francesco dalla Viola, his musician. With Assassino were Moiza, Zudio and one of the valets (the footmen were all left behind). Guarniero brought the cooks Andrea and Turco, Alfonso the carver, one of the *credenzieri*, Priete the sommelier and just one squire, Vicino. Mosto took one of his wardrobe assistants, and Zuliolo brought Panizato. Panizato's main job would be to keep in touch with the rest of the household, who were having a well-earned rest in the inns of Tour-du-Pin. It was twenty-four days since Ippolito had left Ferrara, another world and a lifetime ago. As he rode out of the courtyard of The Angel, newly shaved and smartly dressed, he must have been excited, but he could not have anticipated how the next three hours would determine his future.

4

A Court at War

IPPOLITO JOINED THE royal hunting party somewhere in the wooded hills outside Tour-du-Pin and, during what remained of the afternoon, established a firm friendship with Francis I. His arrival at the French court could not have got off to a better start. Ercole II's ambassador sent a long letter to Ferrara, describing in minute detail the exchange of hand-kissing, embraces and other points of etiquette that were so vital in establishing personal and political relationships in sixteenth-century Europe. Francis I, in his encounter with Ippolito at least, was typically dismissive of the usual formalities of courtly ritual – he was not a ruler who needed his self-esteem bolstered by sycophants. As Ippolito approached and prepared to dismount, the King called twice to him not to get off his horse. Ippolito, unaware of Francis I's informality and determined to behave with proper decorum, did dismount. He removed his hat before kissing the King's hand and murmured some appropriate words of greeting. He was introduced to the King's closest advisers, Anne de Montmorency and Cardinal Jean of Lorraine, who both greeted him warmly. Francis I, impatient to continue the chase and presumably to test Ippolito's hunting skills, then invited his guest to remount and ride beside him, a marked sign of favour. The two men chatted away all afternoon. There was no language barrier: Ippolito spoke French, learned from his sister-in-law and her courtiers in Ferrara, while Francis I spoke excellent Italian, which he had been taught by his mother, Louise of Savoy.

Francis I

Francis I was 45, seventeen years older than Ippolito. He was a jovial giant of a man, self-confident and handsome, and still retained the energy of his youth. There can be little doubt that he genuinely liked Ippolito. The two men shared the same interests – hunting, tennis, gambling and women. Ippolito was fun, irresponsibly so at times, and certainly no sycophant. He must have been a welcome change from the French courtiers with their factional rivalries who competed for favour and influence with the King. Ippolito was a guest and he was family, the brother of the King's brother-in-law – a somewhat broader interpretation of kinship than we are accustomed to use, but very real in sixteenth-century Europe.

Taking his cue from the King's obvious liking for Ippolito, Montmorency perceived a potential ally. Once the party had escorted

Francis I back to the abbey of St-Cyr, where the royal court was lodged, Montmorency offered to take Ippolito to his rooms and invit-ed him to dine that evening. After dinner the two men returned to the King's chambers, where they joined the royal family for the evening's entertainment – music, games and gossip. The Queen of France was Eleanor of Portugal, the sister of Charles V. She was Francis I's second wife and their marriage had been designed to secure peace between the two rulers in 1530. Aged 38, she was small, blonde and plain, and not popular with Francis I. They had no children and the King clearly preferred the company of his beautiful 28-year-old mistress, Madame d'Etampes, who held an increasingly influential position at court. There were five royal princes and princesses, all born to Francis I's first wife Claude, the elder sister of Renée. So Ippolito's first evening at court had a distinctively family flavour and gave him the chance to meet Renée's nephews and nieces: François (aged 18), Henri (17) and his Italian wife, Catherine de' Medici (a week or so off her seventeenth birthday), Madeleine (15), Charles (14) and Marguerite (12).

Ippolito did not get to bed until the early hours of the morning, and he must have been exhausted. After a month of gruelling travel across Italy and the Alps, he had ridden 34 kilometres that morning – say three hours' hard riding along the rough roads from Voiron to Tour-du-Pin. At the inn there he had changed and hosted a lunch party before setting out to join the King. Quite apart from the physical exertion involved in all this, there was also the excitement, and appre-hension, of his first encounter with the French royal family, the unfa-miliar formalities of social life at court, and the effort of meeting so many new, and important, faces. The next morning he wrote a long letter to Ercole II, the first he had written for two weeks, in which he described his favourable reception by the King. Ippolito's optimism was confirmed later that morning when Francis I presented him with three beautiful deerhounds – Ippolito had left his own dogs behind in Ferrara – before the two friends went out hunting again. He spent a week at St-Cyr before leaving, with the King's permission, for Lyon.

A sixteenth-century map of Lyon, showing the city straddling the rivers Rhône and Saône

~

The old city of Lyon had been built high up on a hill overlooking the point at which the rivers Rhône and Saône converge, a strategic position which made it the ideal choice for the capital of the Roman province of Gaul, established in 43 BC. By 1536 Lyon had expanded down the hill to the banks of the Saône and across the river to the promontory between the two waterways. The city was heavily fortified, with walls to the west and north reinforcing the natural defences provided by the rivers to the south and east. The main entrance was across a single bridge over the Rhône, guarded by a substantial gatehouse. It was by this bridge that Ippolito and his household first entered Lyon on the afternoon of 11 April, into the city that was to be their base for several months and that was later to play an important role in Ippolito's career.

With a population approaching 50,000, Lyon was the second city of Francis I's realm, and it had a strong sense of its own identity.

It was a major centre of international trade, its prosperity boosted by tax concessions and other benefits. Many Italian merchants had their shops and offices in the narrow streets that clustered round the twelfth-century cathedral on the west bank of the Saône. Florentine bankers had made Lyon an important financial centre. The city was also famous for its printing industry, and for its intellectuals, providing a haven for writers and free thinkers, among them Rabelais, as well as many Protestant sympathizers. The semi-autonomous civic government had a highly developed sense of Christian duty. This was one of the few cities in Europe where care for the poor had been removed from the Church and put in the hands of a government committee, the Aumône-Générale, which had been set up by businessmen and lawyers in 1534 to provide money for the needy, homes for orphans, and, unusually, subsidies for young boys and girls so that they could become apprenticed to a particular trade or craft. The Aumône-Générale was funded by charitable donations – lawyers were asked to remind their clients of this fact when drawing up wills – and to show that the funds were being properly used, the committee organized an annual Easter parade of all those who had benefited during the previous year. Ippolito would have witnessed the parade himself in Lyon in 1536.

Ippolito and his household arrived in Lyon on the Tuesday before Easter. In a rare reference to his religious beliefs, Ippolito explained to Ercole II that he had gone to Lyon, with the King's permission, in order to 'attend to my soul and go to confession in these holy days'. Easter was the principal festival in the Church calendar and the one time in the year when Christians in sixteenth-century Europe took communion. This celebration of Christ's Last Supper was one of the issues dividing Protestant reformers and traditional Catholics. Catholics believed that the bread and wine they received at communion had been miraculously transformed at the altar into the body and blood of Christ himself – the theory of transubstantiation. Protestants had rejected the miraculous nature of the sacrament, insisting that the bread and wine merely represented the body and blood of Christ. Not all Protestants went so far as one radical reformer, who accused Catholics of cannibalism, but the rift between the reformers and the established Church had begun to widen alarm, ingly across Europe in 1536. Ippolito and his courtiers took commu, nion in Lyon cathedral on Good Friday – Alessandro Rossetto, one of the valets, left ½ scudo in the offertory box in the church on Ippo, lito's behalf. That same day in Ferrara, where the Protestant leader John Calvin had just spent a month under the protection of Ippo, lito's sister,in,law Renée, one of her Flemish musicians was arrested on a charge of blaspheming in front of the Cross during mass. The penalty for heresy was death. Renée pleaded with her husband to pardon the musician but he refused. Their relationship, already tense, now deteriorated dramatically. Ercole was horrified by this public display of his wife's Protestant sympathies. He removed her from their three children – Alfonso, the heir, was now 2½ years old, Anna was 4½ and Lucretia was only 6 months old – and exiled her to Con, sàndolo, one of his country retreats 30 kilometres outside Ferrara.

Meanwhile, Ippolito settled in Lyon and began to receive a steady stream of visitors. The ambassador of Venice paid him a call, as did those of Portugal and England. He got news daily from the court at St,Cyr, including personal messages from the King and Mont, morency. Much of the news concerned the war. During their hunt, ing expeditions at St,Cyr, Francis I had told Ippolito of his plans to send 14,000 Swiss and German mercenaries to reinforce the army holding Savoy. Lyon was full. In addition to those members of the court who were not hunting with the King, there were also many sol, diers – as Ippolito wrote to Ercole II, the city was swarming with armed men. Nevertheless, he seems to have liked Lyon. He certainly enjoyed being rowed across the Saône by the lady bargees, often tip, ping them lavishly with as much as 1 scudo for entertaining him on the short journey. One scudo was a lot of money – it would buy a whole calf or twelve capons in the city markets, or pay for eleven din, ners at the inn where many of Ippolito's household were lodged.

Francis I had arranged accommodation for Ippolito at the

monastery of the Celestines. This was on the east bank of the Saône, across the river from the cathedral and the main commercial centre – hence the frequent trips with the lady bargees. Ippolito does not seem to have paid any rent, though he gave the monks regular presents of fish and eggs, and they certainly profited financially by charging Ippolito the market rate for their wine, which was collected by the sommelier Priete and drunk in large quantities by the household. There was not enough room at the convent for the entire party of 117 men, nor was there stabling for the horses and mules. The animals were divided between three different inns, along with the stable boys and muleteers. Mindful of the extortionate charges made by innkeepers on the journey from Ferrara to France, Ippolito supplied all the fodder himself – a major headache for Jacomo Panizato, who was responsible for finding it. Lodgings also had to be found for over half the household, some in these inns and others in rooms rented from private landlords. They were not comfortable. All the lower levels of the household had to share two or three to a bed. The two chaplains slept in one bed. Zoane da Cremona had to share with Arcangelo, the table-decker, in a room in a private house, and they had to move several times during the following three weeks. The courtiers had their own beds, but even they had to share rooms – Tomaso Mosto shared with Girolamo Guarniero. The only courtier with his own room, and bed, was Alfonso Cestarello, who was now seriously ill. He had been too unwell to leave Tour-du-Pin with the rest of the men and only arrived in Lyon, still in a litter, on Good Friday.

The accommodation might have been cramped but now that they were settled in Lyon, Ippolito's staff returned to the regular routine of palace life. Mosto unpacked the wardrobe chests and sorted out Ippolito's clothes. One of his first jobs was to exchange his scudi for French currency, and he spent 600 scudi on a set of twelve silver plates for the *credenza* from a dealer – unusually, a woman – who had a shop near the bridge over the Saône. Guarniero supervised the unpacking of the rest of the *credenza* silver and the glasses, and planned his daily menus, which were prepared by Andrea the cook and the two *credenzieri*, Zebelino and Gasparino. With Cestarello ill in bed, Zoane da Cremona took over his responsibilities and orga-nized the stocks of non-perishable goods, such as candles, firewood and the contents of the larder. Other jobs were delegated to Jacomo Panizato. Panizato, who, less than a year before, had been working as a painter in Ferrara, was proving to be both efficient and trustworthy. In addition to his job at the stables, where he paid the wages and living expenses of the stable boys and organized all the fodder for the horses, he now took over the tasks of paying expenses to the servants of Ippolito's courtiers and of buying the firewood needed in the kitchen and bedrooms at the Celestines. Zoane gave him cash virtu-ally every day, usually 10 scudi at a time. They normally met in the cloisters of the Celestines – Zoane was careful to record exactly where he gave Panizato the cash – but sometimes in Zoane's room or on the streets of Lyon, and once 'under a church door'.

Panizato also went out for odd items of food but Zoane delegated most of the food shopping to Zebelino and Turco, the second cook who worked under Andrea in the convent kitchen. Shops were open every day, including Sundays, though they did close on Easter Day. Turco frequently went out twice – in the morning to buy food for lunch and again in the afternoon to get supplies for dinner. One of the kitchen boys also went out twice a day to collect fresh bread from the bakers. Zoane himself continued to shop for the important ingre-dients – fish and meat. The fish he bought from the market stalls along the banks of the Saône, and for meat he particularly favoured one butcher called Jacques – recording his name as Giac in the ledger – who delivered his supplies to the Celestines by cart.

The range of food available in Lyon was enormous. And now, for the first time, we know exactly what Ippolito and his household ate at home. Because they were based only temporarily in Lyon, there was no point in drawing up contracts with local suppliers, so all the groceries, meat, poultry, fish, fruit and vegetables, firewood, candles and other necessities, were itemized in Zoane's account book.

Food items	Total cost (in scudi)	Days bought
Meat and poultry	28.04	9
Wine	24.21	n/a
Fish	22.71	7
Bread	16.07	13
Cheese	7.92	4
Fruit and nuts	3.27	11
Animal fat	2.73	6
Sugar	2.16	3
Salad and vegetables	2.04	11
Oil	1.81	3
Flour	1.73	4
Eggs	0.93	4
Spices	0.72	5
Honey	0.60	2
Salt	0.54	3
Lentils and rice	0.39	3
Vinegar	0.31	6
Milk	0.16	2
Sweets	0.13	1
Total	116.47	
Non-food items		
Firewood	8.06	9
Plates etc.	7.32	8
Candles	4.42	5
Laundry	0.62	2
Total	20.42	

Shopping in Lyon for two weeks, 11–24 April

Zoane was catering for fifty-three men – Ippolito eating at his own table and the household eating in the staff dining-room. As at

the Palazzo San Francesco, the stable boys and muleteers ate separ/
rately with a daily allowance to cover the cost of their food, and there
was a similar arrangement for the courtiers' servants. Zoane's expen/
diture during the first fortnight in Lyon totalled nearly 137 scudi,
which works out at an average of just over 1¼ scudi per man per
week, or 5½ scudi a month.

The daily diet of Ippolito and his household emerges from the
ledger with prosaic clarity. The largest items of expenditure were fish,
meat, bread and wine, the basic ingredients of each meal. The bread
was fresh – bought daily except on Easter Sunday, one of the rare
occasions when the baker was closed. The choice of fish or meat was
dictated by the Church, not by personal taste. Zoane bought fish
every day during Holy Week. Lyon was a long way from the sea and
they ate mostly freshwater varieties, such as carp, pike and shad, with
occasional treats such as trout and small eels, and a salmon for Ippo/
lito and his guests on Good Friday. By contrast the celebrations for
Easter Day were entirely carnivorous, though surprisingly lamb was
not on the menu – the sheep was mutton. Jacques delivered a whole
cart of meat to the Celestines on the Saturday afternoon, and his bill
came to 4¾ scudi:

¼ ox	1
2 whole calves	2
1 sheep	0.75
4 kids	1
Total	4.75 scudi

Jacques the butcher's bill
for Easter Saturday

With Lent over, the household returned to the regular rhythm of
eating fish only on Fridays and feast days, though Ippolito also ate fish
for lunch on the Saturday after Easter. For the rest of the week they
ate meat, cooked in the lard and other animal fats that now also

reappeared in the ledger. Zoane must have got to know Jacques quite well – most days the butcher delivered what seems to have been a standing order of part of an ox, one calf, one sheep and one kid.

Other items were bought according to the requirements of Guarniero's menus, and Turco's shopping list varied daily. The only spice he purchased that fortnight was saffron, suggesting that they had brought stocks of other spices from Ferrara – these must have run out by the end of April when he started buying ginger, pepper, cinnamon and cloves. One surprisingly frequent purchase was vinegar, which he bought several times in tiny quantities. Most of his shopping consisted of fresh fruit and vegetables. He bought salad and herbs (particularly parsley and mint) most days, along with a selection of other vegetables, such as onions, garlic, beet greens, leeks or spinach. The fruit available during April was limited to oranges and apples, and a lot of raisins. The nuts were mainly almonds, which the cooks used for sauces and puddings. Once the weather turned warmer the fruit and vegetables in their diet changed as new varieties ripened. Turco found the first artichokes of the year on 6 May: they were astonishingly expensive – five for 1 scudo – but by the end of the month he could buy fifteen for the same price. The first strawberries appeared on 15 May, bitter morello cherries on 25 May, peas on 27 May and sweet cherries the day after. There were also special purchases. The braces of pigeons were for the falcons, while the sweets – anise comfits – were probably a treat for the young pages. Some of the sugar was given to Tomaso Mosto to starch Ippolito's shirts, while more sugar, as well as almonds and capons, were bought to tempt the delicate appetite of the convalescent Cestarello.

∾

After a fortnight in Lyon Ippolito must have been impatient to return to court. Finally, summoned by Montmorency, he left to join Francis I, who was now hunting in the countryside west of Lyon. The week he had spent with the King at St-Cyr could hardly have prepared him for the extraordinary peripatetic lifestyle of the French court. Francis I spent most of the year travelling around his realm, rarely staying as much as a week in any one place. If he did stop for longer, it was usually for pressing political reasons or because he was ill, a frequent occurrence. To add to the confusion, the plans to move were not made far in advance. In his letters to his brother, Ippolito frequently comments that he does not know how long he will remain in a particular place – in others he mentions a plan to move but adds the proviso 'if the King does not change his mind'.

The itinerary of Ippolito's first month at court gives some idea of the exhausting schedule of those living with the King. Ippolito left Lyon on Sunday, 23 April, and headed west to St-Rambert (now St-Just-St-Rambert), a small town at the head of the Loire valley, 80 kilometres from Lyon. This was an easy two-day journey and they arrived in St-Rambert on Monday, in time to join the royal party hunting that afternoon. They hunted again the following day and spent Tuesday night in Montbrison, a larger town about 20 kilometres away, where they stayed for three days. On Friday, Ippolito rode back to Lyon with the King. He spent Saturday night at the Celestines and returned to St-Rambert on Monday, 1 May, for more hunting.

At this point the King fell ill – hardly surprising after such an active week – so on Tuesday the court moved back to the walled medieval town of Montbrison. Ippolito, and presumably Francis I, much preferred Montbrison to St-Rambert. It was larger, and its shops, while not as varied as those in Lyon, were sophisticated enough to stock cinnamon, ginger and other imported spices.

After a week convalescing in Montbrison, the King was sufficiently well to resume his punishing schedule. On 9 May the court moved off to Pommiers, another walled town 35 kilometres away, where Ippolito spent five days hunting with the King. Then they spent one night (14 May) at Montbrison on their way back to St-Rambert, where they stayed for six days. Ippolito wrote to Ercole on Saturday, 20 May, 'Since I last wrote we have stayed in the Lyon area, sometimes in one village, sometimes in another, and I have been with the King. We leave St-Rambert today and will lunch at the hunt,' adding, 'then if the King does not change his mind, we go back to Lyon.' Ippolito expected to be back in Lyon on Sunday night, but the King delayed his departure for a couple of days, and they finally returned late on Tuesday.

The logistics of this way of life required a great deal of organiza-tion. As many as 10,000 people travelled around the country in the wake of the King, staying in royal palaces and castles, abbeys, major cities, small towns and even in villages. Only about 2,000 of them held official posts in the royal household or those of the Queen and other members of the royal family. There were also armies of lawyers, secretaries, bookkeepers and other officials who manned the various departments of state, as well as hundreds of soldiers of the King's bodyguard. Ippolito was just one of several guests – others included the King and Queen of Navarre – who were attached semi-permanently to the court, each travelling with their own staff. There were also officially accredited ambassadors and their entourages from all the major states of Europe, many of whom were Italian. And there were the unofficial hangers-on – the tradesmen, artisans and itinerant entertainers who made their livings by supplying the court with goods and services, as well as the inevitable hordes of beggars subsisting on alms. It is unlikely that all these people were with the King on this particular hunting expedition – many must have remained behind in Lyon – but it must have been quite a challenge for the King's foragers to find suitable accommodation for the royal party in St-Rambert, Montbrison and Pommiers.

Ippolito himself seems to have adapted well to the unstructured rhythm of life at the French court. His letters contain no hint of exas-peration, or even mere annoyance, at the lack of forward planning. However, it must have been hard on those members of his household who preferred the regular routine of working in a palace. When Ippolito set out on Sunday, 23 April, to join Francis I at St-Rambert, he took only a few essential members of his staff – his secretary

Antonio Romei, Assassino the Master of the Chamber, Zudio the chief Chamber servant, and Moiza the barber. He also took Andrea the cook and Gasparino, one of the *credenzieri*, together with two kitchen boys to assist them. Panizato left the same day but travelled separately with the mules carrying Ippolito's luggage – and he spent most of the following week in the saddle, riding back to Lyon with orders and messages, and returning with cash for fodder and food. Another party set out from Lyon on Wednesday, 26 April, including Tomaso Mosto with the wardrobe, and Guarniero with the rest of the kitchen and dining staff. They took with them a large quantity of spices and sugar, bought that morning in Lyon, as well as eighty-seven new pewter candlesticks. Vicino, Ippolito's favourite squire, also left that day – his departure was recorded in Zoane's ledger because he had forgotten to pay ½ scudo he owed to an innkeeper and Zoane had to settle the bill for him. Zoane and the rest of the household left a week later to join Ippolito at Montbrison. Only Cestarello, still ill in bed, stayed behind with his servants and Ippolito's doctor to care for him.

Zoane took with him two large chests containing all the larder stores. These chests, made of wood and reinforced with iron bands and padlocks, were new and had caused a lot of trouble. They had originally been commissioned by Zoane from a carpenter in Lyon, who made the pair and then demanded more than the agreed price. The carpenter – Zoane did not give his name in the ledger – refused to negotiate and Zoane refused to pay. In the end Matteo, one of the muleteers, was sent out to organize another pair, presumably from another carpenter. The journey to Montbrison was particularly unpleasant for Zebelino the *credenziero*, who had been put in charge of the mules carrying the chests. Two of the mules got into difficulties on the road over the hills to Yzeron, where Zebelino's horse lost a shoe, and they finally arrived at Montbrison a day later than the rest of the party. After two nights in Montbrison the household had to repack before leaving to follow Ippolito and the King to Pommiers. This town was too small to accommodate any more than Ippolito's essential staff and most of the men lodged in private houses in Arthun, a village about 6 kilometres away. On top of the travel, they still had their work to do looking after Ippolito. In each unfamiliar town they had to find new butchers, fishmongers, grocers, bakers, wine merchants and laundresses, and, in Arthun, arrange for all the purchases to be transported to the court up the road.

~

Meanwhile, Ippolito settled down to court life, which suited him enormously. His official duties were minimal. Most mornings after breakfast he met Ercole II's ambassador to discuss affairs of state and to report items of news he had picked up during the course of the previous day. Once or twice a week he wrote to his brother – Ercole complained frequently that he wanted more news. In fact Ippolito did not usually write these letters himself but instead dictated them to his secretary, who transcribed all the political gossip into code before Ippolito signed the finished copies with his distinctively large and untidy scrawl. The rest of his time he could devote to pleasure, and to networking, furthering his career through his powerful and influential friends. He spent a lot of time hunting with the King, chasing deer and boar with hounds or using his falcons to bring down pheasant. There were no tennis courts in the rural backwaters of Montbrison and Pommiers, but there was plenty of time for games and gossip. Ippolito was a regular gambler at the card-table. One of his gaming books has survived and shows that quite large sums of money changed hands – often 50 or 60 scudi in a single session. He played two or three times a week on average, and although he does not seem to have played on either Easter Day or Christmas Day, he certainly played throughout Lent and on Sundays.

Ippolito's friendship with the King opened many doors. He went hunting with the royal princes and the King of Navarre, Francis I's brother-in-law. He was also popular with the ladies. He gambled at cards with Madame d'Etampes, Francis I's mistress, and

One of Ippolito's coded letters. The basic code was relatively simple, with letters transposed in blocks of four (ABCD are encoded as DCBA). But there were several embellishments to confuse the unauthorized reader. Vowels could be indicated by the accents above the letters (the grave accent is an 'e'), or by numbers (6 is also an 'e'). Greek letters were used to indicate important people – δ is Francis I

was a regular guest at the dinner table of Francis I's sister Marguerite, the Queen of Navarre. He was assiduously cultivated by Mont, morency, Grand Master of France and head of Francis I's house, hold, a position he was exploiting to build up a powerful faction at court. Montmorency was 43 years old, stern, authoritarian and hugely wealthy. He loved hunting but does not seem to have been much of a gambler – he only occasionally played cards with Ippolito. More fun, and Ippolito's principal companion at the card, table, was Montmorency's chief ally, the 38, year, old Jean, Cardinal of Lor, raine. Like Ippolito he came from an old aristocratic family – his two brothers were Antoine, Duke of Lorraine, and Claude, Duke of Guise. He had also started his career young, becoming Bishop of Metz at the age of 10 and a cardinal at 21, something which Ippo, lito must have envied.

Like all courts of the period, the French court was a hive of intrigue and rivalry, fuelled above all by gossip. Out hunting, round the card, table or the dining, table, and at the regular after, dinner enter, tainments in the King's chamber, these men and women chatted – idle talk about the day's hunt, rumours of scandal, whispering cam, paigns to discredit those in power, and serious discussions about high politics. That month in Montbrison and Pommiers, the news was dominated by the progress of the army in Italy. Francis I had ambassadors in England, Germany, Spain, Rome, Venice, Florence, Ferrara, Mantua and many other Italian states, all of whom sent lengthy official reports back to France several times a week to inform the King of their hosts' opinions of the war, and of Charles V. Their counterparts at the French court were doing exactly the same, interpreting the rumours according to their own political agendas and evaluating the evasive responses Montmorency gave to their questions regarding Francis I's plans. Some of course, were better at this than others.

The French ambassador in Ferrara was the source of one rumour that directly affected Ippolito: his brother's loyalty to France. Ercole II's decision to exile Renée, coupled with the fact that he had sent his other brother, Francesco, to join Charles V's court, had made the ambassador suspect that Ercole was planning to change his allegiance from Francis I to the Emperor. While they were at Montbrison Francis I challenged Ippolito with this rumour. Ippolito staunchly defended his brother, arguing that Ercole had only sent Francesco to the imperial court to keep in touch with the other side. In reality the Duke had little choice. With the war between Francis I and Charles V threatening to escalate, he had to plan for the possibility of an imperial victory. (Even Ippolito assisted the opposition – his factor in Ferrara sold wheat that summer to Charles V's troops, for which Ippolito received 235 scudi.) Justifying his brother's behaviour towards Renée was far harder. The King sent a thinly veiled warning via Ippolito that Ercole II's loyalty would be judged by his treatment of his wife. Renée was, after all, a royal princess, the daughter of Louis XII, Francis I's predecessor. 'You could not give the King a greater sign of your service and friendship than to treat her with love', wrote Ippolito after his meeting with the King, adding that Francis I 'assures you that everything you do for her is as if you do it for the King himself.'

The diplomatic network, and the expatriate community,

generated mountains of correspondence and made a significant con-
tribution to the profits of the paper-making industry. Ercole wrote
frequently to Ippolito and sent him copies of ambassadors' reports
received from Rome, Spain or elsewhere which he thought would be
of interest. To safeguard against loss, a duplicate copy of each letter
would be sent by a different route. Ambassadors' reports could run
to fifteen or twenty pages, and they were also duplicated. Often
attached to the official reports were several pages of news-sheets, outlining the less significant stories circulating in that particular location. These news-sheets read rather like local newspapers, with lists
of marriages and deaths (though not births – surviving early childhood was still hazardous), the arrival and departure of notables, and
incidental news items, such as reports of a particularly aggressive
eruption of Mount Etna or the information that the Spanish galleons
from Peru had anchored in the Canaries to await gunships to escort
them safely to Seville. All this correspondence was carried by road.
The letters between Ippolito and Ercole usually took a month to
arrive, consigned to men travelling between the two courts, often
diplomats or trusted friends, who did the journey at much the same
rate as Ippolito had done in March.

The royal mail was much faster. Francis I had a very impressive
postal service, using a chain of couriers and horses to send letters to
France at speed. News from Ferrara frequently reached Ippolito more
quickly via French couriers from Italy than it did from his brother. It
was Montmorency who told Ippolito one morning in Montbrison
that Ercole II had fallen off his horse and been knocked unconscious.
The news had arrived in Montbrison via the French ambassador in
Rome. At first, everyone had been very worried, but the Duke had
recovered quickly. Ippolito had to wait more than three weeks to
receive news of the accident from Ercole himself.

The month Ippolito spent hunting with the King west of Lyon
was particularly eventful. With the French and the imperial armies
facing each other across the border between Savoy and Milan, Pope
Paul III decided to intervene and persuaded the two rulers to negoti-

ate a truce. Francis I sent the Cardinal of Lorraine to Siena for talks with the Emperor. The meeting took place on 24 April and, late in the evening of 27 April, a courier arrived at Montbrison with a letter from the Cardinal: the negotiations had broken down. Lorraine's letter was urgent and the speed at which it travelled from Siena to Lyon, and then a further 80 kilometres across country to Montbrison, was impressive even by modern standards. It took only seventy-two hours to cover over 800 kilometres – an average of 11 kilometres an hour, requiring a change of horse every three or four hours and several changes of rider.

With the breakdown in negotiations, events moved rapidly. The day after the letter arrived, the King interrupted his hunting to return to Lyon with Ippolito and the court for urgent consultations with his advisers. On 3 May Ippolito reported that Admiral Chabot, who was in charge of the French troops in Italy, had been removed from his post. This was a coup for Montmorency. The Admiral was one of his chief rivals at court, and though Chabot retained the position of Governor of Burgundy, it was Montmorency himself who was promoted as head of the army. The Marquis of Saluzzo, Ippolito's host of six weeks earlier, was appointed as the new lieutenant-general in Italy. Saluzzo did not last long, however, though for different reasons. Within a fortnight of the breakdown of the talks at Siena, Charles V reopened the war and invaded Piedmont. Francis I ordered Saluzzo to fight, but on 17 May Saluzzo, who had signed a secret alliance with the Emperor, defected.

The crisis did not stop Francis I hunting. The day before they left Montbrison for Pommiers the court was gripped by a piece of real scandal sent by Jean de Dinteville, Francis I's ambassador in England. Less urgent than the report from Siena, it took six days to cover the 900 kilometres or so from London. Dinteville's news was that the King of England had arrested his wife, accused her of adultery with one of his courtiers, as well as with her spinet-player and her brother, and had locked them all up in the Tower of London. Henry VIII had in fact arrested Anne Boleyn on the advice of his chief minister,

Sir Thomas Cromwell, after the May Day jousts in Greenwich, accusing her of adultery with Sir Henry Norris, one of the jousters that day. The news, according to Dinteville, was greeted with joy across the country. At the French court it instantly generated speculation as to whom Henry VIII would marry next. Nobody doubted Anne's guilt, nor that she would be executed for her crimes. Henry VIII had long exploited the rivalry between Francis I and Charles V for his own ends, and both rulers knew that an alliance with him could tip the balance of power in Europe in their favour. Ippolito discussed all the available options, French and imperial, with the King, who was planning to offer his daughter Madeleine. The princess, Ippolito reported to his brother, was ill, but she 'showed great happiness and evidently improved with this news'. If Ippolito's tone was that of the broadsheets, then the papal ambassador typified the tabloid approach. Paul III's representative in France was Rodolfo Pio da Carpi and he reported Anne Boleyn's execution in gruesome detail, including the fact that she had had to watch her brother being hung, drawn and quartered before her own beheading. Scurrilously, Carpi added that Henry VIII had been in danger of being poisoned and that the real father of his daughter by Anne (Elizabeth) was actually a peasant.

Ippolito arrived back in Lyon on Tuesday, 23 May, lodging again at the Celestines. 'We expect to stay seven or eight nights', he wrote to his brother, 'and then go to La Côte-St-André so long as the plan does not change, which easily might happen.' The plan did change. The court stayed in Lyon for nearly a fortnight and, instead of going to La Côte-St-André, went hunting around Cremieu in the middle of June before returning to Lyon for most of July.

Ippolito meanwhile continued his charm offensive with the royal family. He gave the two princesses, Madeleine and Marguerite, expensive rosaries of gold beads which had been filled with musk and ambergris. Mosto had had these rosaries made by a goldsmith in Lyon and gave him forty-five gold rosary beads from the wardrobe to use for the commission: a little drawing preserved between the pages of one of Ippolito's account books shows four different designs for the rest of the beads, presumably drawn by the craftsman. Ippolito also gave two of his own rosaries – one ivory, one gold – as presents, each, according to Mosto's notes in the margin of the inventory of the wardrobe valuables, to 'someone known to Ippolito in Lyon'. Rosaries were invariably given as presents to ladies, and Mosto's diffidence about naming the recipients suggests that Ippolito was planning to embark on an affair.

He also began to entertain the royals. On the first Sunday in Lyon (28 May) he hosted a lunch party for the Queen and her sons, and, presumably, Catherine de' Medici and other ladies at court. The lunch did not take place at the Celestines, which was not grand enough for this event, but the food was cooked there and then transported to the Queen's lodgings. This was a major undertaking for the household, the cooks and Zoane da Cremona (Cestarello was still ill in bed). It was also Guarniero's first opportunity to organize an Italian-style banquet for a largely French audience. We know nothing about the entertainments he staged but a lot about the 46 scudi that were spent on food, a sum that would have covered two months' wages for all those men, including Guarniero, who prepared and served the meal – at a more banal level, it would have paid for forty-six calves from Jacques the butcher. It is clear that Ippolito wanted to impress his royal guests and the menu was appropriately extravagant. Zoane da Cremona spent 6 scudi on sugar, almonds, raisins and spices, all bought from a spice merchant named René. He spent over 5 scudi on cheese and bought six artichokes for 1 scudo. There was a lot of fish, including a large eel, several pike, a salmon, 100 crayfish and even some frogs. Jacques supplied beef, mutton, veal and kid, but Zoane also bought more exotic meat and poultry, including hare, rabbit and goose. The Italian flavour was much in evidence: there was pasta, served with quantities of fresh butter, which cost 1½ scudi, and Italian cheese, also hugely expensive and imported by Italian merchants from northern Italy.

A week later, on 4 June, Ippolito had exciting news to impart to his brother – he sent his letter to Ferrara with Georges d'Armagnac, who was travelling to Italy to take up his post as the new French ambassador to Venice. After just two months in France Ippolito had received the first concrete indication that his career would profit handsomely from Francis I's friendship. The King had promised him the abbey of St-Médard at Soissons (near Rheims). This was a lucrative benefice with an income of 4,000 scudi a year, though he would have to wait until the incumbent abbot, who was very ill and over 80 years old, finally died. Ippolito thanked the King who, 'then replied that this was just a small beginning to what he has in mind for me'. Francis I had a sense of humour: Ippolito added that the King had said, 'if I do not get the abbey then at least I will acquire fame by curing elderly priests who are seriously ill'. Ippolito got the abbey and the King made several more similar offers as the year progressed. When the Archbishop of Arles fell seriously ill in July, Francis I again promised Ippolito the benefice, but this cleric recovered to live another fourteen years. In October Francis I gave him the highly prestigious archbishopric of Lyon, with the same proviso. The Archbishop died on 13 October and the King nominated Ippolito in his place. Both appointments – St-Médard and Lyon – now had to await papal approval.

∼

Illness was a major preoccupation in sixteenth-century Europe, and good health a much-treasured commodity. Having survived the hazards of early childhood, life expectancy, interestingly, was not as low as we might think, at least not among the rich and powerful. Of the hundred or so people mentioned in Ippolito's letters for whom we have reliable dates, the average age of death was 56, though if we exclude those who were executed or assassinated, the figure rises to nearly 60. There were plenty of old men and women in Ippolito's world – Montmorency died at 74 and Pope Paul III at 81, and Queen Eleanor of France lived to the ripe old age of 90. But there were many diseases for which sixteenth-century doctors had no cure.

Malaria, typhus, dysentery and the plague could all be fatal. Others died from septicaemia, the inevitable result of a burst appendix, gangrene from infected wounds or the complications of childbirth. Gout was widespread (Ippolito himself suffered from it later in life, and died of its complications). The sudden death of great men and women had major repercussions on the careers of those further down the ladder, and there was an indecent, almost morbid, interest in symptoms. One news-sheet from Rome included details of the lancing of Cardinal Ercole Gonzaga's boil, while Ippolito's letters to Ercole contained frequent medical bulletins on Francis I's health. While they were hunting around Cremieu in the middle of June, the King had one of his regular attacks of fever. This time, reported Ippolito, it started with a bad pain in his kidneys while they were out chasing deer. That night his temperature rose alarmingly and he spent two days in bed, ill enough to listen, for once, to his doctors who advised him to convalesce properly and not start hunting again as soon as he was out of bed – he cancelled the rest of the hunting trip and the court returned to Lyon.

Ippolito himself does not seem to have been ill during 1536, but many of his household suffered. Cestarello spent five months in bed in Lyon. Zoane da Cremona's ledgers list frequent purchases of capons, sweetbreads, sugar and delicate cuts of veal for the invalid, as well as borage flowers, which were widely regarded as a tonic. Francesco the farrier died in December, and Arcangelo the table-decker in early 1537, though the account books do not record why. Nor do they record the nature of Niccolò Tassone's ailment, though it must have been more troublesome than severe, because he returned, with Ippolito's permission, to Ferrara to recover.

Tassone left Lyon on 19 April and travelled very slowly, taking two months over the journey – he carried an urgent letter for Ercole which Ippolito ordered him to pass on to anyone he met who was travelling more quickly. Eleven more members of the household went back to Ferrara in June. There is no indication that these men were ill, and it is much more likely that Ippolito wanted to cut his expenses. The twelve men, including Tassone, were accompanied by ten servants and three muleteers to take charge of the mules carrying their baggage, making twenty-five in all, and reducing the size of Ippolito's entourage by 25 per cent. In addition to Tassone, Ippolito lost two more courtiers, Provosto Trotti and Scipio d'Este, one of his two chaplains and Besian with his two fellow falconers, who were taking the birds home to rest during their annual summer moult. These seven men remained part of the household, but the other five went back to new jobs or retirement. Two were pages who disappear completely from the documents. Cavreto, the footman whose wife had had a baby shortly before he left for France, went back to take up a job as footman in Duke Ercole's household. The other two, Zoane da Cremona and Moiza the barber, both retired (on full-salary pensions supplied by Ippolito).

Only Cestarello, Moiza and Zoane were replaced. Cestarello's ill-health had made him unfit for the taxing job of major-domo and Ippolito appointed a new one, Alessandro Zerbinato, another Ferrarese aristocrat who arrived later in the year. Cestarello did not retire completely but stayed on in Lyon, where Ippolito appointed him to act as agent for his new French benefices of St-Médard and the archbishopric of Lyon, which were still awaiting papal consent. We do not know the identity of the new barber – he might well have been French – and perhaps he was not satisfactory, because another barber was sent out from Ferrara the following year, poached from the household of Ippolito's younger brother Francesco. Zoane's job was given to Gasparino, one of the *credenzieri*. Zoane recorded the event, rather bleakly, in the pages of his ledger – 'Friday 9 June: Gasparino *credenziero* succeeds in my place as purveyor to the Illustrious Monsignore and starts his job on this aforementioned day.' Like the barber, he too did not last the year, though it is not clear from the ledgers whether he retired or died. His successor was Jacomo Panizato, the ex-painter, whose meteoric rise through the household ranks was far from over.

The letter which Niccolò Tassone took back to Ercole II contained several urgent requests. Ippolito wanted a horse from Ercole's famous stables because, as he flattered his brother, 'yours are reputed to be amongst the best that can be found'. There was also a request, which was passed on to Fiorini, Ippolito's factor in Ferrara, for a large tent – more like a marquee – for travelling with the court. In the middle of July, in the boiling heat of an exceptionally dry summer – so dry that the river Po was almost unnavigable and the peacocks at Belfiore needed feeding because the grass had died – one of the ducal trainers left Ferrara with two stable boys, two muleteers, four mules and two carthorses. They brought not just one thoroughbred horse but two, the second a present to Ippolito from one of Ercole's courtiers, Scipio Bonlei. They also brought the marquee, a large case of Italian cheese, forty-three salamis and two large carved wooden chests from the Palazzo San Francesco, which Ippolito wanted to furnish his apartments in France.

They found Ippolito with the French court at Valence, a town on the Rhône, about 80 kilometres south of Lyon. The court was in mourning. On 10 August the 18-year-old Dauphin had died very suddenly, shortly after drinking a glass of cold water after an energetic game of tennis with his secretary. Although the post-mortem established death from natural causes, rumours soon began to circulate that he had been poisoned by someone in the pay of Charles V, and the secretary was charged with the crime. He confessed his guilt under torture and, although he immediately retracted it, he was publicly executed in Lyon in October. Unfortunately, Ippolito's letters reporting this disaster have not survived, but its impact was soon apparent in a new structure of power at the French court. Francis I's second son, the 17-year-old Henri, was now the heir to the throne and his wife, Catherine de' Medici, the future Queen.

Meanwhile, Francis I was preoccupied with war. In the middle of July, Charles V, having failed to oust the French from Piedmont, decided to invade Provence. Montmorency was appointed to lead the army and he set up camp at Avignon, while the King, together with the court, settled at Valence, from where the camp could be supplied with troops, artillery and food. The French strategy was simple, and devastating. With the imperial armies advancing along the coast from Nice, blocked to the north by mountains and to the south by the Mediterranean, Montmorency's soldiers just destroyed everything edible between Nice and Avignon. They burned the ripening crops, ruined wells and mills, shattered wine barrels and set farm animals free to roam (killing them would have left a ready supply of meat), though they left fruit on the trees and grapes on the vines in the hope that this diet would encourage an outbreak of dysentery in the imperial army. Aix was evacuated and the inhabitants told to destroy anything that could be of use to the enemy. For the people of Provence, this scorched-earth policy must have been appalling, but from a military point of view the strategy was spectacularly successful. Charles V's army, under its general, Anton de Leyva, marched into France and, meeting no opposition, took control of the area. They got as far as Aix, which they captured on 13 August without trouble, but the famine engineered by Francis I soon took hold, as did the dysentery. By early September it was estimated that 8,000 imperial soldiers had died – Leyva himself died on 7 September – and a few days later the army started to retreat along the barren coast back to Italy.

On 9 September, two days after the death of Leyva, but before the imperial army had started to retreat, Ippolito left Valence with the King for the three-day journey south to Montmorency's camp at Avignon. They travelled down the Rhône on a barge, staying the first night at Montélimar, the second at Pont-St-Esprit and the third at Sorgues, where they were met by Montmorency. The following day the royal party made their entry into the army camp at Avignon, about 20 kilometres away. Ippolito reported the entry with great excitement: 'it was a most wonderful sight and I would not ever wish to be deprived of such a spectacle'. The King left Sorgues after lunch with 200 courtiers and an escort of 400 archers. They were met on the road by the new Dauphin, Montmorency, the Cardinal of Lorraine and the Comte de St-Pol. St-Pol was an old friend of Francis I and an experienced soldier. He had been badly wounded and taken prisoner at the Battle of Pavia in 1525 but he had managed to escape with the King of Navarre by bribing the guards. As Ippolito described the entry to his brother, 'although the Cardinal of Lorraine entered in armour, I followed your advice and entered unarmed'. Ercole II had made quite a fuss about this in one of his letters, and Ippolito must have resented the curb on his pleasures, because he added that he had looked as if he had 'left his fleece behind, as if I had been shorn, and it would not have been so bad if at least I had worn leg armour because of the great crush'. Evidently he decided not to be so conspicuous again, and a few months later he commissioned his own suit of battle armour from a Ferrarese armourer.

~

By October the fighting season was over for the year and, having watched the public execution of the young Dauphin's poisoner in Lyon on 7 October, the court set out on its slow progress northwards to Paris. Their leisurely journey left plenty of time for hunting, tennis and gambling, though Ippolito mislaid the bag that contained his gambling funds while they were in Roanne, 80 kilometres north-west of Lyon. They spent a week in Moulins, the seat of the powerful Bourbon dynasty, whose castle contained a tennis court. They also spent several days in the medieval stronghold of Loches – where Ippolito's uncle Ludovico Sforza had died as a prisoner of the French. It was here that the new Dauphin had a serious hunting accident. Ippolito reported the accident to Ercole II in a reply to several coded letters from his brother, which 'I cannot decipher because I am too busy'. He related how he had been out hunting with Francis I and the Dauphin, James V of Scotland and the King of Navarre. The hounds had been chasing a large boar, when suddenly it turned and charged at the Dauphin. He narrowly escaped death thanks to his own bravery and the timely intervention of Navarre, who managed to wound the boar before it could do any serious damage. After more stops at Amboise, Blois, Cléry and Orléans, they finally reached Fontainebleau early in December.

Francis I traditionally spent Christmas, New Year and Carnival in the Paris area, dividing his time between the medieval palace of the Louvre, uncomfortable but central, the château of Madrid, a hunt-ing lodge he had built just outside the old city, and his magnificent villa at Fontainebleau, 60 kilometres south of the capital. This was the season for feasting, and the celebrations in 1536–7 were particu-larly impressive because the whole court gathered in Paris for the wedding of James V of Scotland and Francis I's eldest daughter, the 16-year-old Madeleine. James V was 24 years old, three years younger than Ippolito, and popular at the French court. He had inherited his throne at the age of 17 months when his father, James IV, was killed fighting the English at the Battle of Flodden. His mother was Mar-garet Tudor, sister of Henry VIII, and she came to the wedding. One of the few royal relations not to attend was Madeleine's aunt, Renée – Margaret Tudor objected to her Protestant sympathies. Ippolito com-miserated with his sister-in-law but told her the journey would have been awful: a winter crossing of the Alps was something of which he had first-hand experience.

Ippolito thoroughly enjoyed his first winter in Paris. He, like James V, was popular at the French court, something Ercole II heard not only from his ambassador in France but also from his agents in Rome, who had had the gossip from the French diplomats there. Above all, Ippolito enjoyed the court's grandeur and sophistication. The year before he had spent Carnival in Bologna, and he had been somewhat disdainful of the quality of entertainment on offer. Now he was at the heart of what was arguably the grandest court in Europe, taking part in splendidly regal jousting tournaments and attending masked balls, both of which had been conspicuously lack-ing in Bologna. He reported from Paris that 'the King has jousted every day and held banquets and masques of various sorts in the evening'. On 6 January, the feast of Epiphany, there was a masked ball presided over by the Queen of Misrule who, that particular year,

A game of real tennis

was one of the Queen's Spanish ladies-in-waiting. This traditional upsetting of the normal social structure of the court provided a lot of amusement – Ippolito was particularly entertained by a group of men and women dressed as servants in court livery, who turned out to be the King and Queen of Navarre, Montmorency and Châteaubriand, the Governor of Brittany and one of Montmorency's closest allies at court.

Ippolito could also indulge in that most elitist of sports, real tennis. Francis I had built a tennis court at the Louvre, and two at Fontainebleau, each with tiled floors and dark walls so that the light-coloured ball could easily be seen. The French courts were broadly similar to those in Ferrara but not identical – there was no such thing as a standard court. Ippolito had to master the possibilities of a completely new set of cuts and angles as his ball bounced off the sloping roofs and buttresses of the court walls. Moreover the French had added a refinement to the game in the form of small grilles (*dedans*) set in the wall behind the service court. If a player managed to hit one of these he automatically won the point. According to Ippolito's

gaming book, his most regular opponents were the Cardinal of Lorraine and the two royal princes, the Dauphin and the Duke of
Orléans.

There was also excellent hunting in the royal deer park at Vincennes, on the outskirts of Paris. During the autumn Ippolito had
written to Ferrara to ask for his dogs and falcons to be sent to France.
For some reason, not explained in the account books, their departure
was delayed but eventually, on 27 December, Besian the falconer left
Ferrara with his assistants and kennelmen to escort eight dogs and
twenty-one falcons to France. Several of the birds were new. Some
had been bought in Ferrara but the prized peregrines and sakers had
been acquired in Venice. For Besian and the falconers this was the
third time they had done the trip that year and this particular journey
must have been foul. There was so much snow in Ferrara when they
left that the peacocks at Belfiore had to be given extra grain, and it
took the party ten weeks to reach the French court, by which time the
festivities were over and Ippolito had left Paris. These trips became an
annual event for Besian. He returned to Ferrara the following May,
for the seasonal moult, and left again for France in September,
making sure this time that he arrived for the start of the season.

Dogs provided Ippolito with an excellent excuse for networking.
Ercole II was particularly keen to acquire some good hunting dogs.
By good, he clearly meant large — size mattered more to him than
breed. Throughout the summer Ercole chided his brother — one
could even say nagged — for failing to find any. For once, Ippolito was
not being lazy. During the summer the court had been too busy with
war but, as soon as the fighting season was over and the hunting
season under way again, Ippolito did all he could to procure animals
large enough for Ercole's taste. Plenty of people, especially those
belonging to Montmorency's faction, were evidently happy to oblige,
and Ippolito's letters home were littered with references to those who
had agreed. The Cardinal of Lorraine had promised some, as had
his brother, the Duke of Lorraine. Châteaubriand was sending a
dog and a bitch from Brittany. Even James V promised to send some

when he got home to Scotland. The King had produced a particularly nice dog, 'very good after boars', but Ippolito decided not to
send this one to Ercole II, claiming, somewhat suspiciously, that the
animal was too old.

Montmorency was characteristically prompt: by the middle of
January he had produced two dogs, one of which, Ippolito informed
his brother, was 'good for wolves and I think you will like it', and
another that he had seen run after 'a deer which I killed in the park at
Vincennes, where it ran very well'. He had also received one from St-
Pol, which was 'not the type you are expecting but St-Pol recom-
mends it as particularly good after boar, and I have seen it go
strongly'. These dogs were sent off to Ferrara. 'Today', Ippolito
wrote on 20 January, 'I am sending the dogs from St-Pol and Montmorency and I hope they arrive for you to enjoy them during Lent,
especially one from Montmorency, which is a good size.' Sadly the
journey was too much for them and they arrived in bad shape, much
to Ercole II's disappointment.

Ippolito was rapidly gaining a reputation for extravagant generosity with his presents to the French court. Such liberality was rather
more than he could afford. Mosto had to sell five of Ippolito's medals
to a goldsmith in Paris for 25 scudi in part payment for two rosaries
and a pair of gold-embroidered sleeves which the goldsmith had supplied for Ippolito to distribute as presents to ladies of the court. Many
of the presents were his own treasured possessions. Francis I received
Ippolito's entire collection of 215 antique medals as a New Year present. The horse which Ercole II had sent the previous summer had
been much admired, especially by one of the Dauphin's courtiers,
Gaucher de Dinteville, who was the younger brother of Guillaume
and Jean, Francis I's ambassador in England. As Ippolito phrased it,
Gaucher was 'a gentleman and a good friend of mine and in very
good standing with the Dauphin, so I gave the horse to him and I am
sure that, even though I am not able to enjoy it myself, I could not
have made a better investment at this court'. Presents, as Ippolito
knew, were excellent political currency. When Francis I admired the

other horse, which had arrived in France that summer (a present to Ippolito from Scipio Bonlei, a ducal courtier in Ferrara), Ippolito instantly gave it to the King. This horse was called The Turk and Francis I lent it to Montmorency for a jousting contest against the Dauphin which took place during the wedding festivities. Montmorency won, largely, he claimed, because of the exceptional bravery of the horse.

Not everyone at court liked Ippolito, however. His popularity inevitably generated jealousy, and one man in particular was determined to ruin his chances of acquiring a cardinal's hat. Rodolfo Pio da Carpi was the papal ambassador in France and he had a personal axe to grind. His family had been evicted from their state by Charles V for insisting on maintaining their loyalty to France, and the Emperor had given this tiny fief to Ippolito's father, Duke Alfonso, in 1530. Carpi could do little to stall Ippolito's success in France, but he had considerable influence in Rome and seized every available opportunity to discredit Ippolito at the papal court. One such opportunity occurred just before Christmas when he overheard a conversation between Ippolito and Cardinal Jean du Bellay, the Archbishop of Paris. The topic was Ippolito's appointment as Archbishop of Lyon. Ippolito asked the Cardinal if he had any news and du Bellay warned him that the Pope was unlikely to give his consent. According to Carpi, a violent argument ensued, in public, which culminated in Ippolito accusing du Bellay of insulting his family. Carpi also reported that a few days later, again in public, Ippolito accused du Bellay of cheating at cards. Carpi surely exaggerated both incidents – Ippolito's anger was directed towards the Pope, and he was soon gambling with du Bellay again. However, Carpi's dislike clearly affected his judgement when he used this incident to prove to Paul III that Ippolito's popularity was on the wane. 'It should be said that Ippolito has come to be disliked by all men at this court', Carpi wrote, adding, 'it is true that the King quite likes him but, having the whole court against him, I cannot but judge that things will go badly for him.' How Carpi must have crowed when, just a few days after writing this letter, news arrived in Paris that he had been created a cardinal and Ippolito had not.

Ippolito's campaign for a cardinal's hat had started in earnest in late October when he sent his secretary Antonio Romei to Rome as a kind of personal ambassador to lobby on his behalf at the papal court. Romei could exploit two factors in Ippolito's favour. First, Ippolito was now Francis I's prime candidate. Second, Paul III owed a debt of gratitude to Pope Alexander VI, Ippolito's grand-father. As a lowly but ambitious clerk in the Curia, Paul III had lacked the right connections until his beautiful sister became the mis-tress of Rodrigo Borgia. When Rodrigo was elected Pope, he chose Paul III as his new papal treasurer and made him a cardinal, thus launching not only his protégé's spectacularly successful career but also the fortunes of the entire Farnese dynasty – quite a debt. There was evidence that Paul III had not forgotten. In the Christmas Con-sistory of 1536 Paul III had created ten new cardinals, but he had also reserved two names *in petto* (literally, in the breast). From Rome Romei reported back to Ippolito and Ercole II that one of these names was widely rumoured to be that of Ippolito.

Paul III maintained a dignified silence for six weeks before finally confiding to the French ambassador that one of the reserved card-inalates was indeed intended for Ippolito. But there was one signi-ficant, and troublesome, condition. Ippolito would not get his hat until Paul III had resolved a long-standing dispute with Ippolito's brother regarding the ownership of Modena and Reggio. These two cities were imperial fiefs and traditionally part of the Este duchy but they had been captured in 1512 by Pope Julius II, who had incorp-orated them, with imperial approval, into the Papal States. Ippolito's father had snatched them back in the power vacuum that followed the Sack of Rome, an action immediately declared illegal by Pope Clement VII. Much to the annoyance of Ippolito, and Ercole II, Paul III had decided to enforce his predecessor's policy, despite the fact that Charles V had recognized the Este as the legal owners of the cities.

Paul III

Paul III was 68 years old but, despite his age and an excessive bias in favour of his children and grandchildren, he had not lost his faculties. He was a wily old bird and a very astute politician. He knew he was unlikely to get Ercole II to surrender Modena and Reggio, with their highly lucrative incomes, but he intended to squeeze as much profit, financial and political, as he could from the settlement of the dispute. He needed money badly, not least to finance an enormous programme of artistic patronage to promote his authority as Pope. This included not only an ambitious series of fortifications to defend the Papal States against the Turks, who were harrying the Italian coast, but also two of Michelangelo's most famous works – his *Last Judgement* in the Sistine Chapel and the hugely expensive rebuilding of St Peter's.

Ercole II d'Este

Paul III's condition for granting Ippolito's hat put both brothers in a difficult position. Ercole II, as stubborn as the Pope but not so clever, deeply resented having to pay anything at all for the privilege of owning what he considered to be part of his birthright, even if it would help his brother. Ippolito had to be careful not to push his brother nor to appear to put his own personal agenda ahead of family loyalty. 'You will have heard from Romei in Rome', he wrote to Ercole on 5 January, 'that the only reason I was not made a cardinal is because I am your brother, but I would rather be that than have one or a hundred cardinalates.' Diplomatically, he urged the Duke to exploit Paul III's affection for their grandfather and to come to an agreement with him, because the Pope was old and 'his successor might not be so amenable'. The situation did not augur well for Ippolito's hat.

~

Ippolito's life in France during 1537 is sparsely documented. None of the ledgers kept by the members of staff with him have survived – though all the books kept by Fiorini in Ferrara are extant. Reading the letters between Ippolito and Ercole II, as well as the diplomatic correspondence between Rome and Ferrara, and between Rome and France, it is clear that the focus that year shifted away from pleasure towards politics and war. With the worst of the winter weather over, the fighting season opened in early March. Ippolito was about to experience war at close quarters. This year Francis I's target was northern France and the recapture of Artois and St-Pol, two counties on the Flemish border which had been seized by Charles V's troops the summer before, in an ineffective attempt to lure the French away from Provence. The court left Paris in late February for Amiens, which was to be the base for the campaign and where the Queen and the rest of the court now settled. The King and his army, and Ippolito, continued north towards the border. Many of Ippolito's friends were actively involved in the fighting – Francis I's general was Montmorency and among the army commanders were the King of Navarre, St-Pol, the Duke of Guise and the Dauphin. They invaded Artois in early March and initially met with little resistance, but their advance was halted at the castle of Hesdin, a heavily fortified stronghold garrisoned by 700 imperial troops.

On 20 March the new Ferrarese ambassador arrived to take up his post in France. Alberto Turco had left Ferrara on 29 January and it had taken him seven weeks to reach the army camp outside Hesdin. Despite the battle raging a few kilometres away, the formalities of Turco's official reception were observed and he presented gifts to the court on behalf of Ercole II. Mindful of the need for good relations with Francis I's new heir, the Duke had sent the Dauphin an expensive suit of armour and a horse. These presents were not as welcome as they might have been. The horse took three weeks to recover from the journey and the armour was for jousting not war – the Dauphin asked Turco if Ercole II could provide him with a suit of battle armour. Ippolito was more fortunate. Turco had brought large quan-tities of goods for him from Ferrara. One wooden crate was packed with 175 metres of velvets and satins (in black, purple and dark orange), bought in Venice for over 350 scudi. There were also two new violins, which had been specially made for Ippolito in the ducal castle workshops, two new swords with elaborate black and gold hilts, together with a spare sword blade, two ornamental sleeves that had been made in Mantua as presents for ladies at court, and four new white linen shirts, specially embroidered for him by Sister Sera-fina. Turco's predecessor left for Ferrara, taking another consignment of dogs which Ippolito had found for his brother. These included two Breton hunting dogs from the Cardinal of Lorraine and a bitch from the Duke of Guise, 'which he says is very beautiful and that is a great pleasure to me because he is someone who likes dogs very much'. Châteaubriand had also sent two from Brittany, a dog and a bitch, but the bitch died on the journey and the dog arrived too late – Châteaubriand promised to replace the bitch as soon as he could. Unlike the first batch, these all arrived safely in Ferrara, but Ercole was still not satisfied and complained that they were not large enough.

On 26 March, despite the heavy rain and strong winds, Turco went out with Ippolito to see the siege of Hesdin – war was very much a spectator sport. The ambassador wrote to Ercole II that, in his opinion, the French had little chance of victory. The castle, he reported, was only slightly smaller than the stronghold of Milan, and it was widely believed to be impregnable. It had now been under siege for a week and so far every attempt to breach its walls had been repulsed by a hail of artillery from the imperial troops inside. Attached to his official report was a personal note for the Duke. He had found the camp filled with pretty girls, but he assured his master that, 'Even though I wanted to send for one, I did not because I would not sin in marriage ... Your Excellency knows how the Devil tempts me in this more than anything else, and God alone knows how hard it is for me to resist, but I have promised my wife in Fer-rara.' Ippolito had no such restrictions on his behaviour, but Turco makes no mention of his activities in this particular field.

A few days later Montmorency approached the castle to offer the imperial troops their lives if they surrendered, and promising to cut their throats if they remained obstinate. They refused to surrender and Montmorency launched a major attack. The French breached the walls with a mine, which they detonated in a wine cellar, only to find another wall behind. The science of explosives was still in its infancy, and mines were very unreliable weapons. Several French mines fired into the castle did not explode immediately and the imperial soldiers hurled them down on to the troops attacking the wall below, each killing about thirty men. The French, however, ably led by Montmorency, did not give up. Turco was full of praise for the French commander and for the industry of his soldiers, who 'never stop hauling their artillery and making all those attempts which you have to do if you really want to seize such a place'. One day in early April, a special envoy arrived from Paul III to deliver a long speech in front of the castle urging the French to stop fighting and sign a truce. Francis I took no notice of this bizarre interruption and, after meeting his captains, ordered the army to push the can-nons right up to the base of the walls, despite the fact that the troops could easily be picked off by the imperial arquebusiers on the castle ramparts. A lot of men died – neither Turco nor Ippolito mention how many, though both were there watching the proceedings – but after three days the French managed to collapse about 9 metres of wall. This was enough to allow the soldiers to enter the castle, and to enable the cavalry, led by Montmorency, St-Pol, the Duke of Guise and the King of Navarre, to charge. Hesdin finally fell on 13 April.

By early June the court had returned to Fontainebleau. With the campaign in northern France largely successful, Francis I's priority now became the rescue of his garrisons which were still holding out in northern Italy. Ippolito expected to stay just a few weeks in

Fontainebleau before heading south to Lyon. He complained that it seemed very empty without Montmorency and the Dauphin, who had remained behind with the troops in northern France, but he was delighted to find that he and his household were to be lodged in the Dauphin's vacant apartments. His new barber arrived from Ferrara during June, along with his new suit of battle armour, and one of his courtiers, Provosto Trotti. However, their stay at Fontainebleau was much longer than expected. Francis I fell seriously ill at the end of June – indeed he was so ill that his doctors would not let him hear the news of his daughter Madeleine's death shortly after her arrival in Scotland. He recovered very slowly, and it was not until early September that the court left Fontainebleau for Lyon and Italy.

The garrisons in Italy were successfully relieved by Montmorency in October and the following month Francis I decided that Piedmont was secure enough for an official visit. By now the autumn rains had signalled the end of the fighting season. Francis I had recovered what he had lost to Charles V the year before, but the war had been cripplingly expensive for both rulers. It has been estimated that Francis I spent 2,500,000 scudi on the 1537 campaign. He owed 50,000 scudi to the bankers of Lyon, and 100,000 scudi to Ercole II, money which the Duke badly needed to settle his affairs with Paul III. Ercole badgered both Turco and Ippolito to ask Francis I to repay the debt, but, as they reminded him, this was hardly the time to ask the King for money for anything other than war. With the two rivals almost bankrupt, Paul III seized the opportunity to intervene and this time successfully persuaded both sides to agree to a truce, which was signed on 16 November.

Meanwhile, Ippolito's career prospects were faltering. Throughout the year Paul III had been bombarded with letters from Francis I and speeches from the French ambassador promoting Ippolito as the King's candidate for a cardinal's hat. The Pope continued to insist on settling his dispute with Ercole II first. Part of the huge sum he was demanding was the price of Ippolito's hat, which, in March 1537, stood at 10,000 scudi. In June, rumours started to circulate in Rome that Paul III had raised the price of the hat to 40,000 scudi. Romei dismissed these rumours as malicious gossip, but it is clear that they were started deliberately and that they originated from inside the Vatican. However, Ercole II still showed no sign of yielding to the papal demands, despite pressure from Ippolito, from Romei and from Francis I himself – and the Pope refused to compromise. Later that summer Paul III infuriated the Duke by appointing his teenage grandson to take charge of the negotiations. If this was intended as a slight on Ercole, it certainly succeeded. Cardinal Alessandro Farnese – known as the Cardinalino, the little cardinal – was still three months short of his seventeenth birthday, and this was his first public role. Romei reported, perhaps a little acidly, that Alessandro had been having lessons in politics and geography, and knew the names of all the countries and rulers of the world.

It was not just the cardinal's hat that was causing difficulties for Ippolito but also his benefices. Charles V, angry that Francis I's candidate for a cardinal's hat also held the position of Archbishop of Milan, a city under his authority, decided to sequestrate Ippolito's income. In June Paul III gave his formal refusal to Ippolito's nomination as Archbishop of Lyon. Cardinal du Bellay's warning had proved correct. The Pope argued that it was unprecedented for someone who was not a cardinal to hold two archbishoprics, particularly two such important sees as Milan and Lyon (there were only fifty or so archbishoprics in the whole of Europe). It has to be said that Paul III was under considerable pressure to refuse this appointment. A new and very vocal generation of cardinals were gaining support in Rome for their demand that the Pope reform the Church. One of their main targets was the widespread tenure of multiple sees. Alienating the reformers would have been political suicide for Paul III, and, with a show of the greatest reluctance, he agreed to a compromise arrangement, suggested by Francis I, whereby Lyon and the French abbeys would be given to the Cardinal of Lorraine, who was already Archbishop of Rheims and

Narbonne, and who promised to transfer the benefices to Ippolito at a later date.

The situation was exacerbated by Cardinal Carpi, who continued to do what he could to damage Ippolito's reputation. That summer he reported to Paul III that Ippolito had insulted the Pope during a conversation with Francis I. The King immediately denied the story, calling it 'a deceitful tale'. Paul III recalled Carpi to Rome and, much to Ippolito's relief, replaced him with a new ambassador. 'At least the poisonous tongue of Cardinal Carpi has ceased now that he has gone,' wrote Ippolito to his brother, 'but he will certainly do what he can to impede our business with his ill will.' Ippolito was right. As soon as he got back to Rome, Carpi joined forces with the reformers, who were delighted at his apparent conversion to their cause. At a meeting with the Pope, they persuaded Paul III that to make Ippolito a cardinal as part of such a large financial package would leave him open to charges of simony, another target of their radical reforms.

In September Ercole II made a final offer to Paul III. He proposed the sum of 170,000 scudi to settle the issue of Modena and Reggio, and 12,000 scudi for Ippolito's hat, though he told his ambassador that he would go up to 15,000 scudi for the hat, if necessary. The Pope rejected the proposal. The Duke then raised his offer for Ippolito's hat to 30,000 scudi and still Paul III refused to agree. Ercole II would not raise his offer further and Paul III's staff at the Curia suddenly became very reluctant to meet the Ferrarese ambassador, Francesco Villa, giving a stream of rather thin excuses – they were too busy (in a meeting), they did not have the case notes with them, and so on. The negotiations had reached deadlock and the Duke recalled his ambassador to Ferrara for urgent consultations. The two men discussed various tactics, in particular, the idea of dropping the demand for Ippolito's hat and settling the Modena and Reggio business without it. Villa then returned to Rome and rumours started to circulate that Ippolito's hat had indeed been removed from Ercole's agenda.

The news soon reached Ippolito in France and, although the Duke continued to reassure his brother that he would do no such thing, he was in fact considering this option very carefully. He wrote to Ippolito denying the rumours and blamed the breakdown of the talks on Paul III. He promised Ippolito that he had ordered Villa to do all he could to come to an agreement with the Pope, and also to reassure the French envoys that he was doing everything possible to make Ippolito a cardinal, adding, 'so long as it is not simoniacal'. This was a telling escape clause – Ercole II was hoping that the accusation of simony would provide him with the excuse he needed to avoid paying the 40,000 scudi that Paul III was demanding for the hat. This letter survives only as a draft and, intriguingly, it reveals that Ercole had initially intended to tell Ippolito the truth – that he had indeed ordered Villa to exclude the price of Ippolito's hat from the settlement, using simony as his excuse. However, he thought better of including this vital piece of information and it was crossed out of the draft. Nevertheless, Ippolito must have suspected that his brother was no longer as loyal as he had hoped.

5

Domestic Affairs

I PPOLITO TRAVELLED A long way in 1537. By the end of the year he had ridden 2,500 kilometres and seen more of France than most of the country's inhabitants. He celebrated New Year in Paris, spent the spring with the French army fighting in northern France and then returned to Fontainebleau for the summer. In the autumn he rode south to Lyon and crossed the Alps into Italy, accompanying the King on his royal progress through Piedmont, before returning to France and riding south-west to Montpellier, not far from the border with Spain, where he spent Christmas. He sampled the sophistica-tion of a royal capital, the excitement of violent but victorious battle, the luxury of a magnificent royal villa and hunting park, and, twice, the discomfort of mountain travel. It is hard to imagine a greater con-trast to the regular routine and provincial perspectives he had left behind in Ferrara. Nevertheless Ferrara was home, and the source of the wealth that enabled him to live, in some style, at the French court. Although the ledgers kept by his household in France in 1537 no longer exist, the account books charting the management of his properties in Ferrara that year have survived. These ledgers were kept by Jacomo Filippo Fiorini, ex-painter and ex-guardian of Ippolito's wardrobe, who had been left in Ferrara to run Ippolito's affairs during his absence. The scope of Fiorini's job, together with his accountant's eye for precise detail, make these ledgers a mine of infor-mation, providing fascinating glimpses into the everyday lives of all sorts of people with whom Fiorini had dealings – not just merchants,

shopkeepers and artisans, but also bargemen, carters, casual labour
ers and even the destitute. The ledgers also tell us a lot about Fiorini
himself, and his relationship with Ippolito.

One cold morning early in February 1537 Fiorini gave 345 kilos of
wheat (old wheat, worth about 5 scudi) to a widow called Domicila
di Sabadini. Her newly wed daughter had been abandoned by her
husband, a builder, because Domicila had not been able to pay the
agreed dowry. 'I was moved by compassion,' Fiorini wrote, 'and
because God will reward Monsignore [Ippolito] and safeguard him
from ill fortune, I gave her 20 *stara* of the old wheat so that this young
girl can return to the world with honour.' This was not a very large
amount of grain – that same day Fiorini gave 23 *stara* of wheat to
Provosto Trotti, one of Ippolito's courtiers, as the monthly allowance
Ippolito provided for him and his two servants. One hopes that
Domicila, her deserted daughter and even the mercenary son-in-law
all benefited from Fiorini's gesture. Fiorini certainly believed that
Ippolito would gain from it, when God honoured his side of the bar
gain. But the episode reveals much about Fiorini himself, not least the
meticulous way in which he recorded the details to justify this unex
pected item of expenditure. It illustrates his basic decency and loyalty,
his care for Ippolito's welfare and how his master looked in the eyes of
the world, and also his unconscious recognition of the unfairness of
some of the laws that governed the society in which he lived. It was
rare for Fiorini to allow a personal note to creep into his ledgers – he
was much more at home dealing with sums rather than emotions.

Ippolito had been fortunate in his choice of steward (his title was
factore, a word that translates directly to the Scottish 'factor'). Fiorini
was hard-working, conscientious and honest. He lived in rooms in
Ippolito's villa at Belfiore, on the northern edge of the city, and was at
work in his office in the Palazzo San Francesco six days a week, often
seven. During 1537 he worked on thirty-six out of the fifty-two Sun
days and on many major Church holidays, including Easter Day
and Christmas Day; he even worked on 23 April, the day most citi
zens of Ferrara took to the streets to celebrate the feast of their patron

saint, St George. Every transaction, income or expenditure, was minutely detailed in his notebooks in his precise and legible hand-writing. On the first day of every month he started a new notebook — A4-sized exercise books bound in blue card — carefully writing the page number in the top right-hand corner of each spread. He began by listing Ippolito's income on the first page and then left five or six empty pages before starting on the expenditure. He made remarkably few errors, which is impressive given the complexity of some of the transactions, though he did occasionally enter an expenditure item under income, or vice versa, and had to cross the entry out, with firm clear lines, before inserting it correctly.

Each entry follows the same formula. Fiorini recorded the date, the people involved, the sums received or paid out, the goods or ser-vices involved, often an explanation of why the transaction had taken place and, where relevant, the prices. If he found bookkeeping boring and repetitive, it does not show. His assistant, Tomaso Mor-ello, then collated the cash transactions from Fiorini's notebooks (ignoring some of Fiorini's detail) into a large leather-bound ledger to provide neat final accounts. These were audited by the ducal accountants, one of whom was Tomaso's father Piero, who had worked on Ippolito's books since 1524 and had doubtless been instrumental in getting Tomaso this post. Both father and son turned out to be crooks. Piero had managed to extricate himself from a charge of fraud earlier in his career in the ducal administration and only escaped a death sentence by persuading Ippolito's grandfather, Ercole I, to pardon him. He got his job back but the old Duke's trust in the family proved seriously misplaced. In 1543 Tomaso was arres-ted for fraud. While he was incarcerated in the castle prisons — where he was fed at Ippolito's expense — Piero, who was still working at the age of 74, decided on drastic action and set fire to the ledgers in his office in the castle. During his trial he was forced to confess that he had been embezzling ducal funds. I have not found any evidence of dishonesty in the ledger Tomaso compiled in 1537 but he did make some very bizarre mistakes: there is a 31 June for example, and in

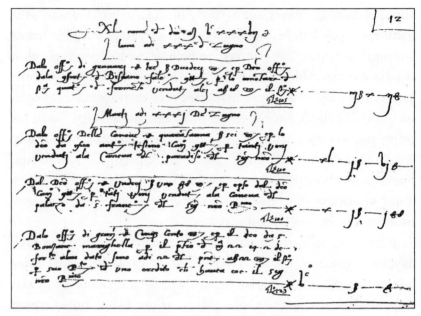

Tomaso Morello's ledger, showing his entries for 30 and 31 June
(xxx and xxxi de Zugno)

mid-March he got muddled with the days of the week, following Friday, 23 March (which was correct) with Thursday, 24 March. These were not the sort of errors that Fiorini would make.

Fiorini's job carried considerable responsibility. He was not just Ippolito's bookkeeper but also his treasurer. It was Fiorini who received the income from Ippolito's assets in Italy, and paid all his bills. He did Ippolito's personal shopping in Ferrara and arranged for these purchases to be sent to France. The upkeep of both the Palazzo San Francesco and Belfiore were in his charge, as were the staff who had remained behind in Ferrara: Marcantonio the cellar-man, Carlo del Pavone the larderer, Francesco Salineo the flour official, Francesco Guberti, who managed the wood store and acted as Fiorini's personal assistant, Antonio da Como, who had been

Ippolito's *credenziero* and was now a general factotum, Francesco the gardener at the Palazzo San Francesco, and Tomaso, who looked after the gardens and the poultry at Belfiore, as well as all the men working in the stables, and the kennelmen and falconers at Belfiore. Fiorini also paid wages and expenses to the families of several mem/ bers of the household who were away in France, such as Andrea the cook, and to staff who had returned to Ferrara, including Moiza, Ippolito's personal barber, who arrived back in June 1536 and con/ tinued to earn a salary until the end of 1538.

However, Fiorini's main responsibility was the financial manage/ ment of Ippolito's estates, stores and granaries (Ippolito owned one granary and rented another at the Po wharves). He had to keep track of every sack of grain, cart of wood, bale of hay and barrel of wine sent to Ferrara. He agreed rates of pay with the bargemen, who shipped the goods, and with the carters and porters, who moved each load from the wharves. Fiorini also had to monitor every sale from each of Ippolito's stores, and to record all in/house transactions, such as the tallow candles taken from the larder to light the cellars, the jugs of oil from the larder to light the lamps in the stables and the brooms the stable boys used to sweep them clean.

Ippolito's income in 1537 came from various sources, all of which had family connections. He had acquired the archbishopric of Milan from his uncle, Cardinal Ippolito d'Este, when he was only 9. Under the energetic administration of Paulo Albertino, his agent in the city, Milan produced a substantial sum in 1537 – the full impact of Charles V's sequestration of his income would not be felt until the following year. The pension Ippolito received from Modena was paid regularly every six months by the Bishop of Modena as part of an agreement with the Pope to compensate Ippolito, who had been refused papal permission to inherit the bishopric after his uncle died. One of the agricultural estates, Bondeno, had also been inherited from his uncle, but the rest of the income – say two/thirds – came from the ducal properties bequeathed to him in his father's will. In addition to the monthly cash allowance his brother was obliged to

	Scudi	%
Archbishopric of Milan	1,599.1	15
Pension on bishopric of Modena	608.57	6
Monthly allowance from Duke Alfonso's will	1,068.57	10
Tax on butchers of Reggio	542.29	5
Tax on live animals entering Ferrara	1,647.74	16
Brescello	2,460.39	24
Agricultural estates		
rents paid in cash 245.01		
sales from estates 802.17		
sales from granary 578.36		
sales from palace stores 146.71		
sales from wine cellar 587.23		
sales from wood store 193.54	2,553.02	24
Total	10,479.68	100

Ippolito's cash income, 1537

pay him, Ippolito received the taxes raised on the butchers of Reggio and on all live animals entering Ferrara. He shared the income from the latter with his stepmother Laura, and they divided the cost of building an office – more like a booth – on the bridge into the city, where the tax was collected. The most lucrative item in his portfolio was the town of Brescello, which provided nearly a quarter of his income. This prosperous little centre close to the duchy's north-western border with Mantua and Milan had a thriving cloth industry, though it is now more famous for its football team.

In his ledgers, Fiorini used the standard silver-based currency of Ferrara – *lire, soldi* and *denari* (1 *lira* = 20 *soldi* = 240 *denari*). He also had to deal with a wide range of foreign currencies, and their fluctuating exchange rates. Ippolito's allowance from Duke Ercole and the tax on live animals entering Ferrara both arrived in Ferrarese coinage, but the butchers' tax from Reggio was paid in local ducats (worth

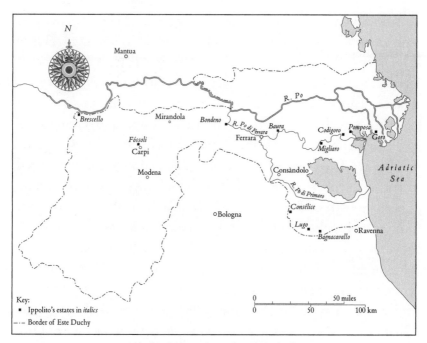

Ippolito's estates in the Este duchy

£3 13s each). Fiorini also received Italian scudi from Brescello
(worth £3 10s each) and money from Milan, which sometimes came
in *lire imperiali* (exchanged at £5 11s to a scudo) but also in various
types of scudi (Milanese and Genoese, and even French). Transporting money in sixteenth-century Europe was a necessary but risky
business. Fiorini preferred to settle bills directly with Ippolito's creditors, but he regularly had to pay these bills to their servants or rela-
tives – and he was careful to note precisely the relationship between
the creditor and the recipient in his ledgers. On one occasion he trusted a barge boy with the salary Ippolito owed to the chaplain at Bondeno, but this was unusual. The income from the estates was carried
by Ippolito's agents, or trustworthy substitutes, on the relatively short
journeys across the Este duchy and delivered to Fiorini in weighty
leather pouches. The dangers were greater outside the duchy. Paulo
Albertino rarely sent cash from Milan but deposited Ippolito's
income with Ferrarese bankers in the city who then sent credit notes

to Fiorini which he could exchange in Ferrara. There was no question of sending large amounts of money to Ippolito in France.
Ippolito got through over 7,000 scudi during 1537, which he withdrew as he needed from the Lyon agent of his sister-in-law, Renée of
France, who was then reimbursed in Ferrara by Fiorini.

The agricultural estates at Bondeno, Fóssoli and Pomposa together with his property in the Romagna made Ippolito a substantial
landowner. Bondeno, which he had inherited in 1520, was a small
parish with rich farming land about 20 kilometres west of Ferrara.
The huge estate of Pomposa, formerly attached to the abbey of Pomposa, gave Ippolito land east of Ferrara across the fertile soils of the
Po delta to the Adriatic coast. In the Romagna he owned woods and
three highly profitable mills at Lugo, Bagnacavallo and Consélice.
Fóssoli, the smallest of the estates, lay 80 kilometres west of Ferrara.
It had been part of the old imperial fief of Carpi until 1530, when
Charles V had evicted the Carpi family and given the state to Duke
Alfonso – Ippolito's ownership of Fóssoli cannot have done much to
improve his relationship with Cardinal Carpi.

The estates were all managed by local agents. The agent at Bondeno was Palamides de' Civali, who administered not only the farm
but also the church, where he paid salaries to the priests and bell-
ringers. Palamides reported directly to Fiorini but the men running
the other estates were supervised by Ippolito's land agent, Bigo
Schalabrino. The name Bigo was the local way of shortening the
name Ludovico, or Lewis – his name translates as Lew Sly, an
intriguing moniker for a man whose job was to keep a watchful eye
on the bailiffs. Pomposa was so large that it required three bailiffs,
based at each of the main towns of the estate, Baura, Migliaro and
Codigoro. They needed Bigo's authorization for any major item of
expenditure, such as shearing the sheep or paying wages to the
workmen repairing buildings on the estates. Bigo spent a lot of his
time on the road. He travelled from Ferrara to Fóssoli most months
to collect the produce and cash amassed by the bailiff since his last
visit – a 160-kilometre round trip – and then on to Pomposa, anoth-

er 54 kilometres each way, where he spent a day with each of the bailiffs there.

About 10 per cent of Ippolito's income from the estates came from rents, though this figure is slightly misleading as some of the rents were paid in goods, which were then sold. Leases for plots of land or houses were drawn up by Ippolito's lawyers and each lessee signed the witnessed contract which laid out precisely how much rent was due and when it had to be paid (the lessee also paid a tax for the privilege of signing the contract). Rents were invariably paid on the feasts of the Annunciation (25 March), St John the Baptist (24 June), St Michael (29 September) and the Nativity – exactly the same as the old English quarter-days of Lady Day, Midsummer, Michaelmas and Christmas. Some of the men who rented Ippolito's land were officials at the ducal court, but most were artisans – barbers, goldsmiths, painters, tailors and butchers – who used their holdings to provide fresh food for their families in town. Some of the plots must have been very small judging by the modest rents: a sack of wheat, three hens or just one capon. Larger plots were leased for money by men like the barber who paid 10 scudi each year for fields at Bondeno or the lawyer who paid an annual rent of 12 scudi for land at Pomposa. Ippolito also owned the inn at Goro, a small town on the Adriatic coast near Pomposa, which he rented out to the innkeeper, appropriately named Andrea Bonamigo (Andrew Goodfriend), for 31 scudi – when the inn burned down in a fire in 1539, it cost Ippolito 23 scudi to rebuild it.

The bulk of the income from the estates came from the sale of produce. Some of it was sold directly on the estates, but most was marketed from Ferrara. All the wine from the cellar at the Palazzo San Francesco, the wood from the store and the grain from the granary came from the estates. Wheat was the largest grain crop grown at Bondeno and Pomposa where it flourished on the rich alluvial soils of the Po plain. This was lush agricultural land, not the thin, dry stony soils where olives were cultivated – Ippolito had to buy his olive oil from the Marche and Puglia, further south. His estates also grew barley and occasionally rye, as well as cheaper grains such as millet, spelt and vetch. Most of the barley, millet and spelt was used as fodder for Ippolito's horses, though the poor ground all these crops, as well as legumes and vetch, to make bread – only the rich could afford white bread made from wheat. The estates produced large quantities of legumes, particularly chickpeas, lentils, beans and broad beans, rotating these crops with wheat (in an age before fertilizers, legumes had the practical advantage of restoring nitrogen to the soil). Flax and linseed were grown at Bondeno and Pomposa, and all the estates produced hay and straw for Ippolito's horses, as well as wine for his cellars. At Fóssoli, where the land was poorer, the main crops were spelt and sheep. Pomposa also supplied livestock – poultry, cattle, pigs and lambs – and the estate's extensive woods produced large quantities of logs for Ippolito's ovens and fires as well as timber for building. The wood was also used as fuel for a profitable kiln at Codigoro which produced bricks and tiles. Even the twigs were useful, bound into brushes and brooms which were sent to Ferrara to clean the Palazzo San Francesco.

All the farming was done by Ippolito's workers – they are called workers (*laboratori*) in the ledgers, not peasants. They planted and harvested his crops, ploughed the land, tended his sheep and cattle, cut the hay, felled the trees, chopped the logs and made the brushes and brooms. However they were not agricultural labourers in the modern sense of the term, nor did they have the independence of tenant farmers. Ippolito did not pay them wages but he did provide them with seeds and with accommodation in houses on the estates, which he was obliged to keep in good repair. He took a proportion of everything they produced. The term used in the ledgers is a tithe (*decima*), literally a tenth, derived from the 10 per cent that the Church originally deducted from all crops grown on its land. By the sixteenth century, however, the *decima* was a euphemism – in practice it was often 50 per cent, the amount Ippolito claimed on the sale of wool and lambs from Pomposa, although the percentage varied for other crops. The workers also had to pay Ippolito seasonal dues – for the workers at Migliaro this meant 100 eggs at Easter and a pig at Christmas. The system was not quite as iniquitous as it sounds. It was certainly unfair by modern standards, but levels of poverty were far worse on the city streets of Ferrara. There is detailed data on what the workers at Pomposa harvested in 1540, how much was taken by Ippolito and how much each worker retained. Marti Bolgarello, one of the eight men working on the farm at Migliaro, was left with grain and legumes worth 23 scudi, while one of his neighbours, Antonio Maria Trova, had crops worth 67 scudi. For both men, this was enough to feed themselves and their families, and Antonio Maria would have had a surplus to sell. However the documents are silent about what happened when a worker became too old, or too ill, to work.

~

The new year in Ferrara began on 1 January – unlike Florence and several other cities in sixteenth-century Italy, where it did not begin until 25 March, the feast of the Annunciation – and winter was the season for feasting at all levels of society. While Ippolito banqueted and jousted in Paris, his staff at the Palazzo San Francesco and the workers on his estates in the countryside also celebrated. January and February were relatively quiet months on the work front both in the city and on the farm. As the agrarian calendar carved on one of the portals of Ferrara Cathedral showed, January was the month when the peasant rested from his labours and ate and drank his way through New Year, Twelfth Night and Carnival, while February was the month to stay indoors in front of a blazing fire. This was good advice – the winter of 1537 was particularly cold.

Much of Fiorini's work was regular and routine. Every few months he settled Ippolito's debts with Renée, paying huge sums to her treasurer to cover what Ippolito had withdrawn from her agent in France – he paid 2,000 scudi to the treasurer on 22 January. Each week he paid alms of 12 *soldi* (worth 2 scudi a year) to the nuns of

*January, showing a man with a large flagon of wine,
from the Door of the Months in Ferrara Cathedral*

Corpus Domini, an allowance that Ippolito had arranged for the convent of which his sister, Eleonora, was Abbess. Every fortnight or so he handed out alms on Ippolito's behalf to various churches to care for the poor – the amount was calculated at a daily rate. Most weeks cartloads of fodder for the horses were delivered to the Palazzo San Francesco – millet, spelt and bran, collected from the granaries, and hay and straw, brought over from the barns at Belfiore. There were the sales from the granary and the wood store to enter, as well as the money received from Marcantonio the cellarer for the sale of wine from the palace cellars. On Saturdays Fiorini paid the weekly wages to Andrea the painter and his team of decorators, who were now refurbishing some of the reception rooms in the Palazzo San Francesco. He also had to remember important Marian festivals and arrange for expensive beeswax candles to be sent from the larder to the church at Bondeno, which was dedicated to the Virgin. The first of these was Candlemas, 2 February, now known as the feast of the

Purification of the Virgin but described by Fiorini as Santa Maria delle Candele. The priests held a special service to celebrate the feast, decorating the church with the white candles that Fiorini had bought in Venice the previous December – the church must have looked very pretty, and the beeswax would have smelt particularly sweet to the congregation, who were used to the fatty animal odour of the tallow candles they burned at home.

At the beginning of every month Fiorini was preoccupied with paying salaries and expenses. All ordinary members of the house-hold, including the stable boys and the staff running the palace, received monthly salaries and, because meals were not provided in the communal dining-room while Ippolito was in France, they were given a food allowance calculated at 10 *denari* a day (just under 4¼ scudi a year). There were salaries and expenses to be paid to the wives of those members of the household who were away in France. The three courtiers who had returned to Ferrara – Niccolò Tassone, Scipio d'Este and Provosto Trotti – also received their salaries from Fiorini but, instead of the standard sum for food, they were each given a variable allowance based on a daily ration of ½ kilo of veal, beef or fish per mouth per day for themselves and their servants. They were all paid for the same quality of fish on feast days but on meat days the courtiers' rates were based on expensive veal while their ser-vants only got cheap beef. However, these men were much better fed than the rest of the household – the courtiers' allowance was over 8½ scudi a year, while a servant's allowance came to nearly 7 scudi. Fior-ini must have had tables to help him work out the mathematical intri-cacies of these expenses. The final sum depended on the number of days each courtier was in Ferrara, how many servants he had, and the amount of Fridays and Church feasts in that particular month.

One of Fiorini's tasks that January was to organize the purchase and dispatch of several crates of goods that Ippolito had requested (see Chapter 4). The crates were to leave on 29 January with Alberto Turco, who was travelling north to Amiens, in midwinter, to take up his post as Ercole II's new ambassador in France. Fiorini got a carpenter to make up the crates and then had them coated in pitch. He packed four new linen shirts, which Sister Serafina at San Gabriele had embroidered, using black silk from the wardrobe given to her by Fiorini, and a lot of materials. Fiorini had been to Venice during December and had spent 363 scudi on 175 metres of velvets and satins which Ippolito had requested. Ippolito might have trusted Fiorini to buy good-quality materials but real luxury goods were outside his steward's area of expertise. The two sets of gold embroidered sleeves and two gold and silver collars *alla francese*, which Ippolito wanted as presents for ladies at the French court, were all commissioned in Mantua by one of his courtiers, Niccolò Tassone, who was reimbursed by Fiorini. Tassone also bought special boxes to protect these delicate and valuable items (one of the collars was not finished in time and had to be sent on later). Similarly it was Tassone who ordered Ippolito's arms and armour, another area with which Fiorini would have been unfamiliar. He commissioned two swords and scabbards from Costantino, a swordmaker who did a lot of work for the ducal court, and bought another in Milan, for 8 scudi, all of which were sent off with Turco. Also in the crates were two violins, which Tomaso Mosto had commissioned on Ippolito's behalf from the ducal workshops before they had left for France the previous March.

January brought other problems for Fiorini, in particular, a spate of petty thefts by boys who had got into the rooms upstairs in the Palazzo San Francesco. To deter further thievery he decided to install a strong gate reinforced with iron bars and a heavy lock at the top of the main staircase of the palace. There were also several outstanding bills to settle. Most suppliers were paid on delivery, but the shopkeepers and small businessmen who were used regularly were invariably paid in arrears. One butcher had to wait over four years to be paid for a calf he supplied, but this delay was exceptional (there was a long dispute about how much it was worth). In January 1537 Fiorini paid the men who had supplied and killed the pigs for the hams, which had been made in December, the farrier's bill for the horsehoes supplied since September, the bargemen's bills for transporting the harvest the previous summer, the saddler's bill dating back to June and one from a cloth merchant, who had still not been paid for materials he had supplied before Ippolito left for France in March 1536.

The season of feasting ended abruptly with the start of Lent which, in 1537, began on 14 February. Fiorini took a holiday to celebrate the last day of Carnival but he was back at his desk the next morning. His ledgers soon reveal the impact of the shift from indulgence to denial that marked the onset of Lent in sixteenth-century Europe. Fiorini doubled the daily quantity of coins he gave to the churches for the poor, who suffered increasing hardship during the winter months. The ban on eating meat during Lent, which must have had an immediate impact on Fiorini's stomach, also affected Ippolito's income. The revenues from the tax on live animals dropped sharply from a high point of 244 scudi in January to an annual low in February of 57 scudi. Fiorini also had more wages to hand out – Andrea the painter and his team decorating the Palazzo San Francesco had worked only fourteen days during January but were paid for twenty days the following month. However, there were advantages – Lent must have simplified Fiorini's task of working out the food allowances for the courtiers and their servants, who would now be given an allowance based on fish every day until Easter.

~

Towards the end of February – while Ippolito was travelling through the mud and rain in northern France – spring arrived in Ferrara. As the weather improved and the days lengthened, the blossom came out on the fruit trees at the Palazzo San Francesco, and green shoots appeared in the vegetable garden. On 24 February, the gardener had enough salad to take down to the Saturday market in the main square in Ferrara – his first trip that year – and he bought himself a new basket for the occasion. It was also the beginning of the year's work on the farms. The shepherds started to wean the lambs that had been born at Christmas and fatten them for the Easter market. Bigo took

17 kilos of vetch over to Codigoro for the lambs on 28 February, together with another 8 kilos for sowing. This was also the season for pruning the vines and for planting legumes. By the end of February Fiorini was recording the dispatch of sacks of chickpeas, broad beans and other pulses from Ippolito's granaries to Pomposa and Bondeno for sowing (the wheat and other grains had been planted in October). In early March he sent linseed to Migliaro for Marti Bolgarello, Antonio Maria Trova and the other workers there to plant for the summer's flax crop. Another sign of spring was the renewal of traffic along the canals and waterways of the Po delta, a welcome sight for the porters and carters waiting at the wharves, who relied on this traffic as their main source of income. Jacomino Malacoda (or as we might say, Jimmie Badtail), whose barges had lain idle for most of December and January, arrived at the wharves on 16 February with a load of broad beans and chickpeas, returning to Bondeno with his craft laden with planks for building. The broad beans and chickpeas were sent on to Pomposa for sowing, carried by other bargees who had made their way upstream to Ferrara laden with firewood. Nearly 100,000 logs, mostly from the woods at Codigoro, arrived by barge for the store at the Palazzo San Francesco during March and April.

Transport was labour-intensive and expensive. Fiorini's ledgers contain extensive data on the transport of produce from Ippolito's estates, not only the names of all his bargemen, and the prices they charged, but also the rates charged by the porters and carters who moved the goods from the wharves. Every cargo had to be unloaded from the barges by hand, loaded on to carts, carted to the stores, unloaded and finally stacked. The cost of transporting one cart of firewood (375 logs) from Codigoro to the store at the Palazzo San Francesco came to nearly 40 per cent of its market value, while the cost of bringing a cart of straw from Bondeno to the barns at Belfiore amounted to over 60 per cent.

Fiorini had to record the arrival of the goods under income, and each of the payments for the various stages of transport under expenditure. The bargemen usually worked on contract. Most of the crops

A cart of wood from Codigoro (market value 47 soldi 3 denari)		
Barge from Codigoro	9s 4½d	
Counting and loading logs into carts	5s	
Carting logs to wood store	3s	
Stacking logs in wood store	1s 4d	Total 18s 8½d

A cart of straw from Bondeno (market value 22 soldi)		
Barge from Bondeno	5s 6d	
Loading bales into carts	1s 6d	
Carting to Belfiore	5s	
Stacking in barn	1s 6d	Total 13s 6d

Transport costs

from Bondeno were brought by Jacomino Malacoda, whose family had been moving Ippolito's harvest ever since he inherited the estate – Jacomino's bill for 21 scudi for the 1536 harvest had only been settled by Fiorini a month earlier. We do not know the size of his barges but they regularly carried loads of 5 tonnes and more, hauled slowly along the Po to Ferrara – a 20-kilometre journey that must have taken the best part of a day. There were also regular bargemen on the Codigoro and Migliaro runs, who charged a higher rate as they had much further to travel. Although Baura was only 10 kilo-metres from Ferrara, Migliaro was 40 kilometres downstream, while the distance to Codigoro was 54 kilometres. Porters and carters were casual labourers and were invariably paid on the day, as were the unfortunate men who had the unenviable task of counting the logs in each shipment, often as many as 10,000.

March was a particularly heavy month for Fiorini. He took just two days off and covered twenty-three pages of his ledger listing items of expenditure – he had only used fourteen in February. The week leading up to Easter – which fell on 1 April in 1537 – was par-ticularly heavy and accounted for eight of these pages. Fiorini and the other staff at the palace were so busy that no one was allowed to go home for lunch – they were fed instead, at Ippolito's expense, on bread and cheese from the larder. One of the days Fiorini took off was Sunday, 25 March, which, in 1537, was not only the feast of the Annunciation but also Passion Sunday. The church at Bondeno needed special decoration for both feasts, as well as for Easter Sunday. Fiorini sent 9 kilos of wax candles (ten large and thirty medium) to Palamides to ornament the church for the Annunciation, a substantial quantity to mark the principal Marian feast in the Church calendar. He also reimbursed Palamides for buying sixteen olive branches, which were hung in the church on the same day to mark Christ's Entry into Jerusalem. The following Sunday, Easter Day, the church was decked out yet again – this time with a rather elaborate and expensive arrangement of wax candles, topped by a cross, to symbolize the Crucifixion, and a statue of the Virgin, to mark the dedication of the church. This arrangement had been specially ordered by Fiorini from Venice and, if the price is any guide, it must have been impressive – it cost 2½ scudi, a sum which would have represented twenty days' work for any carpenter in the congregation or provided seventy chickens for his dinner table. Fiorini also had the first of the year's rents to record, which were due on the Annunciation (Lady Day) – none had arrived by 25 March, but they started to roll in from 5 April. The Easter eggs due from Marti Bolgarello and the other men working at Migliaro – 100 from each of them – all arrived on time, though the bailiff had already sold Antonio Maria Trova's eggs locally and sent the cash instead. Most of these eggs were given to the painters redecorating Ippolito's apartments at the Palazzo San Francesco to mix their colours.

There were presents and alms to hand out in Ippolito's name. Fiorini organized porters to deliver paschal lambs, weaned by the men at Migliaro, to the houses of three of Duke Ercole's lawyers who were involved in sorting out various disputes on Ippolito's estates – one of them also received a large cheese from the larder weighing 24 kilos. There were no Easter gifts for Violante, Ippolito's mistress –

this was a time for duty presents and alms, and Fiorini handed out coins to several 'poor but respectable' widows. One of these widows, who had three children, earned a meagre living doing the cleaning at the monastery of Santa Maria delle Grazie. Another was the widow of the Governor of Brescello, who had been murdered in 1536, leaving her with three small children and pregnant with her fourth – she must have been grateful for the 70 kilos of wheat she was given by Fiorini. The widow of Arcangelo, Ippolito's table-decker who had died recently in France, received a small sack of flour, as did the motherless son of Bagnolo, Ippolito's chief stable boy, who had left his baby behind in the care of his brother-in-law. There was extra cash for the convent of Corpus Domini, and Fiorini gave a pair of shoes to a Sister Cecilia so that 'she will pray every day to God to safeguard Ippolito and keep him healthy and happy'. On Good Friday he handed out coins worth nearly 2 scudi to people making the annual pilgrimage to Loreto, about 270 kilometes away down the Adriatic coast. Loreto was particularly popular with childless women who were eager to pray at the famous shrine containing the house of Joseph and Mary (miraculously transported from Nazareth in the thirteenth century). Fiorini noted in his usual precise way that these coins had been given 'so that God will keep the Archbishop of Milan healthy and that the Madonna of Loreto will safeguard him from misfortune in France where he is at present'.

Fiorini's biggest headache during March and April was Renée of France, who had been allowed to return from exile in the Este villa at Consàndolo – largely thanks to the threats relayed by Ippolito from Francis I. Her relationship with her husband had improved to the extent that she was now seven months pregnant and, with her confinement imminent, she took up residence at the Palazzo San Francesco during April (expectant wives of princes in sixteenth-century Europe were literally confined to guard against accidents, and changelings). There are numerous payments to porters for moving Ippolito's possessions out of the way, and to smiths who fitted new locks to doors and grilles to windows. Renée was a demanding guest. Fiorini himself had to move his office into a makeshift room over the stables. Tomaso Mosto's rooms and the wardrobe had to be emptied and prepared for her ladies-in-waiting, with new glass panes installed in many of the windows. Her cooks, who were all French, moved into the attic rooms under the tiles where Ippolito's footmen had slept. The cooks were not happy with their accommodation – one can hardly blame them – and Fiorini had to get a carpenter to install cloth windows, for which the footmen must have been grateful when they returned. Renée herself moved into Ippolito's apartments (though not his bedroom, which was about to be redecorated) and kept the fires burning with logs from the wood store, for which Fiorini charged her the market price. Shortly after she arrived Andrea and the painters were ready to start redecorating the ceiling of the Great Hall, something which Renée had agreed to, but once the carpenters began to erect the scaffolding for the painters to work on, she changed her mind – as Fiorini politely noted in his ledger – and the porters had to dismantle the half-made structure and take all the wood back to the store.

With Lent over there was meat on the dining-tables once more. Ippolito's income from the tax on live animals almost doubled from 72 scudi in March to 131 scudi in April, and Fiorini once again had to work out the veal, beef and fish allowances for the three courtiers and their servants. Work also picked up on the farms. According to the calendar on the cathedral portal, April was the month to put the cattle and sheep out to pasture on the new grass. By the end of the month it was warm enough to shear the sheep at Lagosanto. Bigo authorized the wages of the shearers and started selling the fleeces to various cloth merchants in Ferrara. The weather was also now dry enough to start building work in Ferrara and on the estates. Bigo decided that a new hay barn was needed at Migliaro and he commissioned a carpenter at Baura to prepare forty-eight planks of poplar, which were then sent down the Po by barge together with several large beams, bought from the ducal stores in Ferrara. At Bondeno Palamides started to rebuild one of his hay barns in preparation for the harvest, while in Ferrara Fiorini commissioned a team of roofers to replace the roof tiles that had been damaged by winter storms and frost at Belfiore and the Palazzo San Francesco.

April was a particularly busy time in the stables. The new foals had started to arrive in March, and the covering of the mares that were in season was about to start. Several extra loads of barley were delivered from the granary – some of this was to nourish the weaker foals, but most of it was to strengthen the stallions for their exertions (there was nothing extra for the mares). The covering season lasted until the end of June and meant a lot of extra work for the stable boys. Fiorini recorded extra measures of oil from the palace larder going to the stables so that the lads could keep an eye on the stallions at night. Working with the stallions was dangerous work: one of the lads got kicked in the shin and needed medical attention. At the end of June the stable boys were each given 1½ kilos of salami and salted hams from the larder – more of a tip than a realistic payment for the extra work they had put in.

Pierantonio, Ippolito's trainer, had returned from France on 10 March in time to oversee the foaling and the covering. He had left Paris on 28 January, the day before the new ambassador had left Ferrara travelling in the opposite direction, and he presumably endured a similarily gruelling winter journey across the Alps (one wonders where their paths crossed). He brought back several horses, including a little bay pony, or jennet (*chinea*), that Ippolito had found as a present for his 6-year-old niece Anna, Ercole and Renée's eldest child. Pierantonio moved into his old rooms above the stables, next to Fiorini's office, and Fiorini added him to the list of courtiers receiving allowances for fish and meat – Pierantonio was not quite as grand as Niccolò Tassone and the other gentlemen, and received beef like their servants rather than veal. One of Ippolito's reasons for sending his trainer back to Ferrara was to acquire some decent horses. Just before Easter Pierantonio went off to Florence, where he spent 37 scudi on a bay which had belonged to Duke Alessandro de' Medici – Alessandro had been brutally murdered by one of his cousins in

January that year and replaced by another, Duke Cosimo I, who seems to have been selling off Alessandro's stables. The horse must have been impressive because when Provosto Trotti saw it, he informed Fiorini, who duly noted the conversation, that if Ippolito did not like the animal, he would buy it himself.

May is one of the best months in Italy – the air is warm, with none of the stifling humidity of summer, the cherries are ripe and there are plenty of holidays. Even Fiorini did not work his usual long hours, and he must have been anticipating the season when he arranged for beeswax candles to be sent out to Bondeno to decorate the church for Pentecost (seventeen large) and Corpus Christi (eight large, eighteen medium). The 'holiday season' started in Ferrara on 23 April when the citizens celebrated the feast of their patron saint. Fiorini had to work that day – a barge-load of 22,500 logs arrived from Codigoro, and 1,000 of them were bought at the wharves. In addition to these two income entries, he also entered two more items incorrectly under income that day, which had to be crossed out and re-entered under expenditure – a new lock and key for one of the feed chests in the stables, and payment to a porter for carrying chests in the wardrobe. In May, however, he took off an unprecedented seven days, including most of the church holidays: May Day (1 May), an old pagan feast which celebrated the start of spring and which was also the feast of his name saints James and Philip, Ascension (10 May), Pentecost (20 May) and Trinity Sunday (27 May), though he did work on the feast of Corpus Christi (31 May).

The month brought two unusual interruptions to Fiorini's routine. On 14 May there was high excitement at the palace when the stepson of Francesco the gardener stabbed a Franciscan friar with a knife. Fiorini offered, on Ippolito's behalf, to pay the barber who treated the wounded man because, as he entered in the ledger, Francesco was a faithful servant and could not pay the barber's bill, which amounted to less than ½ scudo. The following day Fiorini unexpectedly bought three paintings from a pair of travelling salesmen from the Romagna. Fiorini had trained as a painter, so we can

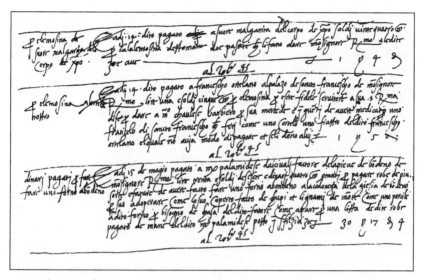

Fiorini's entries for 14–15 May 1537, recording the alms for the convent of Corpus Domini (£1 4s 0d), the sum he paid the barber who treated the Franciscan friar knifed by the stepson of Francesco the gardener (£1 5s 0d), and the money given to Palamides de' Civali to cover building expenses in Bondeno (£30 17s 4d)

assume he knew what he was buying, but the purchase was unusual – he did not buy any other works of art for Ippolito – and, although he recorded the transaction in detail, he did not explain who painted them nor why he had bought them. There is no evidence that Ippolito had requested any paintings, and they were not sent to France but remained in the palace in Ferrara. The largest (about 2 × 1 metres) was a *Supper at Emmaeus*, or, as the more literal-minded Fiorini explained, 'an oil painting with six large figures, *viz* a Christ in the garb of a pilgrim with two Apostles after they had arrived in Emmaeus and were at table with three other figures'. The other paintings, both smaller, were a *Holy Family* – 'the Virgin and Son and St Joseph' – and a painting of 'the battle of Scipio Africanus in oil with plenty of figures and horses'. The total price, 12 scudi, was negotiated by a dealer, who charged a fee. Fiorini then organized the making of frames, which cost almost half the price of the paintings themselves (see overleaf).

Making frames	£ s d	Scudi
Wood for frames	0 14 0	0.2
More wood for frames	palace stores	
Making wooden frames	3 0 0	0.857
Glue	0 1 0	0.014
Nails for the frames	0 5 0	0.071
Nails to attach the canvases	0 6 0	0.086
Decorating frames		
Milan the painter for nine days' work making and gilding plaster mouldings	4 1 0	1.157
Gold for gilding the frames	9 11 6	2.736
Azure blue for decorating the frames	palace stores	
Gum arabic for gilding	0 7 6	0.107
Total	18 6 0	5.228

Frames for three paintings

~

As Ippolito's treasurer in Italy, Fiorini was keenly aware that complications had arisen in his master's pursuit of a cardinal's hat, though he may not have understood all the political complexities involved. His references to Ippolito's affairs were succinct – one courier was paid to take a letter 'which is of importance regarding the trouble the Pope has made'. Fiorini had to pay for couriers to carry urgent letters to Rome and to Milan on several occasions. Couriers were expensive. Fiorini paid 3½ scudi to send a courier to Milan (250 kilometres) and 14 scudi for one to Rome (400 kilometres) – substantially more than he had spent on the three paintings. He was regularly in contact with Antonio Romei, Ippolito's secretary, who was lobbying on Ippolito's behalf at the papal court in Rome. In December 1536 Romei had sent Fiorini a bill for 969 scudi for expenses he had incurred on Ippolito's behalf, and in April another bill arrived on Fiorini's desk, this time for 81 scudi to cover what Romei loosely termed 'negotiations'. Fiorini was also in touch with Paulo Albertino, Ippolito's agent in Milan, where Charles V had ordered the sequestration of the assets of the archbishopric. Niccolò Tassone had spent most of December in Milan, negotiating with the imperial administration on Ippolito's behalf – Fiorini continued to pay his salary while he was away and gave him 37 scudi to cover his expenses, but his daily food allowances, which were paid at the beginning of each month, had to be deducted from his salary after his return.

Fiorini organized several presents to oil the political machinery in Rome and Milan. Ippolito had sent two horses from France with Pierantonio which were to be sent on to Romei to use in Rome – one of these was a jennet, like the one Ippolito had given Anna d'Este, and the other was a Spanish stallion called il Sarto (the Tailor). Sadly, very little of the correspondence between Ippolito and Romei has survived, so we do not know the names of the recipients, but we can assume they were influential at the papal court. The two horses spent a month in the stables recovering from the long journey and being fattened with extra measures of barley – they were sent down to Rome in April. Fiorini, acting on Romei's instructions, commissioned elaborate new harnesses and caparisons for the horses. The black leather harness and saddle for the jennet were commissioned, rather unusually, in the English style (*al inglese*) from a saddler in Ferrara. There were also more prosaic gifts. In June Fiorini sent Romei sixty salamis, a product for which Ferrara was famous. They weighed 52 kilos and, though they were worth little more than 3 scudi, it cost 2 scudi to transport them to Rome (the shipper was not paid until October). Also in June Fiorini sent another twenty salamis together with 6 kilos of candied fruits – citrons, pears and quinces – to Albertino in Milan. Like the salamis, candied fruit was a Ferrarese delicacy, and it had been specially ordered by Albertino to give, as Fiorini noted, 'to imperial court officials in Milan so that he can have successful audiences with these officials about the business of the archbishopric and so that they will not obstruct things at this time when everything is going so badly because of the Pope'.

Despite the logistics of travel in sixteenth-century Europe, there was a constant flow of traffic between Ferrara and the French court, particularly once the snows had melted in the mountains, making the crossing of the Alps less of an endurance test. During April an envoy arrived from Francis I. He was breaking his journey to Venice in order to visit Renée in the Palazzo San Francesco. He was given Scipio Assassino's rooms in the palace and was entertained by Tassone, at Ippolito's expense (the ambassador brought a letter from Ippolito authorizing this expenditure). Tassone hosted three meals for the envoy: they must have been lavish, because the bill he submitted to Fiorini came to over 5 scudi (a year's wages for a stable boy, or the price of forty-seven geese). He also stayed at the palace on his way back in early June when he again visited Renée – now heavily pregnant – and on this occasion Fiorini presented him with 8 kilos of salamis from Ippolito's larder.

Inevitably most of the men, whose journeys between France and Ferrara were recorded by Fiorini, belonged to Ippolito's household. Travellers in either direction meant extra work for him. Departures involved packing crates and dispensing large sums for expenses, while arrivals meant more shopping lists from Ippolito, and names to add to the lists of salaries and food expenses. The first of the spring arrivals was Francesco dalla Viola, Ippolito's musician, who arrived on 7 May with his servant, and they were duly added to the roster of those receiving veal, beef and fish allowances. A fortnight later Provosto Trotti left Ferrara, riding the horse he coveted from the Medici stables, with 80 scudi to cover his travel expenses to Fontainebleau. He took with him several bolts of black satin from Lucca which Fiorini had bought from a merchant in Ferrara (for 59 scudi) and Ippolito's suit of battle armour, which had been ordered the previous summer and had finally been completed by Zanpiero, the ducal armourer. Travelling with Trotti was Ippolito's new Italian barber, Jacomo Casappo, who had been working for Ippolito's younger brother Francesco, currently travelling in the entourage of Charles V – Jacomo's new post would give him the unusual experience of service at each of the rival courts. Scipio Assassino, his two servants and Priete the sommelier all returned to Ferrara in June. The party had left Amiens on 10 March, taking over three months to make the journey. We do not know why Priete was travelling, but Assassino, Ippolito's chief valet and a key member of his household, was unquestionably ill – Fiorini had to pay doctor's bills for him, and an apothecary's bill which came to over 2 scudi. Besian the falconer also arrived at about the same time, bringing his birds home for their annual moult. At the end of August Romei arrived from Rome for urgent consultations on Ippolito's behalf with Duke Ercole. None of these men left Ipplito's service – the only one to do so was Ippolito Machiavelli, one of Ippolito's gentlemen, who returned in September and joined his brother running the family bank.

Francesco dalla Viola had brought a shopping list from Ippolito, and on 10 June Fiorini went off to Venice, taking ten days away from his desk to buy these goods, as well as more beeswax candles for the church at Bondeno. He spent a total of 140 scudi, most of which went on quantities of sewing silks that Ippolito wanted – the purple and white silks cost twice as much as the black. He brought

	Scudi
12.5 kg coloured silk thread	86.80
3.33 m red velvet	17.71
5.33 m red satin	11.81
4 m purple cloth	7.71
65 kg white wax candles	11.34
Transport and expenses	4.74
Total	140.11

Shopping in Venice, June 1537

the shopping back with him to Ferrara by barge, transferring the goods to a cart for the final part of the journey – the cost was consid-erable (though it amounted to only 3 per cent of the total).

June was another busy month for Fiorini. He took only three days off, one of which was 29 June, the feast of the Apostles Peter and Paul. Renée had her baby on 19 June – her fourth child, a girl they called Eleonora, after her aunt and great-grandmother (her birth coincided with the tragic death of Renée's niece, Madeleine, the new Queen of Scotland, whose precarious health had broken down on the long sea voyage from France to Edinburgh). A week or so later, most unfortunately, the kitchen well at the palace became blocked. Renée complained and Fiorini called in a plumber to repair it. He also paid her another 2,000 scudi to cover what Ippolito had with-drawn from her agent in France.

Fiorini was now preoccupied with preparations for the harvest. He bought ink, red sealing wax and new ledgers for the bailiffs on all the estates. The granary sacks had to be washed, dried and mended, and then sent off to Pomposa and Bondeno. There were problems with the mill at Bagnacavallo, and Bigo bought two new millstones from a stone quarry in the north of the duchy, from where Fiorini had to organize bargemen to transport them back to Ferrara and on to the Romagna. Bigo needed materials to repair some of the houses at Fós-soli, and Fiorini organized planks of wood and several sacks of nails from the palace stores. There were also loads of bran and millet to be send out to Bondeno and Pomposa for the tithe-collectors who had started work on 1 June and were supplied with fodder for their horses. A week or so later Bigo had to dismiss the bailiff at Migliaro – we do not know why, but his offence must have been serious for him to be sacked at this critical time of the year. The new bailiff, Domenico da Milano, had been working as a tithe-collector at Bon-deno when Ippolito inherited the estate in 1520 and must have proved

Farmland near Bondeno

trustworthy, despite the occasional errors in his tithe books which Palamides recorded in his ledger. One year there were 4 kilos of linseed and 17 kilos of beans missing from what Domenico should have delivered to Palamides, and another year he forgot to take the tithe on six pigs. More serious theft was punished harshly. Palamides had sacked one of Domenico's colleagues after finding that 70 kilos of chaff and one piglet were missing from his books – produce worth about 1 scudo – and that he had added 2 *soldi* (0.028 scudi) to the price of some sealing wax he had bought.

By 24 June, the feast of St John the Baptist and the traditional start of summer, the grain harvest was well under way. The summer months were extremely busy for everyone employed by Ippolito, in the palace and on the estates. Harvest is the pivot of the year in any agricultural community, the culmination of the previous year's labours and the basis for future hopes. There was no mechanization to lessen the backbreaking labour of manual work.

Ippolito's workers and their families were out in the fields working in the blazing sun for up to eighteen hours a day, wielding heavy iron-bladed scythes and then threshing the grains and seeds from the harvested plants. There was also work for casual labourers loading the crops into sacks and carrying them down to the wharves. One may not have much sympathy for the iniquitous tithe-collectors, but they too had to work much the same hours as the labourers in order to keep track of the crops as they were harvested. They counted every ear of corn, every pod of peas, every ounce of linseed, and detailed it all in their little notebooks. The bailiffs too were busy, recording the details of every load that arrived at the barns and double-checking their figures with those of the tithe-collectors – missing items, however small, were all recorded. The whole enterprise was supervised by Palamides at Bondeno and by Bigo, who spent the summer making spot checks at Fóssoli and the three centres of the Pomposa estate.

The first crop of the year was hay, which in 1537 was ready in early June. By the middle of the month the barges laden with bales had begun to arrive at the wharves in Ferrara. The first sacks of wheat arrived in early July, the first broad beans and chickpeas by the end of the month. The wheat, which had been harvested at Bondeno, arrived in one of Jacomino Malacoda's barges on Wednesday, 4 July. Jacomino was back unloading at the wharves again the following Monday, and then either he or his partner did the journey four or five times a week for the next six weeks. This was a particularly busy period for the carters and the porters, and an unpleasant one, doing heavy manual labour in the stifling humidity of Ferrara during the summer. Each barge had to be unloaded and the sacks piled on to carts and taken to the granaries, where the crops were weighed and stacked, and the empty sacks returned to the wharves. However, even in the middle of the harvest, none of the bargemen, porters or carters worked on Sundays, nor on 15 August, the feast of the Assumption of the Virgin, after which the pace began to slacken. Fiorini, on the other hand, needed Sundays and holidays to catch up with his normal routine after a week spent in the granaries recording the details of the incoming harvest.

Grain yields by our standards were very low. Ippolito's workers got only six grains for every one they sowed, eight if they were lucky with the weather – modern European farmers can expect about fifty – and they needed almost a quarter of their harvest to sow the next year's crop. Their yields were partly the result of poorer quality grain, but also because of the way it was sown. The seeds were thrown across the surface of the fields and then raked over with a harrow. Some of the grains inevitably remained on the surface where they were eaten by birds or blown away by the wind. (Seed drills, which ensured the seed was buried beneath the surface of the soil, were only developed in Italy in the late sixteenth century.) It was therefore important to waste as little as possible. Even the grass in the garden at the Palazzo San Francesco was cut for hay – three times in the summer of 1537; the first crop, harvested on 4 June, yielding just one-third of a cart of hay. For every seven or eight sacks of wheat brought by Jacomino's barges, there was also a sack of chaff, which had to be sieved carefully by hand in the granaries. Hidden in the chaff were grains of wheat and barley to add to the granary stores. The chaff also yielded husks, which were fed to the peacocks, chickens and dogs, as well as the seeds of weeds such as ryegrass and oats that were used as animal fodder.

The 1537 harvest was poor – yet another piece of bad news for Ippolito. Then, as now, the quality of the harvest depended ultimately on the weather. The summer of 1537 was spectacularly wet, affecting both the yields and the quality of the crops. Much of the grain was still damp when it arrived in Ferrara, and one particularly large load of wheat from Codigoro was judged by Fiorini to be 'soaking wet and foul'. At the end of July torrential rain damaged the roof of the granary in Ferrara, flooding the wheat stored there and doing so much damage that some of it was not even fit for chicken feed and had to be thrown away. What a contrast to the year before – in 1536 Fiorini had been obliged to pay Jacomino Malacoda and the other bargees a higher rate than normal because of the severe drought

Crop	Measure	1536	Average 1521–37	1537	% average
Wheat	stara	4,458	2,474	2,015	− 19
Chaff	stara	301	195	227	+ 16
Barley	stara	1,299	508	370	− 27
Millet	stara	1,245	1,237	562	− 55
Flax	mara	n/a	136	272	+ 100
Linseed	stara	n/a	57	45	− 21
Chickpeas	stara	306	32	18	− 44
Beans	stara	255	165	157	− 5
Broad beans	stara	337	258	292	+ 13
Vetch	stara	31	25	17	− 32
Hay	cart	146	58	58	=
Straw	cart	72	51	81	+ 59

Note: the *staro* (pl. *stara*) was a volumetric measure used in Ferrara to weigh crops. In an average year, 1 *staro* of wheat would yield 17¼ kilos of flour, though this figure could vary by as much as 10 per cent in exceptional years. I have not been able to identify the *maro*, the measure used to weigh flax

Harvests at Bondeno, 1536–7

which had left the Po so low that it was impossible to carry a full load on their barges. The 1536 harvest had been exceptionally good but in 1537 the quantities of grain, especially wheat and millet, were way below average, while chaff and straw were well above, another indication of a bad year. The legumes were less badly affected, while the quantity of flax, which thrives in damp conditions, was double that of the previous year.

Bad harvests could be disastrous for agricultural workers and their families who depended on their produce to survive the following winter, but they were not always bad news for those like Ippolito who had large estates that produced a surplus of crops to sell. Poor harvests invariably meant higher prices. In November 1536 the price of a *stara* of wheat had dropped to 19 *soldi*, but a year later it was 24 *soldi* and in 1539, after an even worse harvest, it rose to 57 *soldi*, a price that caused widespread famine.

By September the crops had been harvested, most of the grain and legumes had arrived at the granaries and the wine harvest had begun. The first barges laden with heavy wooden barrels filled with the new wine arrived from both Bondeno and Codigoro on 8 September, the feast of the Birth of the Virgin (described by Fiorini as Santa Maria di Settembre). The day was celebrated in the church at Bondeno by a special service, followed by a harvest supper for Palamides, the tithe-collectors and the priests, though not the workers, at the local inn. With the hard work over for the year, Ippolito's agents now turned their attention to the upkeep of the estate buildings. At Bondeno, Palamides commissioned roofers to lay new roofs on the church, the bell-tower, the tithe barn and several of the estate dwellings. At Migliaro, Bigo Schalabrino authorized Domenico da Milano to rebuild the houses where Marti Bolgarello and Antonio Maria Trova lived. Building was expensive. Palamides spent 8 scudi on tiles alone while Bigo spent over 13 scudi on labour and materials for Antonio Maria's house and nearly 18 scudi on Marti's.

Meanwhile Fiorini was having serious problems with the kitchen well at the Palazzo San Francesco. The first plumber had made some cosmetic improvements but had failed to clear the blockage, and Renée insisted that it be rebuilt. Fiorini had been too busy in July to organize it himself, and Tomaso Morello had taken charge of the project. The work proved to be substandard. In early September part of the new wall collapsed, and the builders had to be called in again. Fiorini also had a lot of work to do in preparation for the departure of a large party who left for France on 23 September. The men included Scipio Assassino, now fully recovered, Priete the sommelier and Besian the falconer. They took with them two more members of staff who were travelling to France for the first time: Carlo del Pavone, the larderer, and Francesco Salineo, who had been appointed as the official in charge of funds for the stables, in place of Jacomo Panizato, who had been promoted to purveyor in France. All were given travelling expenses by Fiorini – 25 scudi for Assassino, 10 scudi each for the others – and they took a lot of luggage with them. Assassino had bought Ippolito a new breviary, expensively covered in black velvet, and, when they stopped off in Mantua, he picked up two swords which Tassone had commissioned there for Ippolito. Besian was returning to France for the hunting season with three new peregrines, as well as new jesses, hoods and lures for all the birds. There were several mules laden with crates of goods for Ippolito, all packed by Fiorini. This time Fiorini had arranged for the crates to be wrapped in cloth, which had been specially waxed, to protect them from the autumn rains. These crates contained all the silk thread and materials Fiorini had bought in Venice in June, as well as several bolts of coloured velvets (84 metres), which Fiorini had ordered from Modena, and taffetas (166 metres), which had been sent from Florence by Duke Ercole's ambassador. Fiorini's entry carefully noted the price of each colour of taffeta – black, dark red, dark orange and black – in Florentine *lire*, and the weights of the bolts in Florentine pounds (the Florentines, confusingly, sold their materials by weight not length). He also packed six new pairs of shoes, made by Ippo‑ lito's cobbler in Ferrara, and three sacks of wheat from the granaries, presumably so that Ippolito could enjoy the Ferrarese delicacies that his cooks had been unable to make with the type of flour produced in France.

A week after Assassino and the others left was the feast of Michael‑ mas, 29 September, and the start of autumn. After a wet summer, the autumn was dry, but though the days might have been hot and sunny, the nights were cold. The signs of approaching winter – the colder weather, the shorter, darker days – are all visible in Fiorini's ledgers. On 1 October, after a break of five months, Fiorini started to dispense tallow candles to the cellars and stables. The next day saw the final cut of grass in the garden at the Palazzo San Francesco.

Fiorini started sending millet to Belfiore to fatten the capons and chickens for Christmas. Sales of firewood from the stores began again. Renée bought 4,000 logs during October, while Fiorini himself took a firebrick made of tufa from the palace stores to improve the fireplace in his office in the palace, and had new glass windows installed in his rooms at Belfiore – this was a real luxury, and one wonders whether Ippolito knew of this unexpected extravagance.

October was one of Fiorini's heaviest months – he took only one day off, a Sunday. He filled in twenty-five pages of expenditure, and three of income, making this easily the longest month in the ledgers. Moreover his assistant, Francesco Guberti, was away for ten days overseeing the loading and shipping of wheat from Ippolito's estates in the Romagna. Although much of the income in October came from rents, due on Michaelmas (29 September), there were still the last loads of legumes and linseed to record, brought from Bondeno by Jacomino Malacoda, as well as 14,234 bricks and tiles from the kiln at Codigoro and 200 brooms from the workers at Migliaro. In the middle of October Marti Bolgarello, Antonio Maria Trova and the other Migliaro workers came to Ferrara to collect seeds to sow for the next year's crop. This must have been quite a holiday – a day out in the big city, away from their daily labour in the fields – and Fiorini provided them with bread to eat on the barge on the way back. Marti went home with 50 *stara* of wheat and 4 of barley, while Antonio Maria took 37 *stara* of wheat and also 4 of barley (though he had to return the barley a fortnight later because he did not have enough land to sow it).

A lot of the expenditure that month related to the transport of wine – payments to the bargemen, carters and porters, and also wages to the two men who were taken on for the month to work in the wine cellars in the palace, storing and sampling the wines. Jacomino Malacoda and the other bargemen also had to be paid for transporting the grain harvest – we can assume that Jimmie Badtail, a small businessman, was grateful not to have to wait until January for his cash, as he had had to do the year before. In addition Fiorini paid the bargeman who had shipped the two new millstones down to the mill at Bagnacavallo in June. One entry recorded 70 kilos of wheat given to the piano tuner who looked after Ippolito's musical instruments at the Palazzo San Francesco, while another recorded the cost (1½ scudi) of mending several windows and door latches that had been broken by the staff of Cardinal Benedetto Accolti, who had stayed with Renée for a few days that month. Renée herself left the palace at the end of October. There was also Ippolito's personal shopping. Fiorini paid 15 scudi to Isaac, a Jewish second-hand goods dealer trading in Ferrara, for a new set of bedhangings embroidered in black and red silk, and there were a lot of bills to settle for the purchase and transport of a new set of Spanish leather wall hangings, which arrived in Ferrara at the end of October.

On 22 October there was an unexpected visitor. Vicino, Ippolito's trusted squire, had ridden the 720 kilometres from Lyon with an urgent letter from Ippolito to Ercole. In the letter, which was short and, very unusually, written in his own hand, Ippolito asked Ercole to listen carefully to Vicino and to believe what he said, 'as if it were me myself'. No doubt Vicino brought news of Francis I's impending trip to Italy – the arrival of the French King in Italy would be provocative to say the least – but the real business concerned Ippolito's unease at the news from Rome. Alarming rumours had reached the French court from Francis I's envoys in Rome that Ercole II had ordered his ambassador Francesco Villa to abandon the demand for Ippolito's hat. It was in order to hear Ercole's side of the story that Ippolito had sent Vicino to Ferrara. In fact, as the Duke told Vicino, it had been Villa himself who had suggested this radical solution in order to encourage Paul III to accept Ercole's offer of 170,000 scudi to settle the dispute over Modena and Reggio, an offer which the Pope had rejected. Ercole insisted, both verbally to Vicino and in the letter Vicino took back to Ippolito, that he had no such intention and that he had rejected his ambassador's advice. But Ippolito knew that Ercole was considering this option very seriously, which put him in a difficult position. He could trust neither his brother nor Villa.

Instead he would have to rely solely on Francis I's goodwill, and the King's influence with Paul III, to get his hat. With these facts in mind, Ippolito had given letters to Vicino to deliver to Fiorini with orders for a lot of expensive presents for the French court. He also gave Vicino a letter for Romei, instructing him to return to Rome without delay. Romei left a week later, carrying a new silver seal engraved with Ippolito's coat-of-arms so he could sign documents on Ippolito's behalf, and 100 scudi from Fiorini to buy perfumed gloves, presents which would be particularly appreciated by their recipients at the papal court.

Vicino also had verbal instructions for Fiorini, of a personal rather than a political nature. Ippolito wanted to give Violante Lam-pugnana some flax and a cartload – 1,250 kilos – of wheat from his granaries. But the gesture was not quite as generous as it seems. Fior-ini's entry for this transaction explains that Ippolito had specified that the wheat was to be from Baura, and not the Romagna. In October 1537 the Romagna wheat was selling for 24 *soldi* a *staro*, while the Baura crop was only making 20 *soldi* – did she know about this and could she tell the difference between the two? On 27 October Vicino went off to Mirandola, about 50 kilometres away, to collect a horse – a roan – which was a present from Galeotto della Mirandola to Ippolito (Galeotto would one day become the father-in-law of Renea, the daughter of Violante and Ippolito). Vicino tipped both the farrier and the stable boy 1 scudo, spent the night in Mirandola and rode back to Ferrara the next day with the horse. It was soon clear that the horse was ill and needed to be treated with a poultice made from pig fat, mercury, verdigris, mastic and incense – Fiorini did not record what exactly was wrong with the animal. Although it was well enough to leave Ferrara with Vicino, it could not be ridden, and Vicino spent 16 scudi on a new horse to use for the journey back to France. After a very hectic ten days, he left on 31 October, and rejoined Ippolito on the royal progress in Piedmont.

Fiorini took the next day off for the feast of All Saints (1 Novem-ber). The month started quietly in Ferrara. The fear, widespread across Italy, that Francis I's arrival in Italy would provoke Charles V to reopen hostilities, proved unfounded, and at last Paul III persuaded the two rival powers to agree to a three-month truce, which was signed on 16 November. Fiorini's accounts show the arrival of the wheat from the Romagna, wine from Fóssoli and Brescello, and firewood from Codigoro, as well as bales of hay and straw brought by Jacomino Malacoda from Bondeno. The poor harvest meant a lot of extra work in the granaries where the damp wheat needed constant attention. Fiorini described it as 'hot' and took on several casual labourers to move the grain around to stop it fermenting. He also had work to do shopping and packing yet another consignment of crates for Ippolito, containing the presents ordered via Vicino. This time there was no convenient party of travellers leaving Ferrara, so Pierantonio took the crates up to Mantua by barge, from where they would be sent to France. This was Pierantonio's third trip to Mantua that year – he had been there in August to collect four horses which were a present from Duke Federigo Gonzaga to Ippolito, and again the following month to collect two more. The three crates contained the usual bolts of material – this time mostly black velvet – and five of Sister Serafina's embroidered linen shirts (she had made a total of nine for him that year).

The presents Ippolito had ordered for France were lavish. On his return journey Vicino had stopped off in Mantua to pay a deposit of 40 scudi on three more sets of embroidered sleeves and collars, which were ready to leave with the crates in December. Fiorini packed two new viols, in specially made leather cases, and 9 kilos of candied fruits, over half of which were quinces, divided between six small stone jars. There was a set of four candlesticks, which Fiorini had ordered from one of the ducal goldsmiths – these had been made with 820 silver coins (worth 82 scudi), and the goldsmith was paid another 14 scudi for their manufacture. Some of the silver was used to make the seal which Romei had taken to Rome and for which the goldsmith had been paid less than 1 scudo. The most expensive present – significantly, in view of Ippolito's situation – was a suit of armour for Montmorency, which was commissioned by Ippolito Machiavelli, now running the family bank in Ferrara. He paid a deposit of 20 scudi to Zanpiero the ducal armourer, on 7 November and must have told him the commission was urgent, because the deposit was double the sum paid for the last suit ordered for Ippolito. Zanpiero worked quickly. By the end of November, just three weeks later, the armour was ready for gilding, and Machiavelli gave him the first of several instalments of gold coins to melt down. The armour was finished by the middle of December and cost Ippolito the sub-stantial sum of 67 scudi (the gilding alone cost 25 scudi). Machiavelli had one last duty to perform for Ippolito that year: on 16 December he attended the christening of Niccolò Tassone's baby daughter, acting as proxy for Ippolito, who had been made godfather.

Another sign of Ippolito's misfortunes was the return of Alfonso Cestarello, his old major-domo, to Ferrara in late November. Ces-tarello had recovered from the illness that had kept him in bed for the best part of six months in 1536. That autumn Ippolito had appoint-ed him to manage the anticipated income from the French benefices to which he had been nominated by Francis I. This proved overly optimistic: all the benefices remained blocked by Paul III in Rome. Ippolito therefore decided that Cestarello would be more usefully employed as his *commissario generale*, taking charge of his affairs in Ferrara. This must have been a blow for Fiorini. Although his job changed little in content, Cestarello ranked higher than him and was now, in effect, his boss. Cestarello's first task was to supervise the ducal accountants doing the audit on Ippolito's books – Fiorini's ledgers as well as those from the estates. The bailiffs themselves spent two weeks in Ferrara and the bailiff from Fóssoli lodged with Fiorini at Belfiore. The work was all done at Cestarello's house in Ferrara, and he asked Fiorini to supply ink and paper, as well as 2 kilos of tallow candles and 200 logs for the fire.

A lot of Fiorini's entries in December relate to the estates. Palamides needed money to pay the roofers working at Bondeno, while Domenico da Milano had to pay the builders working on

Marti Bolgarello's house at Migliaro. One major item was a herd of cattle for the workers at Migliaro, which cost Ippolito 67 scudi. There were twenty-one animals in all, including an ox – a large one, noted Fiorini – and eight dairy cows. Fiorini named all the dairy cows in the ledgers, among them Bride, Little Bride, Gypsy, Rosie, Sparrow and Falcon. A lot of poultry arrived from the estates that month, including over 100 capons which were kept at Belfiore to be fattened on millet for the Christmas market – one of the capons was the annual rent paid by the widow of a carter for a field at Migliaro. The Christmas pigs arrived on 14 December from the workers at Bondeno, Codigoro and Migliaro. They ranged in size from a rela-tively puny 40 kilos to the magnificent beast bred by Marti Bolgarello, which weighed in at 89 kilos (Antonio Maria Trova's pig was one of the smallest, weighing only 54 kilos).

The pigs, all fourteen of them, were made into hams and salamis. No doubt anticipating an increased demand for these Ferrarese spe-cialities to oil the political machinery in Rome and Milan, they doubled the quantity they had made the year before. Fiorini bought another fifteen pigs in the market in Ferrara, which cost 45 scudi and weighed an average of 77 kilos each. The pigs were killed by Piero, a gardener who specialized in this bloody task – he made 2 *soldi* 6 *denari* per pig, earning over 1 scudo for butchering all twenty-nine. The process of making the salamis was supervised by Madonna Laura, Ippolito's stepmother, and the work was done by women at Belfiore, in a room which Fiorini had had specially cleaned for the purpose. Fiorini does not explain who these women were, but possibly this was a task which, like sewing sheets, provided extra work for the wives of Ippolito's staff. The team of women were paid for their thirty-two days' work in pig meat, earning about 4 *soldi* a day, half the rate paid to manual labourers working on building sites. Fiorini also had to organize all the equipment and ingredients needed by Madonna Laura and her women. He bought intestines (pig and ox) to case the salamis, and arranged for candles, firewood, spices and salt to be transported from the Palazzo San Francesco stores. The pork needed a lot of salt (416 kilos), but this was not as expensive a commodity as we are often led to believe. Salt in 1537 in Ferrara cost 9 *denari* a kilo – expensive by today's standards but not excessively so: 3 kilos of salt was worth about the same as a chicken, and a carpenter earned the equivalent of 15 kilos a day.

The pace of work increased as Christmas approached. On 18 December Fiorini entered just three items of expenditure; on Christmas Eve he detailed thirty-three. His first job that morning was to record two jugs of oil taken from the larder to light the lantern in the stables at the Palazzo San Francesco. Later that morning there were deliveries of barley, spelt, millet and bran, and five carts of straw, for the stables. He had several bills to settle with Palamides for work done at Bondeno – the thirty-one beeswax candles Palamides required to decorate the church for Christmas had been sent the day before. He paid a carpenter who had done some small repairs to a door in the palace, and a blacksmith for a new key for one of the rooms vacated by Renée. He settled the farrier's bill for horseshoes supplied since October and the saddler's bill which dated back to February and included the cost of making the English harness for Romei. He paid Piero the gardener for killing the pigs and sent some more tallow candles over to Belfiore for the salami-makers who were working at night. He also paid December salaries to Pierantonio the trainer, Moiza the barber, and Francesco dalla Viola the musician, and sent a cart of straw to Bigo Schalabrino to cover the expenses of his horse.

This was also the day for handing out Christmas presents and alms. Fiorini gave 1 scudo to Ippolito's cousin, Sister Lucretia Borgia, who was Abbess at San Bernardino, and sent sacks of broad beans, chickpeas and beans to several other convents in the city. He gave coins to a preacher who said prayers 'to God to safeguard Ippolito from ill fortune', and to the widow of the Governor of Brescello, 'a respectable woman with three children', who had also received alms at Easter. A tailor, 'a respectable man who is ill and has a wife and two small children', received 13 kilos of flour. Fiorini paid a porter 9 *soldi* to deliver twenty-four pairs of capons from Belfiore to various addresses in Ferrara. Most of them were delivered, four pairs each, to members of the ducal court who had been involved with Ippolito's affairs that year – one of the recipients was Duke Ercole's ambassador in Florence, who had bought the quantities of taffeta Fiorini had sent to Ippolito in September, and another was Scipio Bonlei, who had sent Ippolito the horse that he had given to Francis I for New Year. The porter also delivered four pairs to Cestarello and another pair to Antonio da Como, one of the staff at the Palazzo San Francesco, who, as Fiorini noted, was 'a good and faithful servant and his wife has just had a baby'. There were several presents for other members of the household: one of the stable boys was given 17 kilos of flour for the extra work he had done mending the cart. Easily the most expensive present Fiorini handed out that Christmas was 1,400 kilos of wheat, sent on Ippolito's orders to Alfonso Visconti, Violante's husband. This was worth between 23 and 27 scudi at current prices, depending on the source of the grain – the eight capons received by the ducal councillors were worth less than 1 scudo.

Ippolito's income was never remotely adequate for his extravagant lifestyle. However, he could always borrow on his expectations. In 1537 his income came to 10,480 scudi, but his expenditure that year amounted to 12,603 scudi, over 75 per cent of which was spent either by him in France or by Fiorini on goods which were sent to him from Ferrara.

Place	Item	Amount in scudi	%
Ferrara	expenses	1,229	10
Estates	expenses	1,588	13
Rome	expenses	218	2
France	cash and goods	9,568	75
Total		12,603	100

Ippolito's expenditure in 1537

6

The Business of Pomp

ONE DAY IN late September 1537, while the French court was making its leisurely progress from Paris to Lyon, Ippolito was spotted by the Florentine goldsmith, Benvenuto Cellini. In his auto-biography – a racy and highly subjective account of life in sixteenth-century Europe – Cellini described how he joined the huge crowds of hangers-on who were following Francis I's entourage, and how he singled out Ippolito as someone worth cultivating as a possible patron. Cellini was ambitious and must have noticed that, although Ippolito had several musicians with him, he had no artists in his ret-inue (he did in fact employ two, but both had abandoned their jobs as painters for work with better prospects: Fiorini was now in charge of Ippolito's affairs in Ferrara, and Panizato, who had only been with Ippolito for eighteen months, had already been promoted from an administrative job in the stables to purveyor). Ippolito's back-ground and prospects made him an obvious target for Cellini. He was an Italian aristocrat and he had excellent connections at the French court. Gossiping with his friends in the crowd, Cellini would certainly have heard that Ippolito was Francis I's main candi-date for a cardinal's hat, and he knew that success with Ippolito would bring him directly into the royal orbit. But it was not just Ippolito's rich and privileged background that caught Cellini's eye that day – it was also his appearance.

Appearances mattered in sixteenth-century Europe. For kings and princes, ostentatious display was essential. In modern terms,

Ippolito wore exquisitely cut suits from Savile Row, his watch was a Rolex and he drove a Porsche. Just as we may recognize different designer labels or makes of car, and make judgements about people based on the size of their house or their choice of hobbies, so the people of sixteenth-century Europe had their own ways of assessing appearances. They knew the prices of cheap cloth and fine velvet, could identify a thoroughbred horse from a hack, and could tell the difference between vulgarity and style. For Cellini, as for any other artisan, cook, cleric or courtier in search of a patron, a big spender was a potent magnet. Cellini would have been quick to spot Ippolito's taste for conspicuous consumption.

Ippolito travelled in style. His pack mules and wagons were instantly identifiable by the coat-of-arms embroidered on the cloths that covered his luggage. His footmen were dressed in his personal livery colours of orange and white. His valets wore outfits of black velvet, clothes which Cellini would have been able to see at a glance were valuable enough to be pawned. His horses were caparisoned in black velvet embroidered with gold thread, with plumes of black and white feathers on their heads that shimmered in the autumn sun, and his dogs wore red leather collars studded with silver.

Then there was Ippolito himself, splendidly dressed in silk, velvet and damask – and fur if the weather was cold. His rings were valuable, as were his rosaries, and his hat glittered with gold ornaments. His swordblades were made of the finest Toledo steel and embellished with elegant gilded hilts specially made for him in Ferrara. He did not just look rich. Once Cellini got close to him, he would have been able to smell the citrus and jasmine oils scenting his beard and the expensive ambergris and musk that perfumed his gloves.

Ippolito's extravagance was not limited to his clothes, his accessories and his entourage. There were other areas in which a man of his position was expected to show off his wealth. Ippolito needed furnishings to provide an appropriate setting for his sumptuous dinner parties, and expensive silver for his table. Above all, he was expected to be extravagant in what he gave to others – generous with his alms and tips, and lavish with his presents.

We use the adjectives of magnificence – gold, silver, velvet or damask – to conjure up a visual image of wealth, but we rarely have the opportunity to consider how this image was created or what it actually cost. Thanks to Ippolito's account books, however, we know exactly how much he spent on his clothes and accessories, and on presents, alms and tips. The ledgers might lack the personal touch of a letter but they do allow us to put a precise financial value on the cost of display.

The inventory of Ippolito's possessions, compiled by Mosto and Fiorini in October 1535, before the move into the Palazzo San Francesco, contains a list of his jewels. He took them all with him to France, and Fiorini made a copy of this part of the inventory so that Mosto could keep track of these valuable items. Like most rich and powerful men of his era, Ippolito wore a lot of jewellery, and much of it was gold. He had two gold chains decorated with black enamel, and several rings, three of which contained precious stones – a diamond, a ruby and a turquoise, all set in gold. He owned six rosaries made of lapis lazuli, agate and garnets. These were not functional aids to prayer or indicators of piety but lavish personal ornaments worn for the display of wealth. In addition, Mosto's inventory lists a stock of 181 spare rosary beads and over 275 ornaments to decorate the brims of Ippolito's hats, most of them made of gold and others enamelled in blue, black and white.

Ippolito dressed like a secular prince, not a prelate, in the standard male attire of the non-clerical world. His normal daily dress was a doublet (*giuppone*) worn over a shirt (*camisa*), breeches (*bragoni*) and hose (*calze*), covered by a thigh-length belted tunic (*saglio*). His breeches were normally made of velvet, with hose in matching silk, wool or cotton. His shirt was made of fine linen, and its frills, embroidered by Sister Serafina, showed conspicuously at his neck and wrists. The doublet was a light garment, not unlike a waistcoat, and was made of silk, taffeta or satin. Ippolito's were usually elaborately

Standard male attire of a linen shirt, with ruffles showing at the neck and wrists, doublet, saglio, breeches and hose, and an expensive fur-lined coat

decorated – covered with tiny ornamental pleats, studded with little silk knots, or threaded with strips of velvet. The *saglio* – the word 'tunic' does not carry quite the right overtones of grandeur – was heavier and longer than the doublet, often made of velvet and usually worn open across the chest to show off the tailor's work on the doublet beneath. In winter the *saglio* might be fur-lined. When Ippolito went out he wore a coat, made of damask or velvet, over this ensemble, and in winter he wore a second coat as well, heavier and also lined with fur.

Ippolito owned a great many clothes. It took Mosto and Fiorini four days to compile the list for the 1535 inventory – over 400 items and 611 shoelaces – carefully identifying each garment by colour, material and decoration. By any standards, it was an enormous collection for a 26-year-old, even if he was the son of a duke and Archbishop of Milan. Only forty-three of the items were religious – Ippolito owned eleven archiepiscopal cloaks and capes, five white linen rochets and twenty-seven hats. Sixty-one items were identified as clothes he used for hunting, jousting or dressing up for Carnival or other festivities. Judging by the relative quantities, Ippolito clearly preferred partying to performing his religious duties. His dressing-up clothes included three peasant's outfits, one pair of sailor's breeches, thirty hats and two fleeces which, as Fiorini detailed, he wore as wigs. The most splendid items were his jousting *saglii*. One, in dark red velvet, had a sleeve striped in Ippolito's personal colours of orange and white, while another was made of cloth-of-gold threaded with red velvet ribbons. The bulk of the items were the clothes Ippolito wore every day. His nightwear consisted solely of a bedcap – he had four, all made of fine white linen and embroidered by Sister Serafina with red or black silk. Like most Italian men of that era, he wore nothing else in bed.

Ippolito's hats, shoes, boots, breeches and hose were all made by specialist suppliers in Ferrara. He provided a lot of work for Pietro Maria, the hatter. The inventory lists a total of eighty-six hats, excluding the bedcaps and fleece wigs – two were decorated with peacock feathers and two were made of straw. Most of his boots and

Fine linen shirts	7
Doublets	14
Breeches and hose	11 pairs
Saglii	11
Coats and overcoats	46
Hats	29
Leather boots	5 pairs
Shoes	54 pairs
Bedcaps	4
Handerkerchiefs	102
Gloves	15 pairs

Inventory of Ippolito's everyday clothes, 1535

shoes, including his leather tennis shoes, were made by Dielai the cobbler. Dielai charged about 1 scudo for a pair of leather boots, and roughly the same for five pairs of shoes. Ippolito's everyday shoes had leather soles and black velvet uppers, made with material supplied from the wardrobe, and he got through an average of eighteen pairs every year. His breeches and hose, again mostly black velvet, were made as a single unit by hosiers, who charged around 8 scudi a pair. The hose often needed replacing – ¾ scudo for woollen hose, over 1 scudo for silk.

The only items not made in Ferrara were his Spanish leather gloves. They were a new fashion in Italy, where many people, including Paul III, preferred to wear more traditional gloves made from the soft skin of unborn calves. Top-quality Spanish gloves were still not available in Ferrara and Ippolito had to buy his in Mantua. The gloves themselves were relatively cheap – they cost 10 scudi for a dozen pairs. The real expense lay in the ambergris and musk which were used to perfume them. Ambergris, which comes from the intestine of the sperm whale, cost 417 scudi a kilo; musk, the secretion of the musk deer, was marginally cheaper at 278 scudi.

Gloves

Although the amounts of these aromatic substances needed to perfume a pair of gloves were small, they added 35 scudi to the cost of
twelve pairs, making a price of 2 scudi per glove.

Apart from his shirts, which were embroidered by Sister Serafina, most of Ippolito's clothes were custom-made by tailors, several
of whom worked for the ducal court. One year Assassino had to provide a tailor with candles so that he could work all night to finish a
coat that Ippolito wanted to wear for the St George's Day festivities.
The doublets, *saglii* and coats listed in the 1535 inventory were pre-
dominantly black. Black was the ducal fashion for everyday wear in
Ferrara – expensive but unostentatious, and the colour worn by
courtiers and merchants. It was also the Spanish style, and the look
had been popularized in Ferrara by Ippolito's grandfather, Ercole I,
who had spent much of his childhood at the Aragon court of
Naples. Over half Ippolito's doublets were black – he owned four in

black taffeta, one finely pleated, another threaded with black velvet ribbons. Twenty-one of his coats were black, including a woollen mourning cloak which must have been made for Ippolito when his father died in October 1534. Most of the other garments were red. This was not as monotonous as it sounds. Ippolito wore many different shades of red — a brilliant scarlet, a rich brownish red, a luxurious dark burgundy and a distinctive purple, which was so dark that it was almost black. He was also fond of a dark leonine orange. One of the few items outside this range of colours was a particularly dapper doublet in blue and yellow shot silk. A lot of the *saglii* and coats were decorated with stripes, and many of the coats had slashed sleeves in the same colours — two embellishments which were fashionable in Ferrara. Though the colours of these details were the same, there was contrast in the fabrics — black velvet striped with black satin, dark red damask lined with dark red silk, or scarlet satin trimmed with a scarlet silk fringe.

Soon after his arrival in France, Ippolito decided to add a full-time tailor to his household. Antoine was a Frenchman, though his name is Italianized in the ledgers to Antonio. His importance to Ippolito's image was evident from his salary. Earning 48 scudi a year, he was paid more than anyone else in the household except the salaried courtiers, and received twice as much as Ippolito's chief cook, Andrea. Antoine was also paid a pro rata sum for each item he made — this included not only Ippolito's clothes and furnishings, notably velvet covers for tables and a particularly elaborate set of red satin bed-hangings, but also the cloths embroidered with Ippolito's coat-of-arms that covered his luggage, and clothes for the household. Antoine had to work hard for his money. His bill in 1540 listed 120 items and came to over 212 scudi, making him the highest-paid member of Ippolito's household.

Antoine's first task was a makeover of Ippolito's wardrobe, changing both the style and the colour of Ippolito's clothes to suit the fashions of the French court. Unrelieved black was less popular for those of rank at the French court, and so was the Ferrarese preference for stripes or slashed sleeves, which both looked dated and provincial. All seven doublets and eighteen of the twenty *saglii* that Antoine made in 1540 were coloured. Some were dark orange but most were in one of the various shades of red, lined with the same colour in silk – the preference for colour co-ordination did not change. His coats, however, now had wider sleeves – as the ledger put it, 'in the French style' – and his breeches were longer in the leg. The 1535 inventory lists only a few garments in a distinctively national style. Fiorini described one coat as Milanese and another, in black damask, as German – England does not seem to have had a high fashion profile in sixteenth-century Europe, though it was famous for weapons, armour, hunting equipment and a particular style of harness. It is not clear how far the design of garments carried political overtones. The choice of black in Ferrara may have been associated with Spain but it did not indicate a particular political allegiance. The shoes Dielai made for Ippolito were all detailed as either French or Spanish, and the rivalry between Charles V and Francis I did not stop Ippolito from buying both gloves and sword blades made in Spain.

Antoine also made several extra quilted and fur-lined garments for Ippolito, though this had more to do with the freezing winters in northern France than with fashion. He made several fur-lined coats for Ippolito to wear in the privacy of his own chambers – one in orange taffeta lined with lynx, another in red taffeta lined with sable. There was also a very heavy overcoat – called a *saltimbarcha* – in scarlet woollen cloth with borders of sable and a fox fur lining. In his bill, Antoine specified that it was intended for Ippolito 'to wear over his other clothes when he rides in extreme cold'.

Ippolito may have worn the same type of garments as other men but the quality of his clothes set him visibly apart from the crowd. The fact that he wore a clean shirt every day, even when travelling, was in itself an indication of wealth. The cost of laundering a shirt was small, but it added up to 8 scudi a year, a luxury few could afford. With daily washing the shirts inevitably wore out quickly – Fiorini sent nine new shirts to France during 1537. The decorative details on

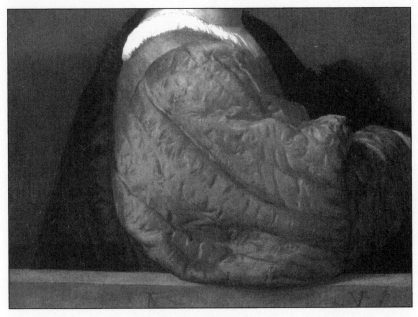

A saglio *with quilted sleeves*

Ippolito's doublets, *saglii* and coats were conspicuously expensive. Pleating, ribbons, stripes, slashes and trimmings all involved a lot of sewing and added significantly to the cost of making a garment. Antoine charged only 1 scudo for a plain doublet but 5 scudi for one with fine pleating across the front. Slashed sleeves, which involved long cuts in the velvet or damask garment and the insertion of material or fur, carried the unmistakable message that the owner was rich enough to waste valuable material. Quilting a garment by hand was a long process and particularly expensive. Antoine charged 1 to 2 scudi for a plain *saglio* but over 14 scudi for a quilted one, and as much as 30 scudi for quilting a coat. Fur was also expensive, and Ippolito wore a lot of it. A fox pelt cost 1½ scudi, a sable 12 scudi and a lynx 13 scudi. The furrier's bill for lining one *saglio* with lynx came to 23 scudi. Not surprisingly the sable and lynx were usually reserved for the exterior of the garment, while cheaper fox fur (and sheepskin) did the practical work inside, keeping Ippolito warm – you needed eight fox pelts to line a *saglio*, but only two sables to trim the edges.

~

Cellini and other onlookers in the crowd would have noticed all these things but above all they would have spotted the quality of the material used for the garments themselves. Expensive textiles were our equivalent of designer labels, and the materials favoured by Ippolito – velvet, silk, taffeta, satin and damask – were all staggeringly expensive. Tomaso Mosto hoarded every scrap of material in the wardrobe, and his ledger detailed each occasion when Antoine dismantled a garment that Ippolito no longer used, listing the precise length of the pieces that went back into the wardrobe to be recycled as trimmings. The *saltimbarcha* which Antoine made for cold weather was trimmed with red velvet from one of Ippolito's old *saglii*. The manufacture of textiles in sixteenth-century Europe was labour-intensive – there were no electric machines or synthetic fibres to simplify production and lower costs. The entire process, from spinning and dyeing the thread to weaving and finishing the cloth, was done by hand. One metre of black velvet could cost as much as 2 scudi, the equivalent of twelve day's wages for a master-builder, and the price of twenty-three plump capons or 1,275 logs for the fire. It took three metres of material to make a doublet (6 scudi), nine for a *saglio* (18 scudi) and over eighteen for a long coat (36 scudi) – and then there was the price of similar lengths of silk to line these garments.

Other factors also influenced the price of textiles. Provenance was important. The best – and the most expensive – velvet and damask came from Venice, while the finest taffetas were made in Florence. Moirés, damasks and other figured fabrics with complicated patterns that were woven in at the loom were more expensive than plain textiles. Colour was another significant factor. Given the importance of appearance, and Ippolito's unerring eye for quality, it should not come as a surprise to find that the black and red which dominated his wardrobe were markedly more expensive than other colours. Orange textiles were as much as 25 per cent cheaper than the same material in black. Black was a hard colour to dye properly, which made it expensive. However, it was not as expensive as the various shades of red which were all dyed with kermes (*cremesino*, from the Arabic, *qirmiz*), a dye made from insect bodies and imported to Venice at considerable cost from the Middle East. The darker the red, the more it cost – a metre of dark red velvet cost about 3¼ scudi, but the same length of dark purple velvet could come to as much as 4½ scudi. These materials were even more expensive in France, where merchants had to pay transport costs and taxes to import Italian fabrics. The length of dark red kermes-dyed damask needed to make a long coat cost 43 scudi in Venice but 59 scudi in Paris. This was why Fiorini sent so much material to Ippolito in France in 1537 – 653 metres of velvet, damask, satin and taffeta, worth a total of 968 scudi.

Although it is impossible to know exactly what Ippolito was wearing that autumn day when Cellini spotted him on the road to Lyon, it is possible to estimate the value of a typical outfit from the account books. The table opposite is based on Antoine's ledger – one of Sister Serafina's shirts, a pleated doublet made of red Florentine taffeta, a dark red damask *saglio* trimmed with velvet from one of Ippolito's old garments, a black velvet coat lined with black taffeta, as well as his usual breeches, hose, gloves and boots. I have assumed that the weather was warm that September, and that neither his coat nor his *saglio* had fur linings, which would have added another 30 scudi to the bill. Even so, the cost of this hypothetical outfit comes to 96 scudi – a sum that would take a carpenter or a builder nearly three years to earn. No wonder Cellini was impressed.

It was not just Ippolito's clothes that provided clues to his rank. There was also his household. The number of those who travelled with him grew steadily during his years in France. In 1536 he had fifty-two men with him, a quarter of whom returned to Ferrara, but by 1539 his entourage in France numbered over sixty. The largest increases were amongst the staff responsible for food and music, a sign of the importance Ippolito attached to entertaining in style. In 1536 Ippolito had only needed two *credenzieri* – he now had three, and three assistants. He added a second sommelier and, in the

Item	Cost of materials	Manufacture	Total in scudi
Fine linen shirt	I	2	3
Taffeta doublet	5	4	9
Damask *saglio*	23	2	25
Velvet coat	44	2	46
Breeches and hose			8
Gloves			4
Boots			I
Total			96

The cost of an outfit

kitchens, where two cooks and a boy had once sufficed, he now had six cooks and three boys to prepare and cook his elaborate dinner parties. Moreover, many of the new men on whom he depended to create an impressive image were French. In addition to Antoine, his French tailor, Ippolito employed two French *credenzieri* and two French cooks, one of whom was a pastry cook from Blois. Most significantly, he took on six new musicians – a bass, two tenors and three boy sopranos, all of whom were French or Flemish.

The visual appearance of the men in Ippolito's entourage had a direct impact on Ippolito's image, and Antoine the tailor made clothes for several members of the household as part of their wages. The falconers and kennelmen were dressed functionally in black fustian jackets, white cotton shirts, red stockings and shoes or boots. Although the jackets cost less than I scudo, their shoes and boots were well-made and only marginally cheaper than those Dielai supplied for Ippolito himself. They were certainly better-quality clothes than they could afford themselves. The valets, footmen and pages – Ippolito's formal retinue – were more expensively dressed in clothes deliberately designed to impress. Assassino and the other valets dressed in black, wearing *saglii* and doublets of black velvet over white shirts, black breeches and black stockings. For formal occasions they changed into orange satin doublets and wore black hats. The white cotton Antoine used for their shirts was of better quality than that used for the kennelmen and falconers, but a lot cheaper than the fine linen of Ippolito's shirts. The doublets were plain, with none of the pleating or other elaborations which Antoine sewed for Ippolito. The velvet was also cheaper, though sometimes the doublets were made from material salvaged from Ippolito's old garments – Antoine took apart one of Ippolito's black velvet coats to make a new *saglio* for one of the valets. The footmen on duty wore doublets striped in Ippolito's colours of orange and white, dark orange breeches, grey stockings, which were patterned with orange and white, and red hats. The pages were even more brightly coloured, in orange doublets and red stockings. All were provided with leather shoes and boots, and travelling cloaks – black cloth for the valets, grey cloth slashed with grey velvet for the footmen and pages. These cloaks were not cheap. One careless page left his behind somewhere between Lyon and Paris, and Antoine spent 8 scudi on the materials he needed to make a replacement.

Above all, it was the size of one's household that was the indicator of rank, and for the most prosaic of reasons – a large household was very expensive to maintain. Ippolito had to pay not only his entourage in France but also the staff running his estates and residences in Ferrara. His annual salary bill came to around 2,400 scudi, but this was only part of the story. Ippolito also had to feed his men, and provide accommodation. The cost of feeding himself and his household in Lyon in 1536 worked out at 5½ scudi a month for each member of the household, or 3,960 scudi for sixty men over a year. On top of this there were the food allowances he paid to the servants of his courtiers, the stable boys and the men who remained behind in Ferrara, which added another 350 scudi to the bill. He also had to pay for stabling and fodder for his horses in France. It is difficult to estimate this figure precisely. We know that he saved money by providing his own fodder whenever possible. Innkeepers charged the equivalent of 40 to 50 scudi a year for stabling and feeding one horse, and the cost of stabling

	Scudi
Salaries	2,400
Food and accommodation	4,310
Horses	1,500
Mules	1,000
Clothes	370
Incidental expenses	20
Total	9,600

Estimated annual cost of Ippolito's household

was only a fraction (2 scudi) of the whole. Assuming he could save 50 per cent on the price of fodder, then the cost of looking after each horse amounted to about 25 scudi a year – and he had at least sixty horses. Then there were the mules that carried his baggage – in 1540 he hired a muleteer and a string of mules for this purpose, and the bill for six months came to 519 scudi. There was also the cost of clothes for his entourage and incidental expenses for the household. The pages and the boy sopranos had their heads deloused every fortnight or so, and their linen, which included a lot of handkerchiefs, was washed at Ippolito's expense. There were also occasional items, such as the rent of sheets or the purchase of medicines for those who were ill. The total, estimated according to these figures, came to 9,600 scudi a year and accounted for the bulk of his income, which in 1537 was 10,479 scudi. Ippolito was living beyond his means.

The most effective way of displaying status in sixteenth-century Europe was to build a magnificent palace. Given his nomadic existence in France, and the uncertainty as to how long he would remain there, this was not an option for Ippolito (it was not until the mid-1540s that he built an elegant little residence at Fontainebleau, complete with tennis court). Ippolito was allocated apartments by the King's foragers, who acted on instructions from Montmorency, and their proximity to the King's chambers was a mark of royal favour. In his enquiries about his future patron's prospects, Cellini might well have heard that Ippolito had spent the summer of 1537 at Fontainebleau, lodged in the suite of rooms usually given to the Dauphin, who was away fighting.

Ippolito may have had little say in the location of his rooms, but he could – and did – ensure that they were magnificently furnished. The walls of his rooms were hung with tapestries brought from Ferrara – Ippolito regularly tipped the King's tapestry men for hanging them. He also owned a set of Spanish leather hangings, stamped with gilded decoration, which were more robust than tapestry, though a lot heavier for the baggage mules. This was another new fashion from Spain and presumably very popular in France, because Ippolito ordered the hangings in May 1536, just six weeks after his arrival at the French court. We do not know how many there were, but they were probably intended to decorate more than one room. They cost 350 scudi, plus another 87 scudi to cover transport and currency exchanges. The hangings were made in Valencia and the commission was handled by a Genoese merchant, Ansaldo Grimaldi, who had trading connections in Spain. The Machiavelli bank in Ferrara paid Grimaldi's bill for the hangings and for their transport from Valencia to Genoa, charging Ippolito 2½ per cent for this service, and Fiorini settled the bill with the carrier who brought the hangings over from Genoa separately.

Ippolito loved expensive fripperies and baubles. He kept the ambergris and musk for his gloves in special silver boxes. He had another little silver box with its own silver padlock, two gilded clocks, one of which sounded the hours, a silver sandbox for blotting letters, three silver dog collars, a set of balances with little silver weights, and twelve pieces of coral. He spent 4 scudi on a silver piccolo for his flautist and 6 scudi on a more exotic purchase, a parrot. Favoured guests might be shown his collection of medals, many of which were antique, and a reliquary – though Mosto did not record what relic it contained.

	Scudi
Hangings	350
Transport Valencia–Genoa	58
Transport Genoa–Ferrara	19
Bank charges	10
Total	437

Spanish leather wall hangings

Ippolito also travelled with a large collection of valuable plate in his luggage – gold cups, silver vases, basins and jugs for his dining-table, and silver plates, dishes and spoons for the *credenza*. Cellini knew that his luxury craft would appeal to Ippolito's tastes. The goldsmith managed to engineer a meeting with Ippolito on the jour-ney to Lyon and persuaded him to commission a silver jug and basin, which he promised would be ornamented with *all'antica* decoration. Ippolito intended to give these items to Francis I, and he paid Cellini an advance for the work. However, Cellini, who was a slippery cus-tomer at the best of times, did not use the money as Ippolito had intended. In his biography he claimed he was sick of France and used the cash to return to Rome, where he had other commissions waiting for him. Unfortunately Paul III had him arrested and imprisoned in Castel Sant'Angelo on a charge of stealing papal jewels during the pontificate of Clement VII. Ippolito had to wait several years for his silverware, and so did Francis I.

The act of giving was one of the most public statements of wealth and power. It is difficult to overestimate the importance of presents, tips and alms in sixteenth-century Europe. Ippolito lost few opportu-nities to distribute largesse to those beneath him in the social hier-archy or to give extravagant presents to those he needed to impress.

His reasons were varied – he gave to buy goodwill or political advantage, to gain merit in the eyes of God or simply to reward good work. Gifts were a valuable and indispensable tool in the political arena: Ippolito and his contemporaries made no distinction between bribes and personal presents. Both were gifts and, depending on the status of the recipient, both were bribes, of a sort – and all required a reciprocal gesture.

The account books that survive from 1536 to 1540 record that Ippolito gave over a thousand items – coins and goods – as presents, alms or tips. His bookkeepers divided his gifts into two distinct categories – alms (*elemosine*) and presents (*donatione,* which included both presents and tips). The money distributed under the alms account included not only that given to the poor and the needy, but also gifts to religious institutions, such as the coins offered during mass or given to the priest who heard Ippolito's confession, as well as the sums donated to the building funds of various churches. Almsgiving in this broad sense was a condition of salvation in the Catholic Church and an obligatory act for all good Christians (it was also one of the teachings of the Catholic Church that was rejected by Protestants). Many of the alms were explicitly reciprocal, and Fiorini's ledgers reveal just how personalized the act of almsgiving could be.

When he departed for France in 1536, Ippolito left behind an army of people in Ferrara praying – quite literally – for his success. One man was paid 6 *soldi* a month (just over 1 scudo a year) to recite daily prayers to God to 'protect Ippolito from the plague and any other illness, and to keep him healthy'. The friars of San Francesco, the church closest to his palace, were given azure and vermilion pigments from the wardrobe so that they could paint the organ in their church in return for prayers for Ippolito's good health. The nun who looked after the tomb of Ippolito's ancestor, Beatrice d'Este, in Sant'Antonio received regular presents of oil and wax for the tomb in the hope that both God and Beatrice would guard Ippolito from misfortune. Her maid, another poor but respectable widow, was also paid to pray to God on Ippolito's behalf. Another nun was given a new pair of shoes — Fiorini specified that they were nun's sandals — because 'she prays to the Virgin every day to guard Ippolito from dis/ grace and to keep him healthy and happy'. During the war in Provence in the summer of 1536 the priests of one church in Ferrara held a special mass to pray for peace, and Fiorini gave them 2 scudi to have prayers said 'to God and the Virgin so that they will guard Ippolito from misfortune', adding, almost as an afterthought, that the priests should also pray 'to bring peace to Christendom'. Even Sister Serafina, who embroidered Ippolito's linen, did her duty. She was given a sack of chicken feed, 'firstly because she prays for Ippolito and secondly because she sews his shirts' (the convent also received money for each shirt she embroidered).

Whether it was deliberate or accidental, a high proportion of the recipients of Ippolito's alms were women. It was mostly nunneries that benefited from gifts of money or beans, chickpeas and wheat from Ippolito's estates. Many of the gifts took the form of charitable aid to assist poor girls entering a convent. Fiorini gave clothes worth 1½ scudi to a Jewish girl who had converted to Christianity and wanted to enter Santa Caterina di Siena. There were new blue bed/ covers, worth 3 scudi, for two girls who entered the convents of San Gabriele and Corpus Domini and who had offered to pray 'contin/ uously' for Ippolito. Entering a convent, like marriage, required a dowry. When his old valet died in 1535, Ippolito was generous with clothes for his four children and financed one daughter to join Santa Caterina Martire. To celebrate her final vows, which she took in June 1536, he paid for a party for her at the convent. This was quite a feast: Fiorini sent cheese, raisins, flour, sugar and almonds from Ippolito's larder, and wine from the cellars, as well as one whole calf, eggs, more cheese, fish, oranges and lemons, all specially bought for the occasion.

Fiorini's ledgers make it clear that alms handed out were given in the expectation that God would reward Ippolito. Equally, the recipients of presents were expected to honour their side of the bar/ gain. Despite the quantity of people praying for him in Ferrara, Ippolito placed far more trust, in financial terms at least, in the tangible relationships of the real and overwhelmingly secular world. Put in this context, it has to be said that Ippolito was not particularly generous with his alms. His income in 1537 came to 10,480 scudi. We do not know how much he handed out in France that year, but Fiorini distributed coins and goods worth a total of just 26 scudi to the poor in Ferrara, and another 22 scudi to monasteries and convents in the city (40 per cent of this to the convent of Corpus Domini, where his sister was Abbess). The total, 48 scudi, would only have paid for enough velvet to make two of Ippolito's *saglii*. The contrast between Christian charity and secular presents was striking. When his aunt, Violante d'Este, died in March 1540, Ippolito had prayers said for her in each of the seven major churches in Rome, a gesture that cost him ⅔ scudo. That was only marginally more than the tip of ½ scudo he gave to the owner of a dog that covered one of his bitches, and a tiny sum in comparison to the 5 scudi with which he tipped Paul III's buffoon.

Tipping was expected for services rendered without charge – and that included entertainment. Fiorini recorded several tips to peasants who returned lost falcons, and one of 10 *soldi* (just over a tenth of a scudo) to a gardener who returned some of Ippolito's peacock chicks that had escaped from the garden at Belfiore – as Fiorini explained in his ledger, the man could have sold them, and no one would have known. Tips were the chief means of negotiating status down the social scale and were often associated with travel and the public display of prestige. Ippolito's standard tip on the road was 1 scudo – this single gold coin had value across Europe and, at a practical level, it was easy accessible in his money bags. It also represented a very substantial sum for many of its recipients – it represented a fortnight's wages for a labourer and would buy twenty-eight chickens, ten geese or 50 kilos of flour.

Ippolito's footman handed out these coins to gate-keepers, guides, couriers and ferrymen and, occasionally, to innkeepers. For the ferrymen who transported Ippolito and his household across the rivers of Europe, this was not the price of the journey, in the sense of a ticket.

There seems to have been no charge *per se* and the system worked well for the simple reason – unimaginable today – that the obligation on the rich to show off their wealth was more effective than any legislation. Staying the night in a private palace involved a lot of 1scudo tips. It was customary to tip all the musicians who had played at the banquet as well as the cooks, the *credenzieri*, the wine waiters and other dining staff, and the officials in charge of the stables, the cellars and the wood stores. Ippolito also tipped the bearer of presents to himself, invariably a member of the donor's household. For all these men, 1 scudo represented a substantial proportion of their wages – and Ippolito's own staff must have benefited in the same way when they distributed presents on Ippolito's behalf.

Ippolito also regularly tipped entertainers who amused him on the road – itinerant players and singers, dwarves and even young girls acting as May Queens. Several of the entries suggest musicians with physical deformities received tips, but these were a reward for delighting Ippolito, not alms for their misfortune. Once again, the tips reveal a fondness for the female sex. The women in Lyon who regularly rowed Ippolito across the Saône or took him for a ride on the river were a particular favourite and received coins for amusing him – they may have sung for him, but it is more likely that he simply enjoyed their flirtatious banter. One unnamed woman, enigmatically, 'accommodated Ippolito in her house for half a day while he was out hunting with the King'. Exactly how she accommodated him was not specified, but she received ¼ scudo – not a large sum, but still worth seven chickens.

Money, in the context of giftgiving, usually moved down the social scale, but goods could move in both directions. Ippolito gave a vast range of goods as presents, to an equally vast range of recipients. Some were thankyou presents, such as the stockings for the Venetian stonecutters who installed the Istrian stone door frames in the Palazzo San Francesco, or the capons he gave his lawyers for Christmas. Others were of a more personal nature. He gave a set of playing cards to his cousin Guidobaldo della Rovere, the Duke of Urbino, and gilded enamel inkwells to his sister Eleonora, Ippolito Machiavelli and the hard-working Fiorini – the quality of the present did not always reflect the rank of the recipient. Violante, the mother of his baby daughter, appears only rarely in the account books. At Christ-mas 1536 she received a barrel of malmsey wine, Ippolito's favourite, and four capons. She may also have been the intended recipient of two valuable rings that Machiavelli took from France to Ferrara in August 1537 and of the eight jars of aromatic carnation petals, made by the nuns of Sant'Antonio and given by Fiorini to an unnamed person, or as he put it, a *persona segreta*.

The largest group of recipients of personal presents were mem-bers of Ippolito's household, who benefited in all sorts of ways from his generosity, over and above their salaries, in return for their loyalty, both past and future. One year he gave Pierantonio the trainer a new set of leather boots, and all his kitchen staff received new jackets, made by Antoine – the cooks' jackets were black fustian, the boys' grey cloth. Favoured members of staff were given his cast-off clothes. Andrea the cook received an expensive dark red satin doublet, lined with matching taffeta, from the wardrobe, while Assassino was given one of Ippolito's old black satin coats, from which the sable lining seems to have been removed, and a sword with an elaborate gilded hilt.

Above all, presents had a political context, like the jars of candied fruits Fiorini sent to Ippolito's agent in Milan to bribe imperial offi-cials who were causing problems in the archbishopric. Not surpris-ingly, the main focus of Ippolito's political gifts was the French court. Success in France was vital to Ippolito, and he worked hard to estab-lish his position at the French court from the day he arrived. His rep-utation for magnificent banquets was reported in diplomatic correspondence, not just to Ercole II, but also to other rulers in Europe. Part of his success was undoubtedly due to his deliberate, and ostentatious, use of conspicuously expensive presents – suits of armour, swords, gold rosaries with aromatic beads filled with musk and ambergris, perfumed gloves and embroidered sleeves, as well as

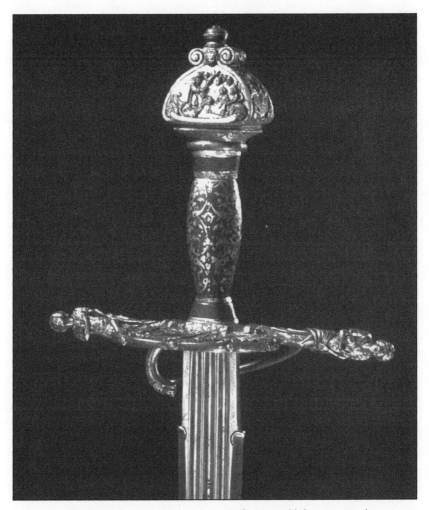

*An elegant late sixteenth-century Italian sword hilt ornamented
with* all'antica *decoration*

embroidered linen handkerchiefs, shirts and bedcaps. He even gave
away his own horses, medals and other treasured possessions. These
presents were far more lavish than those he gave to people back home
in Ferrara. They needed to be. Ippolito expected great favours in
return, not least his cardinal's hat.

The importance of good relations with the French court had
become all the more imperative since October 1537, when Ippolito

first heard the rumours from Rome that Ercole II had decided to abandon the pursuit of his cardinal's hat. His hopes and ambitions now rested largely with Francis I, and with his principal minister, Montmorency. With this in mind he ordered expensive presents for members of the court, including a particularly splendid suit of armour for Montmorency. He also encouraged his brother to help and asked him to send Montmorency one of his prized Ferrara-bred horses. Ippolito must have been disappointed – and a little suspicious – when Ercole replied that he could not find one good enough. Ippolito responded, diplomatically, that this was a pity, and added, 'it would be a good idea to try and please him because he is so important'. Just how important soon became clear. On 10 February 1538 Montmorency was appointed Constable of France, the highest honour that Francis I could bestow on him. Ippolito knew Montmorency's support was essential if he were to realize his own ambitions, a fact that was brought home very forcibly a month or so later when Montmorency used his influence with the King to remove one of Francis I's oldest friends from court. Ippolito wrote, in code, to his brother with the news:

> *Although Admiral Chabot is still Governor in Burgundy, the Duke of Guise was sent there the day before yesterday with letters patent appointing him Lieutenant in the same place, with the authority to appoint and sack as he likes ... it looks like Chabot's career is over and it makes one realize how necessary it is to keep in with people at court because two days ago it was possible to say that he was at the top of the wheel and now, with this disgrace, his career has plunged down to its lowest point.*

Ippolito must have been worried that his own career might do the same.

7

A Court at Peace

THE YEAR 1538 opened badly for Ippolito. His coveted cardinal's hat was under serious threat from several directions. As Francis I's candidate he would have expected, in normal circumstances, to be appointed automatically, but Paul III continued to insist on settling his dispute with Ercole II before agreeing to the honour. The negotiations between Paul III and the Duke had reached deadlock. Ercole refused to pay the 40,000 scudi that the Pope was demanding as his price for the hat, and Paul III refused to settle the dispute without it. The issue was further complicated by the fundamentalist reformers in Rome, aided and abetted by Cardinal Carpi, who had publicly accused the Pope of simony. They had a point – the whole transaction was deeply simoniacal. Ercole II thought, somewhat naïvely, that he could exploit this accusation and so avoid paying the 40,000 scudi. Paul III for his part had no intention of passing up such a large sum of money, and he knew that he could fudge the simony issue by claiming that the 40,000 scudi was just part of the settlement for Modena and Reggio.

To Ippolito the situation must have seemed bleak. Although his brother continued to insist that he was doing all he could to get Ippolito his hat, it was clear that this was not the case. Early in January the French ambassador in Rome reported to Francis I that it was the Duke and not the Pope who was responsible for delaying the settlement and threatening Ippolito's chances of a hat – and, by implication, insulting the King. On 25 January Ippolito sent his squire Vicino back to Ferrara, for the second time in three months, to find out what was going on, and for the next eight weeks Ippolito had to wait as patiently as he could for news.

Early in February the French court arrived in Moulins, the ancient capital of the duchy of Bourbon, and it was here that Francis I invested Montmorency as Constable of France in a magnificent ceremony in the château. The significance of the location would have been evident to all present, including Ippolito. The post of Constable had been vacant since 1523 when its last holder, Charles de Bourbon, had defected to Charles V – he became one of the Emperor's leading generals and died leading the infamous Sack of Rome in 1527. The rivalry between Francis I and Charles V had continued unabated in the intervening decade, and in the two years Ippolito had been at the French court they had fought almost continuously – Ippolito himself had witnessed their battles in Savoy, in Provence and in northern France. They had finally signed a three-month truce in November 1537 but the attempt to convert this into a lasting peace had failed. While Francis I spent Christmas at Montpellier, and Charles V celebrated the festive season just 150 kilometres away at Perpignan, their envoys had been deep in talks at Leucate, a small town between the two courts in the salt marshes of the Languedoc. The envoys could hardly have been more different. Francis I was represented by Montmorency and the Cardinal of Lorraine, members of two of the leading aristocratic families of his realm. Charles V was represented by his chancellor, Nicholas Granvelle, the grandson of a Flemish blacksmith, and his secretary, Francisco de los Cobos, whose origins in rural Andalusia were even humbler.

The talks broke down in early January and Francis I promptly started back to Paris, but his progress was halted by a letter from Paul III. The Pope was desperate for peace between Charles V and Francis I so that the rivals could combine their forces against the Turks who were now threatening the Italian coastline, and he offered to host a peace conference at Nice that summer. Francis I decided to wait at

Moulins while plans for the conference were being made, and the court remained there for two months.

∿

One of the most unlikely, and entertaining, ledgers to survive in the archives at Modena is Ippolito's gambling book for the years 1538–41, which makes it clear that Ippolito spent much of the winter of 1537–8 playing cards. He was rather a successful gambler. The ledger opened on 1 January 1538 with a list of those who owed him money – a total of 456 scudi. Among the debtors were the King of Navarre (171 scudi), Luigi Alamanni (96 scudi), the Duke of Nevers (90 scudi) and the Cardinal of Lorraine (25 scudi). Alamanni was a Florentine who had been exiled for his part in a conspiracy to assassinate Clement VII. He was the only one of the debtors to sign an IOU – the others were perhaps too grand – and the debt was countersigned by a Florentine merchant in Lyon to guaran-tee repayment at the end of July.

The journey from Montpellier to Moulins was a profitable one for Ippolito. During those three weeks he played cards nearly every day and won 550 scudi. By the time they arrived, the Cardinal of Lor-raine's debt had increased to 172 scudi. (Montmorency, on the other hand, was more prompt and repaid the 20 scudi he lost to Ippolito just six days later.)

It was while they were in Moulins in February that Ippolito had an attack of gout, probably the first but certainly not the last, for this excruciatingly painful condition was to plague him for the rest of his life. He was ill for three days and unable to walk, and so spent most of his time playing cards. Perhaps the pain distracted him, because he lost 35 scudi. However, by 2 March he had recovered sufficiently to play tennis in the court at the château and lost 122 scudi to the Dauphin, a sum that included 2 scudi to pay for new balls.

Three days later a courier arrived with an urgent letter from Francis I's ambassador in Rome. The arrangements for the peace

A page from Ippolito's gambling ledger, recording his losses on the left and his winnings on the right

conference had been finalized and he announced that Paul III would leave for Nice on 11 March, the following Monday. Ippolito reported the news to his brother, adding, with some excitement, that 'these three rulers have never talked together'. But the ambassador's letter also contained bad news. Francis I informed Ippolito that the talks between Ercole II and the Pope had finally broken down completely.

March was a difficult month for Ippolito, while he waited impatiently for Vicino's return from Ferrara. His gambling book shows a steady stream of losses – 90 scudi one day, 95 the next, though he did win 60 scudi from the Duke of Etampes, husband of the lovely Madame. On 15 March, a Friday in the middle of Lent, he had to borrow 61 scudi from the Cardinal of Lorraine to pay one of his creditors. Two weeks later the court left Moulins to travel to Nice and they were in Lyon when Vicino finally arrived on 2 April. Vicino brought two letters from Ercole II – one for his ambassador, Alberto Turco, and the other for Ippolito. They contained the startling news that Ercole had persuaded Charles V to champion Ippolito's candidacy for a cardinal's hat.

The deal between the Duke and the Emperor had taken several months to finalize, with letters going back and forth by road and sea between Ercole in Ferrara, his ambassador in Rome, his brother Francesco, who was with the imperial court in Naples, and Charles V in Spain. Ercole II had made the Emperor an extremely tempting proposition. In return for Charles V's help in settling his dispute with Paul III over the ownership of Modena and Reggio, and imperial support for Ippolito's hat, he offered to abandon his pro-French position in favour of a full alliance with the Emperor. Charles V had much to gain. He already controlled most of Italy – Naples and Milan were both under his direct government, and regimes under his protection ruled in Florence, Genoa and Mantua. The extent of Charles V's power in Italy gave him considerable influence over Paul III, who needed imperial support to advance his own dynastic ambitions – negotiations were under way for the marriage of his grandson Ottavio, brother of Cardinal Alessandro, to

Charles V's illegitimate daughter Margaret. An alliance with Ferrara would bring the last major Italian power except Venice into the imperial fold. Moreover, by supporting Ippolito's candidacy, the Emperor would have another potentially useful cardinal as an ally in Rome. The strategy also had advantages for Ercole II. So far Charles V had stayed out of the Duke's dispute with Paul III, but Modena and Reggio were technically imperial fiefs, and the Pope would find it extremely hard to resist imperial pressure to settle on Ercole's terms.

Ercole II's letter to Alberto Turco was long and detailed, and full of instructions. Secrecy about this radical change of allegiance was of the utmost importance. Ippolito was not to be told, and nor was anyone else, particularly Francis I – 'if you see even a scintilla of suspicion in him', wrote Ercole, Turco was to emphasize that the Duke only wanted to satisfy his brother's thwarted ambitions. 'And I want you to keep your eyes and ears open,' Ercole continued, 'and if you hear any rumours I want you to deny them forcefully.' Astonishingly, this detail of the plan did remain a secret – perhaps because it was such an audacious proposal. Turco also had the unenviable task of persuading Ippolito to accept his hat from Charles V. If Ippolito showed reluctance, Turco was to explain that this would anger the Emperor, who would then cause more trouble with Milan and might veto Ippolito's hat. Above all, the Duke urged his ambassador to impress on Ippolito that the Emperor needed an answer as soon as possible.

Ippolito received the news that Charles V had agreed to become his patron with understandable horror. He would get his hat, but if he were to accept it from Charles V, he would have to abandon his loyalty to France. His response to his brother was calculated. He took care to thank Ercole effusively but added, 'I want you to consider what might happen when this is known here. I will be put in a very dangerous position because it will seem that you are allied to Charles V, and I will find myself in greater labyrinths than before, so I beg you not to proceed further in this matter.' What he did not know, of course, was that Ercole II was indeed intending to switch his allegiance.

Ippolito spent April considering his options. He went hunting, lost at tennis to the Duke of Orléans, and lost at cards to everyone except the Cardinal of Lorraine. The court had stopped at La Côte-St-André, about 80 kilometres south-east of Lyon, where Francis I had fallen ill with a bout of fever. The dutiful Turco was also ill and in great pain, but he valiantly made the effort to ride over from Lyon to discuss the problem with Ippolito, though he does not seem to have used the threats suggested by Ercole II to any great effect. Ippolito decided that Francis I must be told of Charles V's offer to be his patron – Ippolito knew nothing about the proposed alliance, although he must have had his suspicions. On 3 May he talked to Montmorency, who informed the King. Francis I demanded to see Ippolito immediately. Later that day Ippolito wrote to his brother: 'On mature reflection I decided to talk to Montmorency, partly because the King is still ill, but also because it will show great confidence in Montmorency.' Ippolito's political skills were improving. 'The King made me understand that he would be most displeased if I accepted my cap from Charles V, so it is essential that I do not.' Then, with a defiant note of triumph, he added that Francis I had also 'promised me that the first favour he would ask from Paul III [at the forthcoming meeting at Nice] would be my hat, and that without it he would not agree to anything else.'

So the rivalry between Francis I and Charles V, which had already transformed the political landscape of Italy, now descended to the question of which of them should take the credit, and ensuing loyalty, for obtaining Ippolito's coveted hat. Whether Francis I would have actually gone so far as to jeopardize peace in Europe so that a 29-year-old princeling could be made a cardinal is debatable, but Ercole II and both his brothers had done their best to ensure that the issue would be central to the negotiations at Nice. The Duke was understandably furious with Ippolito for rejecting Charles V's offer, and for taking so long to reply. He had clearly presumed that Ippolito would agree to the proposal, and had gone further than he ought to have done in negotiating his alliance with Charles V, which now had to be unravelled. There was one piece of good news from Ferrara, however – Renée was pregnant again.

Ippolito did his best to patch up his relationship with his brother and sent him a large bitch from Brittany which Châteaubriand had given him. 'She is like your old Ertus in colour and in size. I think she is very beautiful and should satisfy you for breeding because everyone who sees her tells me that she is one of the most beautiful dogs they have ever seen.' He sent the bitch with Besian, his falconer, who was returning to Ferrara with the birds for their summer moult, 'because he will know how to look after her and how to ensure she does not get too hot on such a long journey'.

Meanwhile, in Nice, the most powerful men in Europe were gathering for the peace conference. This was to be a unique event – the first time for centuries that the Pope, the Emperor and the King of France, together with their courts, had assembled together. Paul III arrived by boat from Savona on 17 May and was forced to lodge in a monastery on the outskirts of Nice because her citizens refused to hand over the castle to Pier Luigi Farnese, Paul III's son and commander of the papal army. Charles V stayed on the imperial galley, which was anchored off Villefranche, just east of Nice. Francis I was the last to arrive and set up his court west of the city, at Villeneuve, in the last week of May. His late arrival was not a political ploy but due to the bout of fever which had developed after an energetic month's hunting in the countryside around Lyon. As Ippolito reported to his brother from Lyon on 26 April, 'the third phase of the fever started yesterday and it was somewhat lighter than the first two, so he will be ready to leave soon'.

The court finally left Lyon on 7 May, travelling by barge down the Rhône to Avignon and then across country via Aix to Villeneuve. After his exertions on Ercole II's behalf, Turco was too ill to travel, and he remained in Lyon in the care of Ippolito's doctor. The talk on the journey concerned the likely outcome of the Nice conference. The Cardinal of Lorraine was convinced that Charles V was serious about negotiating peace. The Emperor had promised him a valuable benefice, and Lorraine claimed that he would not have done so unless he intended to reach an agreement with Francis I. Ippolito was more cautious, and preoccupied about the impact these talks might have on his own career. His gambling book showed modest wins during May. Though he lost 10 scudi to Madame d'Etampes and 4 scudi in a tennis match with the Duke of Orléans, he managed to win 50 scudi off the Cardinal of Lorraine and another 80 off Luigi Alamanni, who repaid his debt with a mule, which Ippolito renamed Alamana. The biggest gaming loss in the ledger – 235 scudi in a single day – occurred at Nice on 6 June, while the peace talks were under way.

Initially, the negotiations were conducted by representatives, with Paul III acting as intermediary. The Pope had audiences first with Montmorency and the Cardinal of Lorraine, then with Cobos and Granvelle, and he hosted a lunch for all four men on 31 May. He then sent his own grandsons to talk to Charles V and Francis I. These meetings were followed by discussions between Cobos, Granvelle and Francis I, while Montmorency and the Cardinal of Lorraine went off to Charles V's galley to talk to the Emperor. Paul III then spoke directly to each of the two rivals and the truce was finally published on 18 June.

The extent to which Ippolito's hat had played a part in the negotiations soon became clear. The day after the signing of the truce, Francis I again visited Paul III and, after four hours of conversation, presented his court to the Pope. One by one, they all kissed the Pope's foot. Paul III, Ippolito triumphantly informed his brother in a letter, 'was very friendly, and told me that I had reason to be infinitely obliged to the King because of what he has done on my behalf'. Later that evening Francis I had a private conversation with Ippolito and told him that Paul III had formally promised him that he would make Ippolito a cardinal. Moreover – a fact which significantly increased Ippolito's hopes for the future – the treaty contained a clause, to which the Pope, the King and the Emperor had all agreed, that compelled Ercole II to reopen negotiations over Modena and Reggio at once and to settle the dispute with Paul III without delay. Ippolito must have been extremely satisfied when he went to bed that night – it would be difficult for either his brother or Paul III to impede his progress now.

Despite its serious intentions, and the oppressively hot weather, the peace conference was also the social event of the year, or even the decade. Gathered in Nice were the courts of all three potentates – courtiers, secretaries, cooks, armed guards, musicians and entertainers (Ippolito gave a hat to Paul III's buffoon, with a valuable crystal of the Fall of Phaeton as a hat badge). Charles V and Francis I may have refused to meet face to face, but there was a great deal of socializing between their courts. Ippolito met his brother Francesco, who had arrived in the Emperor's entourage. Queen Eleanor of France, Charles V's sister, and her ladies-in-waiting spent a day on the imperial galley, escorted by the Cardinal of Lorraine and Montmorency. Charles V gave his visitors handsome presents: jewellery for the ladies and Flemish gold cups, one ornamented with sapphires for the Cardinal of Lorraine, and the other studded with rubies (spinels) for Montmorency. The value of the presents – financial and political – was avidly discussed after dinner that night in the King's chamber. Some thought them worth 60,000 to 80,000 scudi, while others reckoned they were worth as much as 100,000 scudi. Ippolito, sitting firmly on the fence, claimed not to know enough about jewels to judge their value but thought them very beautiful. Whatever their financial worth, it was the Emperor's honour, and his intentions, which were being estimated.

∾

With the conference over, Francis I left Villeneuve on 22 June for Antibes, from where he sailed to Marseille before heading north to Fontainebleau. Ippolito expected the journey to be 'very long and vexatious because of the hot weather', adding, 'and I pray to God to keep me healthy as he has done up to now which is not little considering the many discomforts that I have endured these days we have been at Villeneuve'. The court had got as far as Marseille when Francis I was visited by an imperial envoy, who brought a request from Charles V that the two men should finally meet face to face. The envoy, who sat between Montmorency and Ippolito at lunch, carried a particularly friendly letter from the Emperor, and Francis I not only agreed to meet him at Aigues-Mortes but also sent his own envoy with the keys to Marseille and the offer of a French naval escort for the Emperor's return to Spain. Suddenly, the two men, who had been bitter enemies for decades, were friends. Ippolito's mood on the way to Aigues-Mortes certainly seems to have been optimistic — he won 180 scudi in two days, 70 of them from the Cardinal of Lorraine.

The meeting between the two men went remarkably well, each making use of etiquette to show his trust in the other. They ate alone and had several private conversations 'by a window', as Ippolito observed. And when the Emperor finally embarked on his galley for Spain on 16 July, Francis I made the unprecedented gesture of insisting on coming aboard together with his two sons and his leading courtiers, while Charles V himself made the gesture of standing when the royal party finally disembarked.

The two rulers must have made a study in contrasts — Francis I, tall, handsome, jovial and confident, and Charles V, small, thin and painfully shy, with a long pale face and a pronounced lantern jaw, which he tried to hide behind a reddish beard. Despite his rather unprepossessing appearance, the Emperor impressed all who met him with his grace, his manners and his humility. Ippolito had a brief conversation with him on board the galley and reported back to his brother: 'The Emperor greeted me warmly and spoke to me in particular about my cap, saying he was sure that Paul III would grant it because he had promised to do so once your business is sorted', and that he had graciously added that 'he would feel the same pleasure when I was made a cardinal for the King as he would have if I had been made for the Emperor. In reply I kissed his hands and said

Charles V

I would be forever obliged to the generosity he had shown me and would remain his devoted servant.'

Francis I now resumed his journey north and spent the last week of July in Lyon. On 30 July an unexpected visitor arrived at Ippo-lito's lodgings. Zanpiero, the armourer from Ferrara, had sailed from Genoa with two suits of battle armour, one for the Dauphin and the other for his brother, the Duke of Orléans. Both were presents from Ercole II and had been ordered the year before while the princes were fighting in northern France. The 19-year-old Dauphin was not feeling well the day the armour arrived and could not try his suit on. Perhaps it was just as well, for, as Ippolito wrote to his brother, 'I don't think it will fit him because he has put on weight since he was measured for it, but the suit for the Duke of Orléans does fit and he is very pleased with it, as you will learn from Master Zanpiero.' However, with the war now over, the two princes had little use for battle armour and wanted sets of jousting armour instead – 'white rather than blue', as they requested. Zanpiero took their measurements, and Ippolito then advised his brother that 'you make the armourer work fast to finish them as soon as possible and send them immediately in case the Dauphin puts on more weight'. Zanpiero left a few days later – he had hated the sea crossing so much that he insisted on travelling back to Ferrara across the Alps. Ippolito also had more serious news for his brother. On arriving in Lyon he had found Ambassador Turco gravely ill, and the doctor had warned that 'the poor gentleman is in some danger'. Turco died on 6 August, and Ippolito wrote to Ercole with the news, adding, 'I know you will be very sad.'

The court spent the next six weeks in a leisurely progress through the Loire valley, hunting in various places and staying several days at the royal château at Blois. The start of the hunting season left little time for gambling – Ippolito's gaming book was virtually empty for August, although he did win 50 scudi off the Cardinal of Lorraine on 21 August. In Rome Ercole II and Paul III reopened their negotiations. Now that Paul III's intention to make Ippolito a cardinal had been made public, the pressure was on Ercole II to settle his affairs with the Pope. The basic outline of the settlement had been established at Nice – that Ercole II would pay the Pope to confirm his rights to Modena and Reggio, and in return Ippolito would receive his hat. Now it should simply have been a question of agreeing the finer details. However, the talks did not proceed smoothly and, once again, the Duke started to create difficulties.

The first problem was Antonio Romei, Ippolito's secretary and envoy in Rome. Torn between the need to stay in his brother's good books and the desire to protect his own interests, Ippolito had opted for the latter and, following the advice of Cardinal Alessandro Farnese, had asked Romei to remain in Rome. The young cardinal had a point: Romei's continued presence in Rome and his involvement in the discussions increased the pressure on the Duke to negotiate a settlement. Ercole complained bitterly to Ippolito about Romei, who was interfering, as he saw it, with his own negotiations with the Pope, and ordered his ambassador not to communicate in any way with Romei. The situation deteriorated when the Duke insisted that the draft proposal submitted by the Pope must be completely rewritten, at which point Paul III lost his temper with the Ferrarese ambassador. Ercole then wrote to Ippolito, urging him to ask Francis I to intervene, but the King refused, impatiently dismissing the Duke's complaints as irrelevant and unprofitable. Despite Francis I's reassurance, Ippolito's optimism regarding his prospects began to fade.

Meanwhile the court travelled north to St-Germain, where Francis I was ill again, and on to Picardy – not for war this time, but for a big party at the royal palace at Compiègne. The guest of honour was to be Mary of Hungary, the younger sister of Queen Eleanor and Charles V, and his Regent in the Netherlands, a gesture on Francis I's part to reinforce his new friendship with the Emperor. Ippolito wrote proudly to his brother that the King intended to travel to Compiègne via Soissons, 'lodging at my abbey', but when they got there it was clear that the abbey could not accommodate the whole court. Ippolito had to be content with offering hospitality only to the Dauphin and the Duke of Orléans. Most of the court remained in St-Quentin, while Francis I and his entourage, which included Ippolito, travelled on to the border where they were to meet Mary of Hungary. The Regent, accompanied by some of her ladies-in-waiting, crossed into France to greet the King, a carefully orchestrated gesture of trust on her part. After a chilly open-air lunch – it was early October – the two rulers left to cross the border into imperial territory and to make their official entry into Cambrai, where Mary of Hungary hosted a dinner party for her royal brother-in-law.

The following day they returned to St-Quentin, where Mary was now the official guest, and the party moved south to Compiègne. 'The King spent eight days entertaining Mary of Hungary at Compiègne,' Ippolito wrote to his brother once the visit was over, 'and despite the honours done to her during her entry, I must say that the pleasures of hunting and other pastimes were even greater.' Ippolito had to miss some of the celebrations because of a bad cold but he managed to find time to win 221 scudi at cards and another 19 scudi playing tennis on the court Francis I had built at the royal castle. Mary of Hungary also seems to have enjoyed herself. She famously loved hunting and soon became a great favourite with the French court.

The court spent the rest of October and November travelling slowly back from Compiègne to Paris, hunting in the royal forests that covered the countryside in between. They stayed for several days at Villers-Cotterêts, where Francis I had replaced the old medieval castle with a magnificent new château. While they were there, on 2 November, Besian arrived from Ferrara with his master's falcons. Among them were some lannerets which Ippolito presented to Francis I: 'He liked them very much', Ippolito wrote to Ercole, 'and examined each one carefully'. During the summer, while they had been travelling through southern France to Aigues-Mortes, the King had lamented the lack of falcons in the area, which had once been famous for its lannerets. Ippolito must have boasted of their numbers in northern Italy because Francis I had asked Ippolito to request lannarets from both the Duke of Mantua and Ercole II. The Mantuan birds had already arrived, but Ippolito was pleased to report that the King liked the Ferrara falcons just as much. Ercole, for his part, continued to pester Ippolito for dogs. He now wanted a bloodhound, a particularly rare breed, and started to complain that Ippolito was not trying hard enough to find one for him. Ippolito owned one of these prized dogs himself, 'but because it is not as good as I would wish, it seems wrong to give it to you'.

Illness marred the autumn hunting that year. The King had a bout of quartan fever in the middle of November, and Ippolito could not shake off the cold he had caught in Compiègne. The Chancellor of France died after falling off his mule and news arrived that the abbot of Jumièges was close to death. This last misfortune was a piece of luck for Ippolito, because the King promised the benefice of Jumièges to Ippolito when the abbot died, 'which is an honour because it is worth 10,000 francs, some say 12,000, others 14,000'.

By Christmas the court had assembled in Paris and celebrated a series of marriages. Ippolito listed seven bridal couples, adding that there were 'too many others to name, so that while the King is in Paris he will be almost entirely occupied by weddings'. There were certainly a lot of parties. Ippolito reported that Francis I was now well enough to take part in the jousting, and that he had attended the ball following the marriage of the Duke of Nevers and a Bourbon heiress on 19 January: 'he arrived in a mask and took as much pleasure in the celebrations as if it had been the marriage of one of his own daughters'. There was also good news from Ferrara – on Christmas Day Renée gave birth to a second son, who was named Luigi in honour of his grandfather, Louis XII.

Despite the fun and games, Ippolito must have been depressed. The abbot of Jumièges clung stubbornly to life and, more urgently, the negotiations between Paul III and Ercole II were still unresolved. During the autumn, Ippolito had begun to doubt whether the issue could ever be settled. However, in November a new draft had been drawn up. Although the Duke 'corrected' it, this time Paul III agreed to the changes. This was certainly progress. Ippolito received a copy of the treaty from Rome which made it clear that his brother had finally agreed to pay the price of 40,000 scudi which the Pope had demanded for Ippolito's hat. This was a huge sum of money but, as Ippolito airily pointed out to Ercole, it 'should not impede an issue of such importance to our family'.

In early December, Ercole wrote to Ippolito to say that the final difficulties were being ironed out. But when Montmorency asked the papal ambassador in Paris whether Ippolito's name would be on the list of new cardinals for the Christmas Consistory, the ambassador replied that it would only be included if the negotiations with Ercole II had been finalized. The Duke, however, continued to fuss over several clauses in the final draft and, at the Consistory on 20 December, Paul III once again reserved Ippolito's name *in petto*. After all the trials of the past year, Ippolito was still a cardinal-in-waiting. The papal envoy reported back to Rome that Ippolito had been furious when he heard the news – though he must have been comforted by the fact that at least the papal *in petto* had now been made public.

If Ippolito's gambling book can be relied on to provide evidence of his state of mind, he was not in the best of moods. Despite the fact that he played tennis and cards regularly during December and January, the ledger shows only a small gain over those months, and would have shown a loss had he not won 100 scudi off the King of Navarre. But events were moving fast in Rome, more quickly than even the impatient Ippolito could have anticipated. While he was busy celebrating Twelfth Night and Carnival in France, Ercole II finally signed the treaty. On 22 February – three days into Lent – the Duke sent an envoy to Rome. Alfonso Zuliolo, who was the brother of Ippolito's Master of Stables, took three valuable rings which Ercole II wanted to give as presents to three key officials at the papal court. One of them, a faceted diamond, was for the Datary, the man effectively in charge of the sale of offices. Ercole asked Zuliolo to get estimates of the value of the other two and to give the most expensive one to Paul III's secretary, Marcello Cervini. Now that the dispute had been settled, these officials would have been expecting gifts, and lavish ones at that – the Duke of Ferrara had to display his status.

~

On 5 March 1539, Paul III held a Consistory and officially published the announcement that Ippolito had been made a cardinal. In
Ferrara the news was received with great excitement. A baker in the
city supplied 216 kilos of bread to be handed out to the men and
women who came to the Palazzo San Francesco to offer their con-
gratulations, and Ercole II announced three days of public rejoicing,
inaugurated by a solemn mass in the cathedral. Surprisingly few letters survive from this period of Ippolito's life (maybe he did not write
many), so we do not know exactly when or how he heard the news,
but on 25 March he sent one of his gentlemen, Scipio d'Este, back to
Ferrara with a letter and a verbal message for Ercole. In his reply,
Ercole thanked Ippolito for Scipio's fulsome speech but said it was
quite unnecessary because 'I will always be your loving brother, and
everything one of us does for the other is as if we do it for ourselves'.
Though he had caused his brother much anguish through his stub-
bornness, the Duke now had a significant ally at the papal court. He
ended the letter, 'I congratulate you with all my heart.'

Ippolito had finally achieved his ambition and it was announced,
appropriately, in the gambling book. His biggest single win, 254
scudi, occurred on 27 March, shortly after the news arrived at
Fontainebleau. Ten days later, on the Saturday before Easter, he had
a bad fall from his horse. He was lucky to escape serious injury,
though his bruises kept him in bed for a week. He recounted the
details of the accident in a letter to his brother, and, at the bottom of
the page, signed himself *Hippolyto Cardinale da Este* for the first time.
His status had risen dramatically overnight. In Renaissance society,
cardinals were accorded the rank of princes. Ippolito was no longer
just an archbishop and the younger brother of a Duke. He now had
access to real power, and the chance one day of becoming Pope.

Ippolito was not the only one to benefit from his sudden rise in
status. All the members of his household – Vicino the squire,
Antoine the tailor, Andrea the cook, Besian the falconer, Assassino,

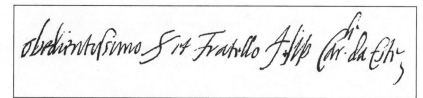

Ippolito's new signature as a cardinal

Mosto and even the stable boys — also acquired greater prestige by being in the service of a cardinal. Back in Ferrara, Fiorini's ledgers no longer referred to Ippolito as the Archbishop of Milan but proudly proclaimed him as The Most Reverend Cardinal of Ferrara, the title Ippolito was to use in future.

Characteristically, Ippolito's new position was soon evident in a marked increase in expenditure recorded in Fiorini's ledgers. Ippolito himself needed more cash. In addition to repaying Renée for the money Ippolito had withdrawn from her bankers in Lyon, Fiorini also had to settle a bill with a Genoese bank for 2,000 scudi which Ippolito had borrowed in Paris (surprisingly, the bank's commission on this loan was only 0.6 per cent, or 12 scudi). During April Fiorini bought falcons, black velvet and a new sword hilt, and gave gold coins worth 105 scudi to various goldsmiths to use to gild some unspecified items for the wardrobe and the stables. He also ordered two new silver seals, engraved with Ippolito's new coat-of-arms — a small one, which was sent to Romei for him to use on Ippolito's documents in Rome, and a large one for Ippolito himself. Ippolito's *credenza*, too, needed to match his new status. On his orders, Fiorini bought a set of silver embossed with the coat-of-arms, now surmounted by a cardinal's biretta with its distinctive hanging tassels. The silver was expensive — the bill came to 386 scudi, though Fiorini managed to negotiate a small discount of just under 4 per cent, which brought the price down to 371 scudi (see table overleaf).

Fiorini also raised the daily sum he distributed to the poor in Ferrara from 4 *soldi* (nearly 21 scudi a year) to 5 *soldi* (just over 26 scudi), and he handed out an exceptionally large sum in alms at Easter that

Item	Weight, per item, grammes	Total price, in scudi
1 gilded sweetmeat plate	1,090	29
2 large silver cups	770	35
1 large silver cup	700	16
4 gilded platters	690	69
2 silver plates	460	24
6 silver cups	440	56
1 large silver charger	420	10
5 silver dishes	370	47
10 silver plates	340	76
1 embossed sweetmeat plate	330	9
12 silver spoons	30	8
4 forks and 2 salt cellars w teaspoons	n/a	7

New silver for the credenza, *April 1539*

year, asking God to guard the new cardinal from misfortune, and to keep him healthy and happy. The recipients – thirty of them, most of whom received about a fifth of a scudo – were all listed in the ledger along with brief details of their situation, status and dependants. Among them were the widow of Domenego the baker (with two sons), the widow of Bigo the rope-maker (with three sons), the widow of Agusto the blacksmith (with several children), and another widow with a daughter to marry. There was money for a carter, described by Fiorini as poor but respectable, for the cleaner at the monastery of Santa Maria delle Grazie, for two crippled old women and for several other women simply described as poor. There were also alms for wives of ex-members of the household, such as the widow of Ippolito's kennelman, who had four children and was ill with a pain in the chest, and the widow of Milan, a porter who had worked in the wine cellars at the Palazzo San Francesco every autumn, and who had died a few days before – she was too poor to bury him, so Fiorini also provided her with 27 *soldi* (⅓ scudo) to cover the cost of his funeral.

Strictly speaking, Ippolito would only officially become a cardinal when the Pope installed him as such in a series of ceremonies in Rome. His original intention was to leave France in early June and spend the summer in Ferrara. He would then go to Rome to receive his hat. There he would also have to face the nightmare of negotiating with the bureaucracy of the Curia. The restrictions that had been imposed on the archbishopric of Milan had still to be lifted, and he had yet to receive confirmation of his rights to the French benefices given to him by Francis I, including the archbishopric of Lyon (assuming the Cardinal of Lorraine honoured his promise to resign the seat in Ippolito's favour). There was much to plan.

The first thing to arrange was suitable accommodation for Ippolito and his household in Rome, and Romei negotiated a lease on the palace of Cardinal Ercole Gonzaga, Ippolito's cousin. He returned to Ferrara in June to collect the 1,000 scudi needed to pay the rent, and for a private meeting with Ridolfo Campeggio, Ippolito's friend and agent, to discuss Ippolito's affairs. The two men stayed at Belfiore on the night of 1 July and Fiorini bought 5½ kilos of fish to feed the men and their four servants, noting in his ledger that 'it was the eve of the feast of the Visitation, which some celebrated and others did not'. There were also four chickens for those who did not keep the vigil, as well as omelettes, salad and pears.

Ippolito meanwhile delayed his departure from France. That summer Francis I's travels around his realm were not dictated by the pressures of war, or the need to negotiate peace, and the court spent April and May hunting in the Seine valley east of Fontainebleau, returning to Paris in June. Ippolito's letters and his gambling book chart the progress of the court through Moret-sur-Loing, where he won 104 scudi at cards, the Abbey of Valuisant, where he won 65 scudi, Courgenay, where he won 10 scudi off Vicino, Château-renard, where he lost 115 scudi, and Montargis, where, as Ippolito wrote, 'we stayed a few days because the King likes the town and indeed it could not be more beautiful'. During the journey news arrived of the death of Charles V's wife, Isabella of Portugal.

Francis I sent an ambassador to Spain to offer his condolences to the Emperor and also, according to Ippolito, who was reporting court gossip to his brother, to enquire 'whether Charles V will remarry, because Marguerite of France would be ideal for him'. Many of Ippolito's letters during this period refer to his efforts to get Francis I – or rather the French Chancellor – to repay a loan of 100,000 scudi, which the King had borrowed from Ercole II to finance the wars against Charles V, and which the Duke now badly needed to pay the Pope for Ippolito's hat. 'For the affection you have towards me and for the gratitude you owe me for your hat, try a little harder,' Ercole urged Ippolito, who replied, 'I can't tell you what an ordeal this business of the debt has become,' adding, 'I am doing nothing else.' Nothing else, that is, apart from hunting and gambling. Despite all his efforts, he failed to extract any cash from the heavily depleted royal coffers.

On 18 July, the King of Navarre paid back 150 of the 271 scudi he owed Ippolito in gambling debts, and the next day Ippolito finally left the court for Ferrara. Mosto, Ippolito's treasurer, was short of cash, and Panizato, who was now purveyor, was given coins from the bulging gambling bag to spend on food and inns on the journey. As he travelled through France with his household towards the Mont-Cenis pass and home, Ippolito must have had mixed emotions. Was he looking forward to a reunion with Violante, and meeting his daughter, Renea? He must have felt pleasure at the prospect of seeing his brother again after three years and excitement about the forth-coming visit to Rome, but also sadness at leaving France. He missed Francis I, and it seems the feeling was mutual, because the King had made him promise to return as soon as possible. The night after they crossed the Alps into Italy, Ippolito wrote to the King, enclosing a poem written by Luigi Alamanni, who had joined the new cardi-nal's entourage as secretary: 'I am envious of those whom Heaven grants the power to cheer themselves up with rhymes and verses, something I have seen you do many times, so Luigi Alamanni has written these lines for you.'

Ippolito left only a few members of his household behind – his kennelmen, who would travel to Italy with the dogs in the cooler autumn weather, and Tomaso del Vecchio, who was to remain in Lyon as his agent in France. For Antoine the tailor, the pastry cook from Blois and the French musicians, this was an exciting voyage into the unknown.

The rest of the household were finally going home, albeit temporarily. Andrea the cook and Zudio the chamber servant would see their wives again, while Bagnolo the chief stable boy, who had left his baby son behind in March 1536, would have to get to know a boy who was now almost 4 years old.

~

Though Ippolito and his household might be looking forward to their return, all was not well in Ferrara. The weather that summer had been terrible – torrential, violent and unseasonal rain – and the harvest had been so poor that everyone expected a real famine. The price of wheat, bran, beans and chickpeas had doubled, while that of broad beans and millet had tripled.

Fiorini was extremely busy, because in addition to his normal workload, he now had to supervise preparations at the Palazzo San Francesco and Belfiore for Ippolito's return. Work had started in the middle of April on rebuilding the stables at Belfiore to accommodate the 100 or so horses that would arrive from France, and on repairing part of the wall of the villa which had blown down in a violent storm. Ten new stable boys were also taken on and the barns at Belfiore were restocked with hay and straw. This was an expensive business. Because of the poor harvest, the hay had to be bought in at 1½ scudi a cart. Eighty-seven cartloads were delivered in July. At the Palazzo San Francesco the builders started to lay out a new walkway through the garden, which had been specially requested by Ippolito. It was to be ornamented with columns and paved with brick, and the painters redecorated the garden loggia. In July the glazier installed 435 new lights in the garden windows at Belfiore and in the upstairs windows at the Palazzo San Francesco, including twenty-eight in the wardrobe. Fiorini also bought 125 metres of black velvet for the wardrobe and restocked the wine cellar. Some of the wine was supplied by Romei, for which he charged Ippolito 19 scudi, but the rest was sent over from Bologna as a present from Ridolfo Campeggio. In order to organize its delivery, Marcantonio the cellarman rode over to Campeggio's estates near Bologna on a horse, which Fiorini hired for six days at 9 *soldi* a day (a total of ¾ scudo), and he took with him a metre of black velvet (worth just over 1 scudo) as a tip for Campeggio's factor.

Stores packed away since 1536 had to be unpacked, and both the Palazzo San Francesco and Belfiore needed cleaning. The rooms were whitewashed and new locks installed on many doors. Fiorini bought eighteen new benches, made from walnut sent over from Ippolito's estates at Fóssoli, and the staff spent several days cleaning the wardrobe cupboards and oiling the wooden tables in Ippolito's apartments. Two boys worked for three days unpacking all the beds, pillows and mattresses, many of which had been eaten by moths and needed repair. Four painters worked a total of forty-four days repainting the coats-of-arms throughout the Palazzo San Francesco, and replacing the panels on the façade of the palace to display Ippolito's new status. Finally, on 29 July, Fiorini spent 23 scudi restocking the spice cupboard and larder with sugar, pepper, cinnamon, ginger, cloves, nutmeg, mace, dates, saffron, pistachio nuts, raisins and almonds, all sent from Venice. That same day he recorded the purchase of 2 kilos of candied fruits – quinces, almonds, pears and, oddly, lettuce – for Ippolito's first meal at home.

Ippolito and his household returned to Ferrara on 7 August. Two days before they had stopped in Mantua, where Ippolito stayed the night with his cousin, Duke Federigo Gonzaga. They then intended to sail down the Po overnight on the ducal barge to Ferrara, but things did not go as planned. 'I know I told you I would be in Ferrara tomorrow morning,' Ippolito wrote apologetically to Ercole on 6 August, 'but it has been raining heavily all day and the weather is so appalling that the Duke will not let me embark this evening, so I have decided to leave at dawn tomorrow, and should be with you by the evening.' Despite the weather, and the famine, Ercole organized a major public celebration to welcome his brother.

Ippolito spent two months in Ferrara. He gambled regularly, though for much smaller sums than was the custom in France, but much of his time was occupied with plans for his trip to Rome. His biggest problem was money. His income from his estates had been affected by the poor harvest, the revenues from Milan were still sequestrated, and his lucrative benefices in France had yet to receive papal confirmation. He could now add the abbey of Jumièges to the list – the abbot had finally died in late August, and Francis I had appointed Ippolito in his place. The journey back from France had also been expensive, and he now had to finance his stay in Rome. There was no question of trying to live within his means and on 27 September he signed an IOU to his brother for a loan to carry him through the following months: 'I declare that I am the true debtor of the Illustrious and Most Excellent Duke of Ferrara, my brother, for 10,000 scudi, and I promise to repay this sum as soon as it is possible for me to do so, and to do all I can to find the money, even if I have to sell my own patrimony to pay the said debt, in faith of which I have written and signed this receipt in my own hand this day.' (This document is one of the rare examples of a whole page of his handwriting to survive.)

Earlier that month Ippolito had appointed a new agent and sent him down to Rome charged with the task of preparing the palace that Ippolito had rented from his cousin, Cardinal Ercole Gonzaga. The palace was almost completely unfurnished and in need of repair. Apollonio Minotto spent 2,353 scudi repairing and restocking the house, and recorded all the details in his ledger. (The ledger was one of two books he bought from a stationer in Rome for ½ scudo – the other, which has not survived, was for recording the use of straw, fodder and other supplies in the stables.)

Minotto's first task was to get the roof repaired, where 150 tiles

The document recording Ercole II's loan of 10,000 scudi to his brother, written in Ippolito's own hand on 27 September 1539

needed replacing. There was also a lot of work to do inside to make the building habitable. Minotto had to organize the replacement of hinges and locks on the doors, buy new window panes, have the chimneys swept and all the rooms whitewashed, and find painters to retouch several of the friezes in Ippolito's apartments. He also paid a carter 9 scudi for removing 200 cartloads of rubbish – the place must have been filthy.

The cost of the building work, repairs and cleaning, which came to 83 scudi, was a relatively minor part of the total. The major expense lay in stocking and furnishing the palace. Minotto's largest bills, a total of 988 scudi, were paid to Leonardo Boccaccio, a Florentine merchant operating in Rome, who supplied wheat and other grain for the larder, and hay, straw and fodder for the stables. Without his own estates to rely on, Ippolito had to buy these goods on the open market, where the impact of the poor harvest had already resulted in increased prices. Wine was another big expense. Minotto spent 515 scudi stocking the cellars with several different types of wine – 151 barrels of rough wine (*vino corso*) for the household, which cost around 1 scudo a barrel, and 163 barrels of a more expensive wine, *vino greco da Summa*, imported from the vineyards near Naples at 2¼ scudi a barrel. The third most expensive item, somewhat surprisingly, was bedding. Minotto had to cater for 100 people, and he spent 358 scudi on mattresses, pillows and bedcovers for the household. Just as Fiorini had done in 1535 for the Palazzo San Francesco, Minotto bought wool and ticking from local merchants and delivered the materials to the mattress-maker. As before, the various ranks in the household were identified by the quality of their bedding – good-quality wool costing 5 scudi a bale for the gentlemen, cheaper wool at 3 scudi for less important officials, and plain cloth pallets for the lowest ranks. Ippolito himself had two particularly heavy mattresses stuffed with expensive white wool, for which Minotto paid 8 scudi a bale.

In early October Fiorini sent several crates of tapestries, including the Spanish leather hangings, carved wooden chests and other pieces of furniture down to Rome. The consignment travelled by water as far as Pesaro, where it was loaded on to a train of mules for the three-week journey overland to Rome. Minotto paid the muleteer the enormous sum of 73 scudi. The cost of hiring a pack mule was just over 2 scudi a month, which suggests that more than 35 mules were needed to transport the goods that Ippolito wanted to furnish the palace. All the utilitarian items, however, were bought by Minotto in Rome. One carpenter's bill, for 69 scudi, listed trestle tables and benches for the staff dining-rooms, large work tables for the larderer and the *credenzieri*, a *credenza*, which would be ornamented with Ippolito's silver, hay racks for the stables, a wooden door for Ippolito's bedroom, a window frame and a knife box. It also included sixty-seven beds — clearly some of the household were expected to share. Fifty of them were ordinary beds, each costing ⅓ scudo, while the other seventeen were made of chestnut planks, for which the carpenter charged ¾ scudo apiece.

Ippolito's next priority during the early autumn in Ferrara was his household, which needed reorganization to befit his new dignity. He had already enlarged the household considerably while he had been in France, adding twenty new posts, notably among the staff involved in dining and entertaining. He now enlarged the household further, adding another twenty positions. The only group that did not increase were the men looking after his dogs and his falcons.

The one new post among the courtiers was that of a second secretary, which was given to Luigi Alamanni, together with a golden hello of 50 scudi. Ippolito appointed two under-trainers to assist Pierantonio in the stables and increased the number of chaplains in his entourage from two to three. The new chaplain, Giovanjacomo Magnanino, had worked for him since 1526 but had remained behind in Ferrara when Ippolito moved to France. Many of the other new members of the household were appointed to help his over-worked staff — there were new assistants for the chief steward, Antoine the tailor and Carlo del Pavone the larderer. To help the *credenzieri*, Ippolito took on a boy whose sole job was to wash the silver, for which he was paid a miserable 4 scudi a year, even less than the stable boys.

There was also a change in the eating arrangements for the household. Ippolito's gentlemen now ate separately, and he took on four men to serve in the second staff dining-room. Most of the other extra

Department	1536	New posts	1539
Gentlemen and courtiers	11	1	12
Chaplains	2	1	3
Wardrobe	2	2	4
Chamber	14	12	26
Dining staff	14	18	32
Musicians	1	7	8
Stables	5	2	7
Dogs and falcons	6	0	6
Total	55	43	98

The Cardinal's household

posts were in the Chamber, where he doubled the number of valets from two to four, and took on an extra servant to help his faithful Zudio. In the clearest sign of his new status, he increased the number of pages attached to his household from three to ten. Most of the men – and boys – in the Chamber were taken on in Ferrara. Ippolito clearly preferred to be looked after by Italians and there were no French staff among his personal servants, though two of the new footmen were from France. Both the new valets were promoted from pages: Diomede Tridapalle, who came from Mantua, had been in Ippolito's household since 1536 and in the party that had accompanied Ippolito on his journey to France across the Col d'Agnel.

Despite the number of new faces at the Palazzo San Francesco, most of the staff who had left for France in 1536 and who had not either retired or died, were still with Ippolito – a striking reminder of the strong bonds of loyalty that existed in sixteenth-century households. Still employed in their old posts were Vicino the squire, Rossetto the valet, Ippolito d'Argenta the footman, and Alfonso Compagno the carver. Andrea the cook continued to reign supreme in the kitchen as chief cook, but he now had far greater responsibilities and more staff to supervise. His old assistant, Turco, was still employed as an under-cook, working alongside four more cooks, as well as three kitchen boys. One of the new cooks was nicknamed Gradasso, the Boaster, but whether there was any friction between the Italians in the kitchen and Ippolito's new French chef and French pastry cook, we have no means of knowing.

Since 1536, there had been two changes to the heads of the household departments. Tomaso Mosto, Scipio Assassino and Ippolito Zuliolo were still in charge of the wardrobe, the chamber and the stables respectively, but Cestarello had been replaced by Alessandro Zerbinato in 1536 and had died in early 1539, unaware that Ippolito had finally aquired his cardinal's hat. The chief steward, Girolamo Guarniero, had retired in the summer of 1538 and had been replaced by another Ferrarese noble, Piero Parisetto. Other members of the household were promoted. Zebelino, who had been one of the *credenzieri*, was now a sommelier. Jacomo Panizato, who had left Ferrara in 1536 as the official in the stables, and had been promoted to purveyor in France, was now given the new post of under-steward, assistant to Parisetto. He was now a key figure in the design and organization of Ippolito's lavish banquets – an extraordinary achievement for an artisan who, in the summer of 1535, had been painting Ippolito's garden walls. Panizato's job as purveyor went to Ludovico Morello, a relation of the infamously corrupt accountants, Piero Morello and his son Tomaso.

On Sunday, 12 October, Ippolito and the household left Ferrara, travelling south to Bologna, across the Apennines to Florence and down the old Via Cassia through Tuscany to Rome. Ippolito must have been excited. This was the last stage in the long journey to acquire his cardinal's hat and his first visit to the city that had once been the capital of a mighty empire and was now the focus of the Christian world.

8

The New Cardinal

IPPOLITO ARRIVED AT the Porta del Popolo on Sunday, 26 October, and, as was the custom, spent that night in a palace outside the
gate before making his official entry into Rome the following morning. Somewhat to his surprise, a papal messenger was waiting at the
palace with orders to escort him to the Vatican that evening for a private audience with Paul III. Ippolito rode unnoticed through the city
streets and spent four hours with the Pope discussing the political
situation in France, before returning to his lodgings outside the gate
for the night. The next day he made his entry, this time formally
escorted by all the cardinals resident in Rome. Ippolito was dressed in
his new red cape, made for the occasion by Antoine the tailor, but he
was symbolically hatless, in contrast to the other cardinals, who were
in full regalia.

Rome in 1539 had a population of around 40,000, much the
same size as Ferrara. Considering its importance, the city was small –
Paris had a population of 200,000 – and it occupied only a third of
the land enclosed by the ancient imperial walls, which had been built
to protect a capital that had once boasted nearly a million inhabitants.
Renaissance Rome was clustered along the banks of the Tiber, a
maze of narrow streets linking the commercial heart of the city by the
Capitol to the focus of papal power across the river at the basilica of
St Peter's. Ippolito's cavalcade made its way through the busy streets,
past shops and warehouses built on the ruins of ancient temples,
churches that dated back to the early centuries of Christian faith, and

St Peter's and the Vatican palace

contemporary palaces whose façades were decorated with the myths and history of antiquity. Rome's past was rich and unique, and, despite its scruffy appearance, the city had an air of grandeur that set it apart from other European centres. Ippolito jostled his way through the crowds of people on the bridge over the Tiber, past the imposing papal fortress of Castel Sant'Angelo, and into the Via Alessandrina, the street built by his grandfather Pope Alexander VI to provide a grand approach to St Peter's and the Vatican palace, the heart of the Christian world. Here, in a fitting climax to a majestic papal cere﹢mony, Paul III formally placed a cardinal's hat on Ippolito's head.

Late in the afternoon Ippolito rode back across the city, still with his escort of cardinals and now proudly wearing his hat in public for the first time. The cardinals accompanied him to his new home, the palace he had rented from his cousin Cardinal Ercole Gonzaga. This was a grand residence in a prestigious location and entirely appropri﹢ate to Ippolito's perception of his new status. It was situated on the Via del Corso, the street that linked the Porta del Popolo with the

Capitol, once the religious centre of the ancient Roman empire where the great Temple of Jupiter had looked out across the Roman Forum. The temple had long since disappeared, but the site was now embellished with some of the most famous bronze statues of anti-quity – the Wolf suckling the twins Romulus and Remus, the Spinario or Thorn-Picker, and the equestrian monument to Marcus Aurelius, which Paul III had moved to the hill the year before. A tax, which had been raised from the owners of all the palaces in the neighbourhood in 1538 to finance street repairs, had assessed Gonza-ga's palace as second only to the Palazzo Venezia, Paul III's summer residence nearby. Ippolito and his escort of cardinals arrived that evening to find its main entrance decked with huge festoons of ivy and myrtle that sparkled with gold sequins. The arrangement had cost 5 scudi, enough to buy ten pheasants or sixty-six chickens.

The palace was certainly grander than the Palazzo San Francesco, but inside much was familiar. Ippolito's own carved wooden chests and other pieces of furniture from Ferrara were now installed in the grand reception rooms and his private apartments. The walls were decorated with his tapestries and his expensive set of Spanish leather hangings (these were so heavy that they had needed five mules to transport them to Rome). The furnishing of the palace had been supervised by Alessandro Zerbinato, the major-domo, who had arrived in Rome a few days earlier. It had been a tiresome business – the tapestries did not fit properly, and a tailor had to be hired to shorten several of the pieces. The whole building was clean and welcoming, thanks to a lot of hard work on the part of Apollo-nio Minotto, who had spent the past two months in Rome transform-ing the empty and somewhat dilapidated palace into a setting that would befit Ippolito's new status.

Ippolito's own apartments were particularly splendid. In addition to the chests and hangings from Ferrara, Minotto had bought several more pieces of furniture for these rooms. He commissioned two cabinet-makers in Rome to make eight chairs – four decorated with bone inlay, four with intarsia – and a local upholsterer had covered them in gold brocade and red kermes velvet, with red and gold fringes. These materials came from Minotto's stores and had been sent down to Rome by Ippolito's agent in Florence. Their price was not entered in Minotto's ledger, but they must have been expensive. The colour theme of red and gold was carried through in other dec, orative details. The door hangings were made of red velvet, bordered with gold brocade and embroidered in gold thread with Ippolito's coat,of,arms. In his bedroom was a small table made by a carpenter in the Via de' Banchi, its modest price of just over 1 scudo carefully disguised by an expensive red velvet cover. Most of the textiles – 70 metres of the gold brocade and 74 metres of the red velvet – had been used to make a magnificent set of hangings for Ippolito's bed. Minot, to had spent over 4 scudi on the bed itself, which he bought from another carpenter in the Via de' Banchi. It was constructed of walnut with metal fittings but was evidently not very well made – one of the iron pieces came loose a month later and the carpenter had to be summoned to resolder it.

Receiving his hat from Paul III was only the first of a series of arcane ceremonies that Ippolito had to undergo to mark this ancient rite of passage. Two days later, on Wednesday, 29 October, he attended his first private Consistory, the regular sessions of the College of Cardi, nals chaired by the Pope. At this first session, Paul III ceremoniously 'closed his mouth' (*os claudit*), forbidding him to speak in Consistory. Ippolito, used to the secular excitements of the French court, was less than impressed with the stultifying ritual of the papal court and he complained to Ercole that the services were 'tedious and long'. His mouth was finally 'opened' on 10 November when, in the last of the ceremonies, Paul III gave him his ring of office and assigned him a titular church. Ippolito was now the Cardinal of Santa Maria in Aquiro, a small church behind the Pantheon, which dated back to the eighth century and had originally been attached to a hospital for

pilgrims. It was not a very prestigious title, as he informed his brother, but 'nothing better was vacant', though he took comfort from the
fact that 'they say it is one of the oldest'. Intriguingly, his companion
at this ceremony was another new cardinal, the poet Pietro Bembo.
Bembo was now 69 years old, but he had once been the lover of
Lucretia Borgia, Ippolito's mother. Paul III, who had a mischievous
sense of humour and certainly knew of the liaison between Lucretia
and Bembo, clearly found the combination irresistible.

The impact of Ippolito's new status was soon apparent. Suddenly, after years of opposition to the establishment of his rights to his
benefices, the difficulties evaporated. Charles V lifted the sequestration order on the archbishopric of Milan and Paul III gave his official approval to the sees and abbeys that Ippolito had received from
Francis I. Ippolito now had an impressive list of titles – Cardinal of
Ferrara, Archbishop of Milan and Lyon, two of Europe's most
important sees, and Abbot of the lucrative abbeys of Jumièges in
Normandy and St-Médard at Soissons. It is a sign of the secular
nature of the Church before the Counter-Reformation that Ippolito
was not ordained as a priest until 1564.

The formal confirmation of his benefices at last allowed Ippolito
to advance the Church careers of some of his courtiers. Tomaso
Mosto now acquired a vicariate in the diocese of Milan and a parish
in Lyon, while Tomaso del Vecchio also received a vicariate in Milan
and a canonicate at Lyon. 'And so, slowly, I am getting there,'
Ippolito wrote to his brother, though he still had to wait for the Curia
to disgorge all the paperwork before he could obtain any financial
benefit.

Marcobruno dalle Anguille, Ippolito's lawyer, came down from
Ferrara in November to oversee this lengthy process and submitted
an itemized bill of 90 scudi which listed over fifty different payments – effectively bribes – made to various officials in the
labyrinthine bureaucracy of the Curia. The notoriously corrupt
papal administration was staffed by men who had bought their posts
and whose income depended on charges that were levied at every

conceivable stage of the process. Each benefice required a *cedula consistoriale*, an official form issued in Consistory to confirm papal agreement to the appointment, in order to start the process of issuing the bull, or papal edict. Each bull had to be written out formally. The cost of writing the bulls for Lyon and St-Médard at Soissons came to 10½ scudi, considerably more than mere payment for a scribe's work. The bulls then had to be registered in the Datary. There were five separate charges for this – the formal request to the Datary for registration, the registration itself, an official examination of the registration, the lead seal needed to fasten the registered bull and, finally, the specially made box in which it was kept. The bulls then all had to be formally settled, a process which required more lead seals, and the titles registered by the notary of the Apostolic Chamber. In the case of the French benefices, copies of the bulls also had to be made by an official dealing with French affairs, and then sent to France.

Meanwhile, Ippolito's household began to familiarize themselves with the chaotic and sprawling city. There seem to have been 100 men in the palace – Minotto had commissioned that number of mattresses and pillows – as well as the stable boys who slept in the stables. Around sixty of these men belonged to the household proper, while the rest were servants of the grander members of staff. Their life in Rome is particularly well-documented in two surviving ledgers. One of these is the wardrobe account book, kept by Tomaso Mosto's assistant, Giovanbattista Orabon, in his neat but rather ornate handwriting. The ledger was valuable – its 200 pages were secured with five red clasps, and Orabon ordered a wooden chest with locks from a carpenter to keep it safe. The account book is a mine of information. Mosto was not only head of Ippolito's wardrobe but also his treasurer, and the book covers far more than just the cost of Ippolito's clothes. Orabon listed Ippolito's income over the first seven pages and then detailed all the sums handed out by Mosto to members of the household to settle Ippolito's bills. For the first time we have precise information regarding Ippolito's expenditure outside Ferrara – the cost of travel, the presents and tips he gave, the alms handed out

by Ippolito d'Argenta the footman, the supplies bought by Assassino and Zudio for the Chamber, the materials, sewing thread and
buttons bought by Antoine the tailor, the advances that Mosto gave
every two or three days to Francesco Salineo to cover the expenses of
the stables and to Ludovico Morello, the purveyor, and even the cost
of delousing the heads of the pages and the boy sopranos. The other
ledger to survive belonged to Morello. It provides a fascinating
insight into his daily routine, shopping for the food needed by the
cooks and *credenzieri* for each day's meals and for more general household supplies.

As the household was settled in Rome for the foreseeable future,
Zerbinato drew up contracts with various tradesmen for regular supplies of meat, poultry, fish, groceries, candles and firewood. They all
charged pro rata for their goods, except for the greengrocer, who had
a shop in the small square in front of the Pantheon and sent salads
and vegetables at a set rate of 10 scudi a month. Zerbinato settled
their accounts each month with funds he withdrew directly from
Mosto. Morello bought everything else, including all the additional
meat, fish and groceries not supplied on contract that were needed for
entertaining. Most days he spent about 2 or 3 scudi on food, though
his expenditure rose to 10 or 12 scudi on the days when Ippolito had
guests – he seems to have given his dinner parties regularly on
Wednesdays. It is clear from Morello's ledger that, although the basic
diet of the household was much the same as it had been in France,
there were significant local and seasonal variations. The fruit he
bought included apples, pears, lemons and oranges, but there were
also more exotic fruits and vegetables that would have been unavail-
able in Lyon during the winter, such as fresh grapes, pomegranates,
fennel and cardoons. Other novelties included a lot of pasta, mainly
lasagna and vermicelli, as well as local cheeses, which Morello just
described as Roman, and southern Italian wines from Ischia,
Naples, Salerno and the Alban hills outside Rome.

The butcher supplied veal, beef, goat and mutton, while the poul-
terer delivered capons, hens, chickens, geese and ducks. Morello reg-

In the Name of God on 7 January 1540 Wednesday in Rome

	Giulii	Baiocchi	Quattrini
For 2 kids	6	0	0
For 6 kids' heads @ 5 *baiocchi* each	3	0	0
For 35 lbs of wild boar meat @ 3 *baiocchi* 2 *quattrini* per lb	8	7	2
For 1 brace of pheasant	10	7	0
For 30 thrushes @ 2 *baiocchi* each	6	0	0
For 8 cardoons @ 4 *baiocchi* each	3	2	0
For 6lbs of grapes @ 4 *baiocchi* per lb	2	4	0
For 100 oranges	1	0	0
For 10 lemons @ 2 *quattrini* each	0	5	0
For 1,200 eggs @ 7 *giuli* 5 *baiocchi* per 100	90	0	0
For transport of above eggs	0	3	0
Total	131	8	2

The currency is Roman:

1 *scudo di moneta* = 10 *giuli* = 100 *baiocchi* = 40 *quattrini*

A page from Ludovico Morello's ledger outlining his expenditure on 7 January 1540

ularly bought items such as sausages, which he found in a shop near the greengrocer at the Pantheon, sweetbreads, giblets, calves' feet to make jelly and sheeps' heads for the dogs. Above all, this was the season for game, and Ippolito feasted on wild boar, hare, pheasant, duck, partridge, plovers, thrushes and other small birds. At nearly 1 scudo each, pheasants were an expensive luxury – Morello could buy seventy thrushes for the same amount.

On Fridays the household ate fish, either freshwater varieties or seafish from the Mediterranean, both of which were supplied by the fishmonger. Morello also bought fish, occasionally eels but mostly large quantities of clams, mussels, cockles and other shellfish, as well as salted anchovies and tuna. Another of his tasks was to take the kitchen knives to be sharpened every fortnight or so, and he bought miscellaneous supplies for the household, including brooms, tooth-picks, kitchen equipment (the French pastry cook's palette knife needed a new handle), and plates for the staff dining-rooms, which seem to have been replaced every month.

Living in Rome must have been a challenge, not only for the Frenchmen in the household who had to use another language, but also for those seasoned travellers from Ferrara. The men had to pay regular visits to the Roman customs house down by the Tiber where a tax was charged on everything entering the city. The officials also demanded payment for opening the crates – the goods sent from Fer-rara by Fiorini, the bales of materials from Florence and the barrels of wine from Ischia. The men also had to learn a completely different set of weights, measures and currency. The local Roman currency was decimal and its principal coin, the *scudo di moneta*, was divided into *giulii* and *baiocchi* – 1 *scudo di moneta* was worth 10 *giulii* or 100 *baiocchi*. Morello kept his accounts in the local *scudi di moneta*, but Orabon preferred to keep his in gold scudi, which were, confusingly, worth 105 *baiocchi* each. Strangers in a strange city, they lacked the influence that had come from being attached either to a royal or a ducal court. They clearly preferred familiar accents in this cos-mopolitan city, and several shopkeepers mentioned in the ledgers came from Ferrara or France. Mosto bought Ippolito's boots and shoes from a cobbler called Alessandro da Ferrara and his breeches and hose from a French hosier, Gian le Mer. Others, including the haberdasher where Antoine the tailor bought most of his supplies, came from northern Italy.

Antoine was especially busy sewing new clothes for Ippolito, whose dress in Rome was markedly more clerical than it had been in France. Although Ippolito continued to wear secular clothes for social events, he needed a cardinal's wardrobe for official occasions, in particular for attendance at the Vatican. There were no doublets or *saglii* in this uniform – cardinals did not show off their figures in tight-fitting clothes but wore long shapeless tunics, cloaks and capes. Above all, their outer wear was bright red, the colour being a badge of their office. Antoine made Ippolito a red consistorial cloak (*capa consistoriale*), its hood lined with red taffetta, and several short ecclesi-astical capes – one in red wool, another in red satin and a third in red damask, for which Antoine charged nearly ½ scudo just for covering the matching buttons. He also made Ippolito a heavy riding-coat to wear whenever he rode across Rome to the Vatican. Mosto bought three new red caps of red cloth from a hatter for Ippolito to wear under his mitre when he attended papal mass – the same hatter also made Ippolito a rather less ecclesiastical confection of black velvet and peacock feathers. The cardinal's hat which Ippolito had received from Paul III was kept in a wooden hat box that Mosto bought from a scabbard-maker in Rome – it was appropriately covered in red leather at a cost of 1½ scudi.

Ippolito's household continued to grow. He took on several new pages from prominent Roman families and increased the number of his valets from four to six. One of the new valets was Pompilio Caracciolo, a member of the Neapolitan aristocracy, who had joined the household as a page several years before. The other was a Roman, Julio Bochabella (his surname translates as Goodmouth), who was taken on specifically to look after Ippolito's gloves. A Flemish flautist joined the household too (in addition to a golden hello of 5 scudi,

Ippolito provided him with smart new clothes, including a black taffeta doublet made by Antoine the tailor, and several pairs of leather shoes).

For the first time Ippolito now added a female member of staff. Agnese da Viterbo was employed full-time to wash his clothes – the rest of the household's washing was sent out to laundries. She received a monthly salary worth 29 scudi a year, slightly less than the squires but without the advantage of bed and board (she was also paid extra for sewing and repairing Ippolito's clothes).

Like all grand households in Rome, Ippolito employed a water-carrier. The ancient aqueducts had been comprehensively destroyed when the city was sacked in 1527, and most of the water used in the city now had to be carted daily from the Tiber. The water must have been clean because Paul III insisted on taking bottles of it with him whenever he travelled.

The most surprising new face at the palace that autumn was the goldsmith Benvenuto Cellini, whom Ippolito had last seen in Lyon in 1537 when he handed over an advance for a commission of a silver jug and basin. Cellini had spent the past year imprisoned in the dun-geons of Castel Sant'Angelo on a charge of stealing papal jewels worth 80,000 scudi, which had been entrusted to him by Clement VII during the Sack of Rome. According to Cellini's autobio-graphy, it was Ippolito himself who managed to obtain his release from the castle one night while he was having dinner with Paul III. Cellini's vivid, and possibly scurrilous, account of the evening describes the Pope indulging in his weekly bout of drinking to excess and, in answer to Ippolito's request for Cellini's release, drunkenly roaring at his guest to take the prisoner home, at once. Whatever the truth of the story, Cellini was released on 24 November, and it was probably a condition of his release that he should move into Ippo-lito's palace. He first appears in the ledgers in January 1540 when Mosto bought him a large wooden table, a supply of charcoal and a small goldsmith's furnace to set up the workshop where he was to make the still-unfinished jug and basin, which Ippolito wanted to give to Francis I. Cellini was not, strictly speaking, part of Ippolito's household – he received no wages, though he did live free of charge in the palace and ate in the staff dining-room. However, he managed to persuade Ippolito to provide money for wages for his two assistants. They were not salaried employees but were paid out of the sundries account, earning a total of 7 scudi a month, a handsome retainer, though a lot less than Ippolito paid either his tailor or his musicians.

∾

It must have taken Ippolito some time to get used to life at the papal court and to a routine that involved far more official duties than he had had in France. His letters home to Ercole refer to endless visits to the Vatican – for religious services, Consistory meetings two or three times a week and lunches with the Pope and his pious ecclesiastical advisers. Cardinals were paid for their attendance in the Consistory, though not very much – Orabon recorded 70 scudi forwarded to Ippolito from the papal banker for his remuneration for the five months he spent in Rome. He was also expected to join his colleagues when they rode to the Porta del Popolo to give a formal welcome to important visitors arriving in Rome. One of his fellow cardinals described him as 'very reserved' – he almost certainly had little to contribute to discussions of the finer details of papal policy – but also 'very sincere and very lazy'.

On his visits to the Vatican Ippolito would have seen the new St Peter's in the process of construction, and the interior of the palace undergoing a major refurbishment: the money Ercole II had paid to settle his dispute with the Pope, and to acquire Ippolito's hat, was being used to magnificent effect. In the Sistine Chapel Michelangelo was half way through painting his *Last Judgement*. This huge fresco above the altar had been started in 1537 and was finally unveiled in October 1541. Paul III was also converting the apartments nearby into a splendid suite of rooms, which included the Sala Regia, a hall for the reception of kings and princes, and building a grandiose staircase to provide access to these rooms from the piazza in front of St Peter's. Ippolito made no mention of the projects in his letters to Ercole, nor did he comment on the Borgia apartments, which he almost certainly also saw. These rooms had been decorated by Pope Alexander VI in the 1490s and contained a portrait of Ippolito's grandfather proudly viewing Christ's Resurrection – one wonders whether Ippolito noticed the ceiling, which was decorated with images that traced the descent of the Borgias from the ancient Egypt-ian deities, Isis and Osiris.

Ippolito's letters to his brother contained regular news from France, some received through personal letters from Francis I, but most of it gleaned from the French ambassadors in Rome. Francis I had been seriously ill during the autumn, but it is not clear what was wrong with him. 'The King', Ippolito wrote, 'has been very ill with a catarrh which descended to his testicles and gave him much pain but thank God it has broken, the catarrh has come out and he is a lot better.' There was also much discussion of Francis I's invitation to Charles V to spend Christmas and New Year in France. Most of the news, however, was second-hand. Life in Rome was far less exciting than it had been in France. High politics and low gossip were replaced by more mundane local issues and, above all, by the exchange of political favours. Ippolito had moved several notches up the ladder of political patronage, and Ercole II began to exploit the advantages of having a brother who was a cardinal, expecting him to use his influence with Paul III on yet another problem that had arisen between Rome and Ferrara – the ownership of some salt-pans on the Adriatic coast. Many of Ippolito's letters deal with his meetings with Paul III to discuss this issue, though it remained largely unresolved.

Ippolito was also expected to help members of the papal court whose clients wanted posts in the ducal administration in Ferrara. Cardinal Guido Ascanio Sforza, another of Paul III's grandsons, wanted the post of governor of Reggio for the brother of his major-domo, while the Venetian ambassador sought a position for a friend of his in Ercole II's army. Cardinal Alessandro Farnese asked

Part of a long leter, mostly dealing with the negotiations Ippolito was conducting on his brother's behalf regarding the Duke's ownership of some salt pans on the Adriatic coast, written in a particularly elegant Italian script

Ippolito to write to Ercole for help in asserting his authority in one of his benefices in the diocese of Reggio where squatters had moved in, sold off much of the produce, pocketed the money and refused to allow Farnese's procurator to take possession. Ippolito's chief musician, Francesco dalla Viola, asked him to intervene with the Duke on behalf of his brother. The brother, who was one of Ercole's musicians, was in prison on a charge of murdering the wife of a colleague after he had caught her in the act of adultery. Ippolito asked Ercole to release Francesco's brother – 'I know little about the crime though I know it is of some importance' – and pleaded with him to consider 'the brotherly bonds between us, and I ask you not out of justice but out of pity for the feelings of the brothers'.

There were problems that required Ippolito's attention in Rome too. His chaplain, Giovanjacomo Magnanino, had started legal action on Ippolito's behalf against a certain Captain Domeneghino without his master's knowledge. 'I am furious', Ippolito wrote, 'and wanted to sack him immediately, but I have decided to keep him on because the process is not far advanced and can be stopped, and also because it is better to keep him in my household, so I have ticked him off, telling him that if he wants to keep my favour he must not only promise never to anything like this again but must also revoke and rescind everything that he has done. He has promised to do so, and it will be a lesson to him, and to my household.'

~

Despite his duties, Ippolito still managed to enjoy himself. His affable nature and his love of gossip seem to have made him popular in Rome. There may have been no tennis but there was plenty of gambling and hunting, and also women. Ippolito began a mild flirtation with the Princess of Salerno, the wife of Ferrante Sanseverino, a distant cousin of Charles V. She sent him a present of some wine and fruit – we do not know exactly why – and Ippolito responded with a lavish gift of black velvet, worth about 24 scudi. The imbalance of this gesture suggests he was expecting something in return. There were also several old companions in Rome – his younger brother Francesco came up from Naples for Christmas, and Ridolfo Campeggio arrived in early December from Bologna. Ippolito's social circle was wide and included not only the Farnese family, members of the Roman nobility and the French envoys in Rome, but also, now that peace had been established between Francis I and

Charles V, many Spaniards. He lost 13 scudi gambling one afternoon with the Spanish ambassador. He was made godfather to the
daughter of Girolamo Orsini, a commander in the papal army, and
gave her a valuable diamond ring as a christening present – Orsini
sent Ippolito a basket of salad a few days later, by way of saying
thank you. He also made the acquaintance of Margaret of Austria,
Charles V's 17-year-old illegitimate daughter. After her first husband, Alessandro de Medici, had been murdered, she was forced to
marry the 13-year-old Ottavio Farnese, younger brother of Cardinal
Alessandro. The union was proving far from satisfactory and there
was much speculation in Rome as to why it remained unconsum-
mated (Margaret finally gave birth to twins, named Carlo and
Alessandro, after their imperial and papal grandfathers, in 1545).

Ippolito's dogs finally arrived from France in early December,
complete with new dog-chains ordered by Fiorini in Ferrara, in time
for them to accompany him hunting with Margaret of Austria. The
outing was not a great success. 'I have never seen worse hunting,'
Ippolito wrote scornfully to Ercole, 'the whole day passed without us
seeing anything, which did not please me, though it was a lovely day
and it was good to have some exercise'. Life in Rome must have been
sedentary by French standards – as a cardinal Ippolito had to ride a
mule in the city – but there was always gossip to keep him entertained. Ippolito spent most of that day talking to Pier Luigi Farnese,
Paul III's son and Margaret of Austria's father-in-law, discussing
which men might be made cardinals by the Pope at Christmas. Pier
Luigi was remarkably candid, and the list he gave Ippolito turned
out to be extremely accurate. The names included Ippolito's cousin,
Enrique Borgia, and Ippolito passed the information on to his brother in a letter that evening. He must have been relieved that it was no
longer his own candidacy that hung in the balance.

The celebrations for Christmas and New Year in Rome were
splendid and, apart from the obligatory religious services, predomin-
antly secular, with masked balls and magnificent banquets hosted by
the Pope, though no jousting. Neverthless Ippolito's enjoyment of

them must have been somewhat diminished by the knowledge that he was missing royal parties and entertainments in France. Charles V had arrived at Bayonne on 27 November, where he was met by the Dauphin and the Duke of Orléans – Francis I was still convalescent – and the two princes escorted the Emperor to Loches, where he met the King. The court then proceeded through Blois, Amboise and Orléans to Paris, where the two old rivals entered the city amid much pomp on 1 January, and finally to St-Quentin, where they parted, with affection, on 24 January. Ippolito sent several presents to France, including a suit of jousting armour for the Dauphin and eight peregrine falcons for Francis I, a gift which cost him not only the price of the birds themselves (70 scudi), but also the expense of sending them to France with a falconer (25 scudi). He must have envied Cardinal Alessandro Farnese, who had been sent by his grandfather, Paul III, as papal legate for this historic meeting (the Cardinal stayed three days as Ippolito's guest in the archiepiscopal palace in Lyon, and wrote to thank him for his hospitality).

By all accounts Ippolito got on well with the Farnese. Pier Luigi gave him a horse and Paul III, in a marked sign of papal favour, offered to install Ippolito as Archpresbyter of St Peter's, a sinecure that had once been held by Ippolito's eponymous uncle. Ippolito celebrated New Year at the Vatican and gave tips of 1 scudo each to the footmen, sommeliers and *credenzieri* of various members of the Farnese family who were present, among them the Pope, Pier Luigi, Ottavio and Margaret of Austria. He also tipped the soldiers of the papal guard at Castel Sant'Angelo, while Cagneto, one of Paul III's buffoons, received 5 *scudi*, and the son of another buffoon, Rosso, who had amused Ippolito so much in Nice in June 1538, was given a velvet outfit made by Antoine the tailor that cost 14 scudi. The boy must have been small – Antoine usually used 3 metres of material for one of Ippolito's doublets, but this outfit only took 1¾ metres. It consisted of a turquoise velvet hat and doublet, turquoise hose and matching breeches made of taffeta threaded with velvet of the same colour and lined in contrasting dark red cloth.

The revelries continued throughout January, finishing only with the end of Carnival and the onset of Lent – Shrove Tuesday fell on 11 February in 1540. Paul III invited Ippolito on several hunting expeditions in the marshes and woods near Civitavecchia. Mosto's ledger recorded a tip to two poor men who found some deer he had killed, which suggests that the Pope's hunts were considerably more successful than the outing with Margaret of Austria. On 7 January, a Wednesday, Ippolito hosted a dinner party for Don Luis d'Avila, Charles V's envoy in Rome. Morello spent 13 scudi on food and the menu included wild boar, a brace of pheasant, thirty thrushes and 100 oranges (see p. 236). He also recorded the delivery of twenty barrels of wine that day. The guests were entertained by music from Ippolito's singers, and one of the pages danced to the accompaniment of two instrumentalists hired for the occasion. There was also a theatrical entertainment one evening in early February when a company of actors staged a comedy at the palace of Cardinal Niccolò Gaddi, a Florentine and a friend of Luigi Alamanni, Ippolito's new secretary. Gaddi may have been the host, but it was Ippolito who financed the performance, giving 75 scudi to the actors for the construction and decoration of their stage.

The Carnival celebrations culminated with a spectacular parade of floats, in which the Roman elite – cardinals, barons and bankers – competed for magnificence. Ippolito, needless to say, commissioned his own elaborate float. The project, which cost 46 scudi, was organized by Ippolito's musician, Francesco della Viola, with the assistance of Cellini. They converted a cart to look like a ship at sea, using real sails rented from a sail-maker's shop down by the Tiber. The cart was covered with old sheets from the wardrobe that had been painted to resemble the ship's hull, while the 'deck' was adorned with festoons of greenery. It was manned by a crew of singing children who, sensibly, were tied to the structure with bands of cloth to stop them falling off, and given apples as a treat. The bill for the project, detailed precisely by Orabon in the sundries account, lists nails, planks of wood, rope,

material for clothes and, finally, a charge of 12 *baiocchi* for disman‐
tling the whole edifice.

Ippolito adapted with enthusiasm to the fashions of the papal
court, in particular to the current revival of interest in antiquity. He
bought antique medals and started his collection of ancient sculpture
with a head of the Emperor Vitellius, which he bought for 20 scudi
– he would later own one of the best collections of antiquities in
Rome. He also commissioned two sculptors to make a bronze copy of
the classical statue of the Spinario on the Capitol, which he intended
as a present for Francis I, and he paid the craftsmen an advance of
100 scudi for their work. Both these deals were arranged by Cellini
who, we can be sure, profited handsomely from them.

Ippolito also decided to rent a villa. The fashion for suburban
villas on the hills above the sixteenth‐century city had been inspired
by the literature of ancient Rome and its descriptions of a cultured
elite retiring from the pressures of urban life to rest and entertain in a
peaceful rural setting where the fresh air provided a welcome contrast
to the noise and smells in the streets below. The famous seven hills of
Rome were largely uninhabited now and the land was cultivated as
orchards and vineyards, or used as grazing for cattle and sheep.
Ippolito rented a villa on the Quirinal, which rose behind the church
of Santi Apostoli, conveniently close to his palace. Though modest
in size, it had a superb position, with views east across orchards and
fields to the Colosseum, and south over the city itself. Ippolito spent
42 scudi making improvements to the gardens, and he enjoyed the
setting so much that he later built his own sumptuous villa on the
same hill.

∾

Ippolito was spending liberally and inevitably he ran out of money.
Although his lawyer had finalized the issue of bulls for all his
benefices, it took some time for his income to come through – the rev‐
enues from Milan did not start until April, and he had to wait until

May to receive the first instalments from his French benefices. 'It is hugely expensive here,' he wrote to his brother on 10 January, 'and I cannot economize very easily because I have to maintain myself and my household at this court where everything is so expensive.' He went on to explain precisely why economies were impossible: 'I need to maintain the expenses of the way of life I have begun, because it seems to me that this is appropriate to my rank and position, and, being a brother to you, it also reflects on your honour, so please lend me some more money.' Conspicuous expenditure was expected of the rich and powerful, and the lack of ready cash was no excuse. 'If I do not have enough money, I shall be forced to borrow.' Ippolito was understandably reluctant to resort to moneylenders in Rome, who were taking advantage of the economic situation and charging exceptionally high interest rates. One of his valets had pawned his expensive black velvet *saglio* in November for 7 scudi and Ippolito had repaid the loan. The interest charge for seventy days, which came to 84 *baiocchi*, worked out at an annual rate of 60 per cent.

Life in Rome was expensive, and particularly so that winter. As a result of the appalling weather during the 1539 harvest, famine was now widespread across Italy. In Ferrara, the poor harvest of 1537 had raised the price of flour to 11 *soldi* a *peso* (over 8½ kilos), but by November 1539 the price had risen to 28 *soldi*. In Rome, where wheat was measured in *rubbia* (1 *rubbio* was equivalent to 2.3 hectolitres), grain prices were also rising. Ippolito paid 8 scudi a *rubbio* for wheat in January and 9 scudi in February. The poor, as usual, suffered the most. Paul III ordered each of the cardinals in Rome, including Ippolito, to contribute 25 scudi a month to a fund which he distrib/ uted among the poor. In January Ippolito wrote to his brother, 'I have pity and compassion for these poor needy people, who multiply here every day.' But the poor were also a nuisance, and he complained that he was jostled by crowds of beggars 'demanding money, so that when I go to Consistory, they do not leave me space to mount my mule'. There were disadvantages to looking rich, and Ippolito felt sufficient/ ly threatened by the violent atmosphere in Rome to buy a small dagger.

Item	Scudi	%
Wheat	1,052	25
Wine	862	21
Butcher	292	7
Poulterer	77	2
Fishmonger	533	13
Spice merchant	278	7
Grocer	277	7
Greengrocer	29	1
Advances to purveyor	380	9
Firewood	234	5
Candles	32	1
Laundry	24	1
Water carrier	3	—
Miscellaneous	33	1
Total	4,106	

Living in Rome, January–March 1540

The surviving ledgers make it possible to be precise about the cost of living in Rome that winter, and to show just how expensive it was for Ippolito to maintain an entourage of 100 men. In the first three months of 1540 he spent 4,101 scudi on food, wine and other household essentials such as candles and firewood, or an average of over 13½ scudi per man per month. That was nearly three times the amount he had spent on the same items in Lyon in April 1536 (see table on p. 99).

Not included in the table above is the cost of maintaining Ippolito's horses. Orabon's ledger records a total of 1,057 scudi spent on fodder supplied between January and March, an average monthly bill for each horse of 3½ scudi, or 42 scudi a year, again considerably more than he had paid in France.

Wheat was easily the most expensive item in Ippolito's outgoings and accounted for just over 25 per cent of the total, but surprisingly this was only marginally more than he had spent in Lyon. Nearly everything was more expensive in Rome – eggs in particular. In Lyon a scudo would buy 450 eggs, but in Rome only 100. On the other hand, oranges, which were grown locally, were significantly cheaper – you could buy 1,050 for a scudo in Rome, but only 270 in Lyon.

The one area where there was a significant difference in the percentage that Ippolito spent on items was in the spice merchant's bills – 7 per cent in Rome compared to only 1 per cent in Lyon – and there was a good reason for this. These merchants also supplied medicines, and nearly 150 scudi of the total bill was spent on 'medicines, syrups and other similar things for those who were ill'. Rome's climate was notoriously unhealthy. Niccolò Tassone was in such poor health that Ippolito gave him permission to go home to Ferrara, and one of the pages, Tebaldo Lampugnano, a relative of Ippolito's mistress Violante, fell seriously ill in November. He had to be nursed by a Madonna Lucretia in her own house for 'three months and seventeen days', as Orabon precisely recorded on 18 March, when he paid her the final instalment of 10 scudi for her labours. In his ledger Morello referred to another ailing page who was given twelve small birds to tempt his appetite, and he also detailed several purchases of kids specifically for the sick. Ippolito himself seems to have been ill in early March, when Zudio bought a length of red flannel to make a compress for his stomach, while Tomaso Mosto had a bad arm and took 5 metres of orange taffeta from the wardrobe to make a rather expensive, and colourful, sling.

～

Lent in Rome was austere. Ippolito curtailed his regular Wednesday evening dinner parties, and there is not a single entry in his gambling book for this period. However, in the middle of March he received a welcome letter from Francis I, asking him to return to France.

Ippolito was flattered and excited. 'I will show you the letter itself when I arrive', he wrote to Ercole, informing him that he was leaving Rome without delay and would stop off in Ferrara on his way to Fontainebleau, 'and you will see how affectionately the King has called me to France.' He added, no doubt to justify his departure, that Francis I had promised that his return to France 'will be of profit to our house', and he immediately dispatched one of his valets, Alessandro Rossetto, with a letter for Francis I announcing his impending return. The letter was sufficiently urgent for Ippolito to pay the substantial cost of post horses for Rossetto. The valet left on 16 March with 160 scudi to cover his travel expenses, and plenty of warm clothes for the journey across the Alps.

Ippolito's sudden decision to leave Rome meant a lot of extra work for his household. In addition to an enormous amount of packing, there were bills to pay and supplies to buy for the journey. Zerbinato settled all the bills with Ippolito's contract suppliers. Morello bought rope, lamp wicks, writing paper, a large quantity of candles, twentythree wine flasks and 1,000 toothpicks. He also paid for the laundering of 1,054 tablecloths on 18 March, settled the bill of Paul III's apothecary for two flasks of syrup for those members of the household who were still ill, and reimbursed Andrea the cook for sharpening all the kitchen knives.

It was decided to split the household in half, with one party travelling directly to Ferrara via Florence, while Ippolito and the other men made a detour via Loreto, where Ippolito wanted to visit the shrine of the Virgin. The Florence party comprised fifty men, nine of whom were too ill to ride and had to travel in a cart. They took with them all the heavy luggage, including the furniture and tapestries sent down from Ferrara to decorate Cardinal Gonzaga's palace, though they left the mattresses and bedding behind, as well as Ippolito's bed hangings. Panizato, who took charge of this party, spent 346 scudi hiring teams of mules, muleteers and their wagons from innkeepers in Rome and Florence, and another 265 scudi on food and accommodation for the party. Morello, who travelled via Loreto with

Ippolito and the other fifty men, and eight mules, spent only 218 scudi on the journey. Cellini, who was also going to Ferrara, refused to travel with the Florence party and insisted on making his own arrangements – according to his own account, he wanted to visit some cousins who were nuns in Viterbo. Mosto gave him 10 scudi to cover his expenses, but they proved inadequate, and when he caught up with the party in Florence, Panizato had to give him another 10 scudi.

On Monday, 22 March, Ippolito made his formal exit from Rome, throwing coins to the poor as he left. The party crossed the Tiber by the Milvian bridge, the site of Constantine's victory over his rival Maxentius in AD 312, and headed north. They spent the first night at Rignano, about 40 kilometres north of Rome, and the next day headed up the Via Flaminia and into the Apennines. Among the party were Ippolito's courtiers, Romei, Alamanni, Mosto (still wearing his orange taffeta sling), Parisetto, Antoine the tailor, Morello and Ippolito d'Argenta, the footman who distributed Ippolito's alms. Carnevale, one of the Chamber servants, had the unenviable task of travelling with the mules several days behind. On Good Friday they arrived at Tolentino where Ippolito visited the basilica of St Nicholas of Tolentino, a thirteenth-century Augustinian hermit much venerated for his charitable work, especially with plague victims. Argenta tipped 5 scudi to the friar who heard Ippolito's confession that day and gave another 4 scudi to the friar who showed him the relic of St Nicholas' head (Ippolito went to confession just once more in 1540, when he celebrated the feast of All Saints in Paris with Francis I). The following day, Ippolito arrived in Loreto, where he spent two nights. He needed his rochet and soutaine on Easter Day, but they were in the luggage travelling with the mules. Mosto had to hire a horse and cart from the innkeeper so that Antoine the tailor could ride back down the road and collect the garments. Ippolito made several visits to the shrine in Loreto, and Argenta left 10 scudi in alms, as well as giving ½ scudi to the doorkeeper and distributing coins worth 1 scudo to the poor in the streets outside.

Once again Ippolito and his entourage fell into the familar and regular routine of the road, spending the five nights of the journey from Rome to Loreto in taverns at Rignano, Narni, Spoleto, Serravalle and Tolentino. At Spoleto they lodged at The St George, which was run by a Ferrarese innkeeper who received an unusually high tip of 1 scudo. For breakfast the next morning, the three footmen were provided with a jug of wine and four bread buns each, while Ippolito and his men ate capon, thrushes and salad, washed down with eighteen jugs of wine (the same men had drunk forty jugs of wine the night before). Like his predecessor Zoane da Cremona, Morello spent his evenings buying food for Ippolito's dinner, as well as supplies for the journey. Every transaction was recorded in his ledger, as were the exchange rate of each currency. The ledger was checked, and signed, every day while they were travelling by Parisetto the steward. It was still Lent, and the diet was mainly fish, but Morello also bought kid most days. At Serravalle he had to pay for broken plates, as well as the usual charges for firewood and candles. On Easter Day in Loreto the party feasted on lamb, capons, pigeon, eggs, cheese, almonds and salad. Morello had to hire napkins and tablecloths for the meal, and he also bought an extra jug of oil to rub into the horses' hooves.

His religious duties completed, Ippolito left Loreto on Monday morning and, for the rest of the journey back to Ferrara, stayed with friends and family. He spent that night at Ancona as the guest of Leonello Pio da Carpi, a kinsman of the Cardinal, who entertained him in impressive style, staging a masque for his benefit. The next morning Ippolito handed out 22 scudi in tips to Leonello's musicians and dining staff, a sum that included a very handsome tip of 10 scudi for the organizer of the masque. He then spent three nights in Pesaro at the court of his cousin, Guidobaldo della Rovere, Duke of Urbino, where the entertainment was primarily musical. Ippolito dispensed 18 scudi in tips to the cooks, the *credenzieri* and the other dining staff, and gave lengths of black velvet, worth about 26 scudi, to two musicians, a lutist and a clavichord player, who had evidently impressed him. They finally reached Ferrara on 8 April, several days later than the party that had travelled via Florence, to find the house-hold frantically busy preparing for the journey to France.

~

At the Palazzo San Francesco, Julio Bochabella prepared eight pairs of Ippolito's gloves, Zudio ordered more soap to wash Ippolito's sheets and shirts, and Jacopo the barber bought six new towels as well as several jars of citrus and jasmine oils for Ippolito's beard. Andrea, the servant to the pages, bought new leather boots and shoes for his charges and a leather case for their supplies, complete with an iron padlock, and stocked up on shoelaces. Diomede Tridapalle, the recently promoted valet, was reimbursed for mending two black velvet *saglii* and for buying new leather boots and shoes. In the stables Pierantonio organized a team of mules, muleteers and wagons to cart all the luggage to Lyon. He also bought several new horses, and swapped a mule called Bimbo for one called Albertino.

In the wardrobe Mosto was extremely busy. Ippolito wanted pre-sents for the French court, and Mosto commissioned embroidered nightcaps, handkerchiefs and fine white linen shirts from several dif-ferent seamstresses. There is no mention in the ledger of Sister Sera-fina, who had done Ippolito's embroidery in the past – perhaps her eyesight had deteriorated with age. Ippolito also needed new clothes, though now that he had left Rome he no longer intended to wear ecclesiastical garb. Mosto ordered two pairs of leather boots and two pairs of black velvet shoes *alla spagnola* from Dielai the cobbler, and paid a woman to mend seven of Ippolito's white linen shirts. He also bought Ippolito a new pair of black velvet breeches with match-ing hose, while Antoine the tailor sewed day and night. He made Ippolito three new overcoats – one in black velvet lined with black taffeta, and two of dark red damask – and a splendid outfit in dark red damask which Ippolito wanted to give to his cousin, the new Cardinal Enrique Borgia.

Ippolito bought himself two new weapons, an arquebus and a
sword, neither of them particularly appropriate for a cardinal. The
sword had an elegant silvered hilt and a scabbard lined with black
velvet. The arquebus, which was ornately inlaid, had been made specially for him in Cremona. Mosto commissioned a holster for the
gun, made of red leather imported from Brabant, together with two
gilded powder flasks, which were covered in green velvet and decorated with green silk tassels and buttons.

During that fortnight, Mosto took delivery of several large con-
signments of textiles and other luxury goods sent from Venice by
Ridolfo Campeggio. They cost 542 scudi and included 50 metres
each of black satin, dark red satin and dark red damask, slightly
shorter lengths of scarlet satin and scarlet damask, a silk carpet, and
ambergris and musk to perfume Ippolito's gloves. Also stored in the
wardrobe during that fortnight was a valuable ornamental collar,
embroidered in gold and red silk, and two expensive rosaries, all
made in Mantua. These were payments in kind from one of Ippolito's gambling partners, who owed him 113 scudi, and Ippolito
intended to give them to ladies at the French court as presents.

At a more mundane level, Mosto ordered a new pair of linen
sheets for Ippolito and bought 100 cheaper sheets for the household to
replace those left behind in Rome. He also bought Ippolito a new
camp bed. This was no utilitarian affair but a substantial four-poster
bed in walnut that could be dismantled for travelling. In addition the
same carpenter made a walnut chest for Ippolito's antique medals and
a round case for his linen. In fact Mosto's ledger detailed a lot of new
luggage. Ercole the saddler covered several flat wooden cases with
black leather for transporting the Spanish leather wall hangings, and
others with red leather for the tapestries. He also covered several boxes
with green leather to hold supplies for the *credenzieri* and the sommeliers. Finally he made two cases for the Chamber: one for Ippolito's
chapel set, the other for his soap.

Cellini was not in the party setting out for France. Ippolito
wanted him to stay in Ferrara to finish the jug and basin, and he gave

him several more commissions to keep him busy over the summer, including a bronze portrait medal. Cellini set up his workshop in a room at Belfiore, furnished at Ippolito's expense with the tools and materials he needed. Orabon recorded the itemized bills sent in for a large table, a whetstone, pitch, soldering wire and lead, and the day before Ippolito left for France, Mosto gave Cellini an old candlestick and 16 scudi in coins, which the goldsmith was to use to make the jug and basin. Cellini remained at Belfiore for the summer and, according to his own account, worked hard on the jug and basin, the medal and an official seal which Ippolito needed as a cardinal. However, he soon got bored and amused himself by taking potshots at the peacocks in the garden. (Ippolito finally summoned him to France that autumn, where he was given gold coins from the cardinal's gambling profits to gild the jug and basin. They were ready in time for Christmas when Ippolito presented them to Francis I.)

The new Cardinal left Ferrara on 20 April. The fine spring weather promised a very different journey to the one he had made four years before. He must have been excited at the prospect of returning to his friends at the French court. He was also to be enthroned as Archbishop of Lyon on the way – the date had been fixed for 17 May.

Ippolito and his household travelled more quickly than they had done four years before, and they took a slightly different route, heading north to Mantua, where they spent two nights with Ippolito's cousin, Federigo Gonzaga, and on to Turin. In Mantua, Ippolito spent 272 scudi on more presents for the French court, buying a new sword with a gilded hilt, several musk-perfumed rosaries with gold beads, and ten pairs of silk stockings. In Cremona Assassino bought bullets for the arquebus and Michiel, one of the boy sopranos, broke his collarbone. The next day they reached Casalpusterlengo, where they were met by Paulo Albertino, Ippolito's agent in Milan, who arrived with 600 scudi due to Ippolito from the diocese. That same day, a courier rode in from Ferrara with 1,400 scudi sent by Fiorini. At Pavia, the second city of the duchy of Milan, Ippolito handed out 3 scudi in alms to several monasteries, and on 30 April, when they arrived in Turin, Zudio paid a laundress to wash eleven of Ippolito's shirts. Turin was now in French hands, and Ippolito stayed with the governor for the May Day festivities, reporting to his brother that he had seen 'a beautiful show' and adding that the people 'all seem to like the King'.

Ludovico Morello's ledger for the journey has not survived, so we know nothing about the inns they stayed in or the food they ate, but the tips and alms handed out on Ippolito's behalf were all recorded by Orabon. In the eleven days they were on the road, Ippolito dispensed 15 scudi in alms and 230 scudi in tips. The tips were given to all sorts of people – 10 scudi to a group of boys who sang for Ippolito on the road, 1 scudo to a monk in Mantua who gave him a basket of lemons, 1 scudo each to the fifty-five musicians who played for him while he was staying with Federigo Gonzaga, and 1 scudo to the innkeeper of The Three Kings at Pavia, where he stayed the night. There were also numerous tips to couriers, to guides and to the men who ferried the household across the numerous rivers that flowed down from the Alps into the Po.

Ippolito left Turin on 2 May and crossed the Mont-Cenis pass into France. The journey over the pass was a great deal easier than it had been over the Col d'Agnel (though this time he bought leather shoes to protect his dogs' feet). Once in France he was greeted in every village by young girls dressed as May Queens, singing and celebrating the arrival of the summer. He also started gambling again. Apart from the record of the expensive collar and rosaries that one of his debtors had sent to repay the 113 scudi he owed Ippolito in April, there had been no entries in his gambling book since the beginning of the year.

Ippolito's enthronement as Archbishop of Lyon was now only a fortnight away, and Antoine had still not finished the clothes that Ippolito's entourage would wear for his official Entry into the city.

Antoine and Orabon were sent on ahead to Lyon with two crates filled with silks and velvets from the wardrobe. In Lyon Antoine started work on new garments for the six footmen, ten pages and three boy sopranos. The footmen needed doublets of grey velvet striped with orange and white, which they would wear with orange taffeta breeches, red hats and grey hose decorated with orange taffeta and threaded with strips of white cloth. Orabon commissioned two wooden shields decorated with Ippolito's coat-of-arms for the footmen to carry in the procession. Next on the list were the pages and the boy sopranos. Antoine made *saglii* for them, also in grey velvet threaded with Ippolito's colours, which they would wear with the orange satin doublets that the tailor had made during the fortnight in Ferrara, while Orabon bought them white leather boots, breeches and hose – grey, orange and white for the pages, and red for the boy sopranos. Finally there were the valets, who were to wear orange satin doublets over black breeches, and hose threaded with strips of black satin.

∼

Ippolito arrived at the gates of Lyon on Sunday, 16 May, where he was met by civic officials and escorted to his lodgings for the night. He was put up in a house called La Guillotière – Orabon referred to it in his ledger as La Gioletiera – then a small village outside the city gates and now a suburb to the east of the Rhône. The following day he made his ceremonial Entry into Lyon, riding a mule and accompanied by his entourage, all splendidly dressed by Antoine. The procession crossed the bridge over the Rhône, guarded by its formidable gatehouse, then made its way through the city streets and across the Saône to the city's imposing twelfth-century cathedral. As Ippolito dismounted, his mule's tail was ceremonially docked, a privilege for which Ippolito had to pay 100 scudi – Orabon laconically recorded in his ledger that 'this was the custom of the place and earlier archbishops had established the price for this service'. Inside the cathedral he was installed with magnificent pomp as the new Archbishop. Ippolito loved the ceremony and all the theatrical and musical enter/ tainments that had been organized for him. In striking contrast to his description of the long and tedious services he had endured when he was installed as a Cardinal in Rome, he wrote enthusiastically to Ercole, describing the beautiful decorations and festivities – 'every/ body was so happy I could not have wished for more', adding that it was 'thanks to God and to you, who I know will be as pleased as I am'.

Ippolito stayed only a week in Lyon, just long enough for his household to reorganize itself and hire another team of mules to transport the luggage north to Fontainebleau, and for Ippolito to be entertained once again by the ladies who rowed him across the Saône. Mosto used the time to commission a seamstress to hem five table/ cloths and three dozen napkins, and to buy new leather boots for Pompilio Caracciolo, two of the pages and one of the boy sopranos, whose boots, new in Ferrara, had worn out on the journey. He also bought Ippolito a new pair of black velvet breeches and hose, dec/ orated with silk fringes, which Antoine had to let out because they were too tight. The tailor now started work on a new set of bed hang/ ings for Ippolito, made of the red satin that Mosto had brought from Venice and embellished with silk fringes and gilded sequins bought specially in Milan. The hangings were lined with expensive rose/ coloured Florentine taffeta and sewn with silk thread purchased from a haberdasher called Matheo Paris.

While his household worked, Ippolito spent his time paying offi/ cial visits and dispensing alms – 20 scudi to the Hôtel/de/Dieu, the city's hospital, 6 scudi to the cathedral priests and 1 scudo in coins to the poor. He also handed out tips worth 53 scudi to buffoons, musicians, including a group of Italian viola players, and the lady bargees. On 21 May, Tomaso del Vecchio delivered 4,000 scudi to Mosto, revenues from Ippolito's abbeys of Jumièges and St/Médard which were owed from 1539. Ippolito's financial problems were beginning to recede. He left Lyon the next day, reporting to his brother that 'everyone here has tried to persuade me to stay, but I have had letters from Rossetto in which he repeats that the King is most anxious that I go to court'.

On the journey through the Loire valley, Ippolito suddenly decided that he required new clothes for his arrival at court. In particular, he wanted two coats of red damask, one short and one long, and both with wide French sleeves. There was not enough red damask in the wardrobe for both garments, so Antoine the tailor was dispatched to Paris with post horses to buy the extra materials needed, and to make the garments. He was then to ride back south again to meet them before they arrived at Fontainebleau.

Early on the morning of 29 May, Antoine set off with two crates of materials and a guide. Shortly after leaving, one of the crates broke open and he had to buy nails to repair it. Then the next day he had to stop again because the ropes holding the crates had begun to fray and needed replacing. It took him three days to cover the 315 kilometres to Paris, and he changed horses eighteen times. He got to Paris on Tuesday, 1 June – Ippolito was at La Charité-sur-Loire that night, having covered only 107 kilometres in the past four days – and went straight to the shop of Philippe Legie, a prosperous textile merchant, who charged him 51 scudi for some red Venetian damask and another 14 scudi for several smaller pieces of velvet and taffeta. For the next three days Antoine sewed and sewed, and on the Thursday he had to return to Legie's shop for more supplies. On Saturday he left Paris and rejoined the household at Nemours, about 80 kilometres south of Paris, bringing the finished clothes with him.

For the footmen Antoine had made six Spanish-style coats in grey cloth, decorated with wide stripes of orange velvet and threaded with rings of white taffeta. He charged Ippolito over 7 scudi for these garments, which suggests that they involved a lot of work, but only 2 scudi for the three coats he had made for the boy sopranos, which were of red cloth, bought from Legie for 10 scudi and trimmed with black velvet from the wardrobe. Antoine had also found time to make a black fustian doublet for the pastry cook and a new orange satin doublet for one of the pages. Ippolito's clothes were decidedly not those of a cleric. Antoine had made two doublets, one in red Venetian satin and the other in finely pleated red Florentine taffeta. There were two new *saglii*, one in brown velvet trimmed with red taffeta for riding, and the other in red Venetian damask also trimmed with red taffeta, which was clearly intended for social occasions. Finally there were two new coats, both of red damask: the long coat had wide French-style sleeves, while the short one was edged with brown velvet and lined with red taffeta. Antoine had also trimmed a brown velvet hat with red taffeta and peacock feathers. Ippolito must have looked splendid, and very expensive – the cost of the materials for these garments came to 210 scudi.

Ippolito arrived at Fontainebleau on 6 June and his enthusiastic reception by the French court was graphically described by Ercole's ambassador.

> *He found the King was still in bed and as soon as he had dismounted, without quenching his thirst, he went straight to the King's bedchamber, where the ushers allowed him to enter, and the King was extremely pleased to see him – so it is said, though no one else was in there with them – and Ippolito stayed with him for two hours. The King then rose, gave Ippolito permission to go back to his own chambers and asked him to return to lunch. When Ippolito left the King's bedchamber he went to that of Catherine de' Medici, who had only just got up – I was with him and saw she was overjoyed to see him. Both of them went to the room of Madame d'Etampes, who was still in bed, and they were warmly welcomed and spent half an hour with her. He then went to visit the Queen and Princess Marguerite, and to the audience chamber where he saw the Queen of Navarre and the Cardinal of Lorraine. When he got back to his chambers he was visited by Cardinal Tournon and others, then he changed and went to Mass with the King. Afterwards they had lunch together alone. The Cardinal of Lorraine lunched with Madame*

d'Etampes and the King of Navarre lunched with the Chancel-
lor. Montmorency was away the day Ippolito arrived, but when
he returned he greeted Ippolito as warmly as the others.

Ippolito had returned laden with presents for the court. They
were graded according to the status of the recipient and were distributed by Alessandro Rossetto over the following month. On 10 June,
Rossetto presented Ippolito's gifts to Queen Eleanor and to Marguerite, Francis I's only surviving daughter. The Queen received two
ornamental collars, embroidered with gold and red silk, one of
which had been made in Mantua and the other in Milan. The Mantuan collar was one of the items Ippolito had received in April in lieu
of a gambling debt. For Marguerite, Ippolito had brought two pairs
of orange velvet slippers embroidered with silver thread, two pairs of
matching stockings and a peacock-feather fan. A few days later it
was the turn of Madame d'Etampes, the King's mistress. Rossetto
presented her with two pairs of perfumed gloves, a pair of fine linen
sleeves embroidered with gold and green silk, two embroidered linen
nightcaps and six linen handkerchiefs, three of which were embroidered with gold and green silk, three with gold and red silk. For
the Cardinal of Lorraine Ippolito had brought two fine linen shirts,
which had been embroidered in Ferrara with dark red silk, and
twelve matching linen handkerchiefs. The Duke of Orléans received
a pair of perfumed gloves and three linen nightcaps, worked with
gold, scarlet, dark red and green silks. For the Dauphin Ippolito had
a fine sword with a hilt ornamented with silver, which he had bought
in Mantua. A month later the Dauphin gave Ippolito a superb chestnut horse and paid the new Cardinal the striking compliment of
having the gift presented by his personal squire – Ippolito tipped the
squire the enormous sum of 70 scudi, an amount that reflected
Ippolito's pleasure at the honour done to him by the Dauphin, and
his delight at receiving such a handsome animal. For the King
Ippolito had only the promise of Cellini's jug and basin, and the
copy of the Spinario, neither of which were ready, but he gave him

his own sword with its beautiful silver Spanish-style hilt because, as Orabon succinctly noted in his ledger, 'the King asked for it'.

There is no mention in the ledgers of what he gave Catherine de' Medici or the Queen of Navarre, nor St-Pol, who presented Ippolito with fourteen dogs, including two prized Brittany hounds, a week after his arrival. Nor is there any mention of a present for Mont-morency who gave Ippolito a magnificent mule when he returned to court. There were, however, several presents for Ippolito's favourites among the ladies-in-waiting. One married lady received four pairs of silk stockings, while another, unmarried and evidently a particular favourite, was given two embroidered nightcaps, a pair of embroi-dered sleeves, a pair of perfumed gloves, a peacock-feather fan and one of the musk-perfumed rosaries that Ippolito had acquired as part of that gambling debt.

A week or so after his return Ippolito received another token of Francis I's friendship, and one that reminded him, with a most plea-surable emphasis, that he was back in an environment which suited his temperament far better than the male-dominated court in Rome. The King took Ippolito, together with the Cardinal of Lorraine and Montmorency, to visit Madame d'Etampes in her private apartments at Fontainebleau. They found her in her bath, and not alone. Also in the bath were Marguerite, Francis I's 17-year-old daughter, and three ladies-in-waiting. All the women were naked, though only their breasts were visible above the water. The men were delighted and, according to the Ferrarese ambassador, who reported the incident, they 'spent a long time joking with the ladies'. This was obviously a regular event, and probably engineered by Madame d'Etampes for the King's entertainment. The ambassador showed no shock in his report, using the incident as proof that Montmorency was still in favour with the King – but it was also a sign that Ippolito himself had really arrived.

Epilogue

I PPOLITO'S FRIENDSHIP WITH Francis I continued to prosper. In August 1540 he was appointed to the Privy Council, and the following year the King gave him more lucrative French benefices, notably Chaalis, a Cistercian abbey in the royal forests north-east of Paris, which provided an annual income of 10,000 scudi. Montmorency was less fortunate. The ruthlessness with which he had engineered his rise to power had made him many enemies. In 1541 he was forced to retire to his estates, while the Cardinal of Lorraine and the Guise family were sidelined. The peace negotiated between Charles V and Francis I at Nice did not last and by 1542 they were fighting again, a struggle that the Emperor continued to wage with Francis I's successor until he retired exhausted to a monastery in Spain and abdicated in 1556.

Francis I died on 31 March 1547, aged 52. Almost his last words were to Ippolito, whom he called to his deathbed and thanked for being one of his greatest friends. The new king, Henri II, engineered a palace revolution, sacking most of his father's ministers and banishing Madame d'Etampes from court. Ippolito was one of the few favourites to remain, a testimony to the friendship he had taken such pains to establish with the former Dauphin. Montmorency, who had also worked hard to acquire the Dauphin's support after he had lost favour with Francis I, now returned to power as chief minister, while the Guise family were rewarded with high offices.

In May 1549 Ippolito left France for Rome to take up the important and influential position of Cardinal-Protector of France, in charge of Henri II's interests at the papal court. (He returned only once more to France, as papal legate to the Colloquoy of Poissy, in 1561.) His reception in Rome was magnificent – Ippolito wrote, in French, to Henri II that 'all Rome assembled at their windows or on the streets to watch me pass'. Paul III was still alive and now 81, though Pier Luigi Farnese had been assassinated by imperial agents in 1547. The Pope died that November and Ippolito had his first experience of a papal conclave, in which he was the French candidate for the papal throne. Despite the large sums of money spent by Henri II to secure Ippolito's election, the bid failed, largely due to the implacable opposition of the imperial faction. Even so, Ippolito continued to enjoy Henri II's favour until the King died in a jousting accident in 1559. After the death of the Cardinal of Lorraine in 1550, Henri II gave him the archbishopric of Narbonne to add to those of Lyon and Milan, and in 1552 he appointed Ippolito as his governor in Siena.

Ippolito's household returned with him to Italy in 1549, and many took this opportunity to retire, notably Antonio Romei, Ippolito Zuliolo, Pierantonio the trainer, Zebelino the sommelier and Andrea the cook. Panizato had died in 1544, and others simply disappeared from the ledgers during the 1540s, including Assassino, Vicino the squire, Ercole Zudio, Antoine the tailor and Fiorini. Marti Bolgarello was still labouring in the fields at Migliaro in 1545 but there is no mention of Antonio Maria Trova. Ippolito's salary list for 1551 recorded a household of 133 men with him in Rome, only nine of whom had been with him in 1540. Scipio Piovena, the valet whose black velvet *saglio* Ippolito had retrieved from pawn, had taken over from Assassino as head of the Chamber and Julio Bochabella continued to look after Ippolito's gloves. Another valet listed was Diomede Tridapalle, who had been on the original journey to France in 1536. When Tomaso Mosto retired in 1553, Tridapalle took over as Master of the Wardrobe, while Mosto's responsibilities as treasurer were given to his assistant and bookkeeper, Orabon.

Ippolito spent most of the rest of his life in Rome, apart from four years when he was banished to Ferrara by Paul IV (1555–9). This

Pope, who had been one of the reformist cardinals so opposed to Ippolito's acquisition of a red hat, accused him of attempting to buy votes in the conclave. Ippolito returned to Rome in August 1559, as soon as he heard of Paul IV's death, in time for the conclave, which lasted four months. It was while he was locked up in the Vatican in October that he received the news of his brother Ercole's death.

Ippolito's career spanned seven popes and he witnessed the transition of the Church from the worldliness of the Renaissance to the religious austerity of the Counter-Reformation. However, he took little notice of the new moral climate and continued to spend ostentatiously. He became one of the leading cardinals in Rome, his magnificence matched only by that of Cardinal Alessandro Farnese, who remained vice-chancellor of the Church. The two men were to become rivals as patrons of the arts, in the pursuit of power, and for the Papacy itself.

Acknowledgements

A MONG THE MANY people who have offered support and shared their ideas and expertise with me, I want to thank Simon and Dottie Ain-scough, Tricia Allerston, Giles Bancroft, Andrew Barclay, Peter Barrowcliff, Janie Bell, Gina and Hugh Birley, David Boothroyd, Sheree Branch, James Brown, Suzy and Humfrey Butters, Melissa Chapman, Lucy Churchill, Thekla and John Clark, Annabel Cottrell, Chris Cuddihy, Lizzy Currie, Cees De Bondt, Flora Dennis, Luc Duerloo, Edward Eden, Peter Finer, Redmond Finer, Milo Goslett, Allen Grieco, Richard Goldthwaite, Guido Guerzoni, Charles and Liz Handy, Chris and Paula Hollingsworth, Elizabeth Hollingsworth, Rosamund Hollingsworth, Charles Hope, Keith and Averil Humphries, Sam Ives, Anna Keay, Julian Kliemann, Robert Lacey, Sally and Liam Laurence Smyth, Meg and Fred Licht, Adrian Lyttleton, Philip Mansel, Ann Matchette, Anna di Majo, Elisabetta di Majo, David Medcalf, Jonathan Miller, Luca Molà, Reinhold Mueller, John Onians, Dee Parte, Kate Petty, Nigel and Clare Reynolds, Glenn Richardson, James Roberts, Jengo Robinson, Nick and Cres-sida Ross, Hugo Rowbotham, the late Lorna Sage, Toby Salaman, Henry Say-well, Richard Schofield, Rupert Shepherd, Alice Simon, Benet Simon, David Starkey, Simon Thurley, Stefano and Carla Tucci, Thomas Tuohy, Camilla and Johnny Vivian, Rose Vivian and Steve Wharton.

I would also like to thank Evelyn Welch, Mick O'Malley and my other col-leagues on the Material Renaissance project, as well as all those who participat-ed in our conferences, and the Getty Grant Program and the Arts & Humanities Research Board who funded this research project at the University of Sussex (2000–3).

I owe a particular debt of thanks to the staff at the Archivio di Stato in Modena for all their help with my research. Finally I want to thank Gail Pirkis and the staff at Profile Books for their faith in the book.

Sources and Bibliography

M OST OF THE material I have used to write this book has come directly from Ippolito's papers in the archives at Modena, hardly any of which have been published. For reasons of space, it has not been possible to include individual references to the sources, but I have given a list of the ledgers and boxes of letters used, with a brief outline of what each contains, for those wishing to consult them. Some of the documents and references are published in my articles (see Hollingsworth 2001 and 2004 in the Bibliography below). A list of notes with page references follows, citing secondary sources used, together with suggestions for further reading. All these books and articles are listed in full in the bibliography at the end.

Archivio di Stato di Modena

CDAP   Camera Ducale, Amministrazione Principi
CDAF   Cancelleria Ducale, Ambasciatori Francia
CDAR   Cancelleria Ducale, Ambasciatori Roma
CS   Casa e Stato

CDAP, vol. 834: the final accounts for 1537, collated from Jacopo Filippo Fiorini's ledgers (see 973 and 974) by Tomaso Morello. They cover Ippolito's income in cash and crops from his estate at Bondeno and his expenditure on the estate, salaries to his employees, his clothes, and other expenses.

CDAP, vol. 870: the ledger kept by Apollonio Minotto detailing his expenses repairing and stocking the palace of Cardinal Ercole Gonzaga in Rome in September–November 1539.

CDAP, vol. 884: the ledger detailing Ippolito's income from his estate at Bondeno for 1521–9, and his expenditure on clothes, salaries and other household expenses in those years.

CDAP, vol. 899: the list of Ippolito's salaried employees for 1528.

CDAP, vol. 900: the list of Ippolito's salaried employees for 1529.

CDAP, vol. 901: the list of Ippolito's salaried employees for 1535–6.

CDAP, vol. 902: the list of Ippolito's salaried employees for 1540–41.

CDAP, vol. 921: the ledger charting the management of the estate at Bondeno for 1529–60, detailing all the crops grown, and the revenues from rents and sales, as well as the expenses incurred by Palamides de' Civali in running the estate (the ledger was kept by his assistant).

CDAP, vol. 924: the inventory compiled by Jacomo Filippo Fiorini and Tomaso Mosto of Ippolito's possessions in 1535, prior to the move into the Palazzo San Francesco. It is divided into various sections detailing table linen, furniture, candelabra, mattresses, copperware, books, wax, clothes, stockings, chests, textiles, armour, sheets, sugar, materials, hangings, pictures, valuables, furs, boots, pigments and caparisons for his horses.

CDAP, vol. 925: the copy, made by Jacomo Filippo Fiorini, of the section of the inventory (vol. 924) dealing with Ippolito's valuables, which Tomaso Mosto took to France. There are entries in the margins showing when and where Mosto disposed of several items in France. (This document has been recently published in Occhipinti – see Bibliography below.)

CDAP, vol. 935: the wardrobe accounts for 1540, listing all Ippolito's income and the expenditure undertaken or authorized by Tomaso Mosto. The book was kept by Mosto's assistant, Giovanbattista Orabon, and is divided into ten sec‑ tions: income, purveyor's expenses, stables' expenses, alms, Ippolito's clothes, Ippolito's personal expenses, household expenses, presents, travel and salaries.

CDAP, vol. 945: the accounts kept by Ippolito's bailiffs managing the estate at Pomposa for 1538–72, detailing all the crops grown as well as the expenses incurred in managing the estate.

CDAP, vol. 949: the ledger kept by Ippolito's purveyor, Zoane da Cremona, for Ippolito's first journey to France in 1536. It opens on 12 March, the day before they left Ferrara, and details all he spent on food, inns and other expenses up to the end of June 1536.

CDAP, vol. 950: the ledger kept by Ippolito's purveyor, Ludovico Morello, from 1 January 1540, when the household was living in Rome, and covers the expenses of the journey home to Ferrara in April.

CDAP, vol. 973: the series of monthly notebooks kept by Jacomo Filippo Fiorini detailing Ippolito's income and expenditure in Ferrara from January 1536 to July 1537 (six of the nineteen monthly notebooks are missing – March–April 1536, September–November 1536, January 1537).

CDAP, vol. 974: Jacomo Filippo Fiorini's monthly notebooks for October 1537, December 1537, January 1538 and March 1538.

CDAP, vol. 975: Jacomo Filippo Fiorini's monthly notebooks for February, April, July and November 1539.

CDAP, vol. 997: the ledger kept by Jacomo Filippo Fiorini detailing the expenses of rebuilding, redecorating and stocking the Palazzo San Francesco in 1534–5. The ledger also lists Ippolito's income, including the sums received from his father's will, as well as the costs involved in making salamis. Some of the material in this volume dealing with the rebuilding and redecorating of the Palazzo San Francesco has been published by Toselli (see Bibliography below).

CDAP, vol. 999: Ippolito's gaming book, listing both the amounts he won or lost, the location of the games and, occasionally, the names of his opponents.

CDAP, vol. 1009: details of the houses and plots of land Ippolito rented out at Bondeno and Pomposa during 1532–4.

CDAP, vol. 1023: this 'volume' is actually a box containing a large quantity of loose papers and notebooks belonging to various periods of Ippolito's life. One of the items is a small ledger detailing Jacomo Filippo Fiorini's expenditure on Ippolito's clothes in 1530–1.

CDAF, vol. 14: reports to Ercole II from his ambassadors in France, 1537–8.

CDAR, vol. 38: reports to Ercole II from his ambassadors in Rome, and from Antonio Romei, Ippolito's secretary, 1537–9.

CS, vol. 79, docs. 1645–xix: letters from Ercole II to Ippolito, 1536–40.

CS, vol. 145, docs. 1709–i: letters from Ippolito to Ercole II, 1535–6.

CS, vol. 145, docs. 1709–ii: letters from Ippolito to Ercole II, 1537.

CS, vol. 145, docs. 1709–iii: letters from Ippolito to Ercole II, 1538.

CS, vol. 145, docs. 1709–iv: letters from Ippolito to Ercole II, 1539.

CS, vol. 145, docs. 1709–v: letters from Ippolito to Ercole II, 1540.

Notes

Chapter 1

p.4　On Lucretia, see Erlanger; Mallet; for contemporary descriptions of the marriage celebrations in Ferrara, see Zambotti, pp.313–15; Diario, pp.281–3; Zerbinato, pp.40–1

p.4　On the Borgias, see Mallett

p.5　On the shield of Mary Magdalen, see Zambotti, p.327

p.5　For more details of the Este family, see Tuohy, pp.1–25

p.8　On the cat flaps, see Tuohy, p.84

p.8　On Alfonso d'Este as a patron of the arts, see Hollingsworth 1996, pp.229–31; on the Bacchanals for his *camerino*, see Hope 1971; Goodgal

p.8　On the recipe for gunpowder, see Zambotti, p.327

p.8　On the revenues of the Este duchy, see Guerzoni 2000, pp.94–7

p.10　On Duke Ercole's addition to Ferrara, see Tuohy, *passim* p.10 On the hunting park (*barco*) and hippodrome, see Tuohy, pp.146, 343–4

p.10 On painted façades, see Tuohy, pp.195–7

p.10 On the Jewish communities in Ferrara and Venice, see Davis & Ravid; Leoni

p.11 On diet in sixteenth-century Ferrara, see Cazzola; Mazzi; Faccioli; see also Grieco 1996

p.12 On the plot to assassinate Duke Alfonso, see Zerbinato, pp.60–5

p.12 On court festivities, see Tuohy, pp.234–76

p.12 On the Epiphany food presents, see Mazzi, pp.165–6

p.12 On the Easter celebrations in 1502, see Zambotti, p.349

p.13 On Duke Ercole's church-building programme, see Tuohy, pp.367–95

p.13 On the Este court, see Guerzoni 2000, pp.79–105

p.14 For contemporary accounts of the St George's Day celebrations, see Diario, pp.178, 200, 269; Zambotti, pp. 251, 259, 289, 304, 338, 358; see also Tuohy, pp.239–43

p.14 On theatre at the Este court, see Tuohy, pp.257–64

p.14 On music at the Este court, see Lockwood

p.14 On tennis in the Renaissance, see website www.real-tennis.nl (I am grateful to Cees de Bondt for this reference)

p.15 On Lucretia Borgia and Isabella d'Este as patrons of music, see Fenlon 1980; Fenlon 1990; Prizer; on Isabella and the arts, see Hollingsworth 1994, pp.221–3; Hollingsworth 1996, pp.291–2

p.15 The letters between Lucretia and Pietro Bembo are published in Shankland; on the relationship, see Erlanger, pp.209–45

p.16 On the attack on Giulio, see Erlanger, p.259

p.17 On Belfiore, see Tuohy, pp.342–52

p.17 On Laura Dianti, see Bestor

p.19 On Renée and her French household, see Franceschini

p.19 On banquets, see Strong; Mantovano; Baraldi

p.20 On peasant food and the new fashion for salads, see Grieco 1991, 1996

p.21 On the banquet Ippolito gave for Ercole and Renée, see Messisbugo, pp.31–42; Strong, pp.129–31

p.23 On Alfonso dalla Viola, see Haar

p.23 On the rivalry between Francis I and Charles V, see Richardson

p.23 On the Sack of Rome, see Pastor, vol. 9, pp.388–423; Partner 1976, pp.30–3; Chastel; for a contemporary eyewitness account, see Cellini, pp.69–79

p.23 On the dispute over the cities of Modena and Reggio, see Pastor, vol. 10, pp.88–9, 97 p.24   On the background and career of Paul III, see Pastor, vol. 11, pp.1–40

Chapter 2

p.25   This section of Duke Alfonso's will is published in Toselli, p.48

p.25   On the leopard, see Toselli, p.48 n.68

p.26   For the single biography of Ippolito based on the extensive archival sources, see Pacifici

p.26   On the palace and its history, see Tuohy, pp.328–32; Olivato

p.28   On the fashion for merlons, see Tuohy, p.188

p.29   On the building industry in Renaissance Italy, see Goldthwaite 1980

p.29   For an example of these painted wooden ceilings, see plate in Olivato, p.227

p.30   On the ducal household, see Tuohy, pp.30–43; Guerzoni 2000, pp.73–88; on Ippolito's household in 1566, see Hollingsworth 2000; on other Renaissance households, see Grieco 1999; Peruzzi

p.30   On 'family' and *famiglia*, see Sarti, pp.31–3

p.31   For a table of the families working at the ducal court, see Guezoni, pp.253–316

p.32   Fiorini described himself as a painter (*pictore*) in the ledger he kept of Ippolito's wardrobe expenses for the years 1530–1 (CDAP, vol. 1023); Thieme-Becker (vol.12, pp.2–5) lists various members of the Fiorini family active as painters in Ferrara, including a Giacomo Filippo, aged 22–25 years old in 1496. If this is indeed Ippolito's Jacomo Filippo, he would have been in his mid-sixties in 1536

p.37   On Panizato's career as a painter, see Thieme-Becker, vol. 24, p.197

p.38   On Ferrara as an equestrian centre, see Tuohy, p.241

p.39   On second-hand traders, see Allerston

p.43   On the ducal agent Pisanello, who bought tapestries in Venice, see Rosenberg

p.44   On the furnishing of Renaissance palaces, see Thornton; Sarti; see also the various articles in Ajmar; Fantoni *et al.*

p.45   On precious objects in the Renaissance, see Syson & Thornton

p.45   On Giovanni da Castel Bolognese, see Vasari, vol. 5, pp.371–5; Robertson, pp.35–45

p.45   On Palma Vecchio, see Mariacher

p.45   On Titian's *Venus of Urbino*, see Hope 1983

p.47   On hygiene in the Renaissance, see Sarti, pp.195–201

p.47   On the movement for Church reform, see Dickens; MacCulloch

p.48   On Cardinal Lorenzo Campeggio, see Pastor, vol. 9, pp.87–8; Chambers 1966 *passim*

p.49   On games, see Guerzoni 1995
p.49   On jousting, see Anglo, pp.227–70
p.50   On hunting, dogs and falcons, see Cummins
p.51   On the Officials of the Mouth, see Grieco 1999; Guerzoni 2000 pp.81–4
p.52   On *malvasia*, see Lancerio, pp.331–2
p.57   On Renaissance diets, see Braudel, vol. 1, pp.183–227; Grieco 1996; see also Sarti, pp.148–91
p.58   For the estimate of 1 kilo of bread a day, see Hurtubise, p.67 & n. 100
p.59   For the recipes, see Messisbugo
p.59   On treatises on food, cooking, etc., see Grieco 1996
p.61   On the identity of Violante Lampugnano, see Pacifici, p.273

Chapter 3
p.71   On the poor in Renaissance Europe, see Cohn; Zemon Davis 1968
p.72   On innkeepers, see Nigro
p.82   On Ferrante Gonzaga, see Hollingsworth 1996, pp.297–9
p.84   On Guillaume de Dinteville, see note on p.121
p.89   On women in Renaissance society, see the various articles in Davis & Farge

Chapter 4
p.91   On Francis I, see Knecht 1977; Knecht 1994; Richardson, pp.12–14 & *passim*
p.91   The ambassador's report describing Ippolito's reception by Francis I is published in Pacifici, p.413
p.93   On the royal family and Madame d'Etampes, see Knecht 1994, *passim*
p.95   On the Aumône-Générale, see Zemon Davis 1968
p.95   On the Protestant Reformation, see MacCulloch; Mackenney 1993, pp.129–72; Dickens, pp.9–18, 29–44; McGrath; on transubstantiation, see Goering
p.96   On the arrest of Renée's musician, see Pacifici, p.38; Prosperi, pp.273–4
p.103 On the French court, see Knecht 1994, pp.117–23
p.105 On gambling, see Guerzoni 1995
p.105 On hunting at the French court, see Richardson, pp.43–4
p.106 On Montmorency, see Knecht 1994, pp.329–41, 385–97; Greengrass
p.106 On Cardinal Jean of Lorraine, see Jouanna *et al.*, pp.866–7
p.106 On games at the French court, see Wilson-Chevalier
p.107 On ambassadors and diplomacy, see Russell, pp.67–89
p.109 On Chabot and Saluzzo as lieutenant-generals in Italy, see Knecht 1994, pp.333–4

p.109   On Anne Boleyn's arrest and execution, see Starkey, pp.568–83

p.110   Carpi's letter is partly published in Pacifici, p.36 n. 2

p.115   On the death of the Dauphin, see Knecht 1994, p.337

p.115   On Catherine de' Medici, see Knecht 1998

p.116   On the war in Provence, see Knecht 1994, pp.334–7

p.116   On François de Bourbon, Comte de St-Pol, see Jouanna *et al.*, pp.649–50

p.118   On Francis I's palaces, see Knecht 1996, pp.187–93; Blunt pp.15–36, 49–61; Knecht 1999; Babelon; Chatenet

p.119   On Jean de Laval, seigneur de Châteaubriand, see Jouanna *et al.*, p. 902

p.119   On Francis I's tennis courts, see Bondt

p.121   There were four Dinteville brothers: François (Bishop of Auxerre), Jean (seigneur de Polisy), Guillaume (seigneur d'Echenay) and Gaucher (seigneur de Vanlay); see Jouanna *et al*, pp.764–5; Brown

p.122   Cardinal Carpi's letters to Paul III about Ippolito and Cardinal du Bellay are published in Pacifici, pp.43–5nn

p.122   On Cardinal Carpi, see Franzoni *et al.*

p.123   On the background of Paul III, see Pastor, vol. 11, pp.1–40

p.123   On the dispute over the cities of Modena and Reggio, see Pastor, vol. 10, pp.88–9, 97

p.124   On Paul III as a patron, see Hollingsworth 1996, pp.45–59

p.126   On the war in northern France, see Knecht 1994, p.339

p.128   On gunpowder and warfare in sixteenth-century Europe, see Hale 1998; Hall

p.129   On the war in northern Italy, see Knecht 1994, p.340

p.129   On Francis I's expenditure on war, see Knecht 1994, p.340

p.130   On Cardinal Alessandro Farnese, see Robertson

p.130   On Paul III and the reform of the Church in Rome, see Pastor, vol. 11, pp.133–73, 182–4, 190–2; Dickens, pp.97–101

Chapter 5

p.134   On alms in sixteenth-century Europe, see Zemon Davis 2000, pp.167–208

p.134   On poverty, see Cohn; Kamen, pp.167–93

p.135   On Piero Morello's career and the fire, see Guerzoni 2000, p.146 & n. 279; on Tomaso Morello's imprisonment, see CDAP, vol. 836, *passim*

p.139   On banking in Renaissance Italy, see Roover; Lane & Mueller; on currencies, see Cipolla; Grierson et al; Spufford

p.140   On agriculture, see Braudel, vol. 1, pp.104–67; Fussell, pp. 94–114 p.151   On a royal confinement in sixteenth-century England, see Starkey, pp.504–8

p.153   On Duke Alessandro de' Medici, see Hale 1977, pp.119–126

p.163   On grain yields, see Bullard

p.163   On the development of seed drills, see Fussell, p.102

p.173   On the salt industry in Ferrara, see Guerzoni 2001

Chapter 6

p.175   On Cellini's meeting with Ippolito, see Cellini, pp.183–4; on Cellini, see Pope-Hennessy

p.176   On Ippolito and display, see Hollingsworth 2001, pp.171–3

p.177   On sixteenth-century dress; see Pizetsky; Newton; Sarti, pp.192–213

p.180   On Paul III's taste in gloves, see Bertolotti p.199 & *passim*

p.185   On the silk industry, see Molà *et al.*

p.186   On the shades of kermes red, see Newton, pp.18–19; Lowe 1993, p.230

p.188   On Ippolito's household in 1566, see Hollingsworth 2000.

p.189   On Ippolito's palace at Fontainebleau, known as La Grand Ferrare, see S Frommel, p.223

p.191   On the commission for the jug and basin, Cellini's return to Rome and his arrest, see Cellini, pp.184–93

p.191   On Ippolito's presents, tips and alms, see Hollingsworth 2004 (which includes archival references to many of the items discussed in the following pages); on the act of giving in general, see Zemon Davis 2000

p.198   On the career of Philippe Chabot, see Jouanna *et al.*, pp.685–7

Chapter 7

p.201   On gout, see Porter & Rousseau

p.203   On Charles V, see Richardson

p.209   On the meeting between Charles V and Francis I at Aigues-Mortes, see Knecht 1994, pp.386–7

p.209   On Charles V, see Richardson, pp.14–20 & *passim*

p.211   On Blois, see Babelon, pp.76–105; Knecht 1994, pp.134–7

p.212   On the meeting between Mary of Hungary and Francis I at Compiègne, see Knecht 1994, pp.387–8; on Mary of Hungary, see Doyle; on Mary as a patron of the arts, see Hollingsworth 1996, pp.310–11, 320

p.214   On the death of the Chancellor, Antoine du Bourg, see Jouanna *et al.*, p.771

p.215   Excerpts from the papal ambassador's letter are published in Pacifici, p.53 n. 3

p.215 On Marcello Cervini, later Pope Marcellus II, see Pastor, vol. 14, pp.1–10

p.221 On famine in Ferrara, see Mazzi

p.227 On cardinals' households in the early sixteenth century, see Lowe 1993, pp.236–44

Chapter 8

p.229 On the custom of staying outside Porta del Popolo, see Shearman

p.229 On Renaissance Rome, see Partner 1976; Stinger

p.230 On the Via Alessandrina, see Lowe 1991; C Frommel 1988, p.50

p.231 On the history of the Capitol, see Krautheimer; C Frommel 1988, pp.62–4

p.231 For the tax levied on the residents of the Corso, see Lanciani

p.233 On Pietro Bembo's career, see Partner 1990, pp.141–4, 220; as a patron, see Hollingsworth 1996, p.37

p.233 On the Curia, see Partner 1990

p.235 On food in Rome, see Hurtubise; Hollingsworth 2000, pp.120–3

p.235 For an account of the wines available in Rome, written by Paul III's sommelier, see Lancerio

p.238 On cardinals' clothes, see Lowe 1993, pp.230–1

p.239 On Paul III's preference for Tiber water, see Pastor, vol. 13, p.404

p.239 For his own account of his release, see Cellini, p.230

p.240 On the income cardinals received for attending Consistory, see Chambers 1966, pp.295–7

p.240 For the description of Ippolito, see his entry in *Dizionario Biografico Italiano*

p.240 On Paul III as a patron of art and architecture, see Hollingsworth 1996, pp.45–59

p.241 On the Borgia apartments in the Vatican, see Hollingsworth 1994, pp.273–5

p.244 On Margaret of Austria, see Lefevre

p.244 On hunting around Rome, see Coffin, pp.111–45

p.245 On Paul III's buffoons, see Dorez, pp.54–8; Pastor, vol. 11, p.353

p.246 On Carnival celebrations in Rome, see Pastor, vol. 11, pp.349–57

p.247 On villas in Rome, see Coffin; Hollingsworth 1996 pp.35–6, 66

p.247 On Ippolito's villa on the Quirinal (Palazzo Montecavallo), see C Frommel 1999, pp.28–47

p.252 For Cellini's account of his journey from Rome to Ferrara, see Cellini, pp.240–5

p.256 For Cellini's account of his stay at Belfiore, see Cellini, p.246

p.257   On the clothes for Ippolito's Entry, see Hollingsworth 2001, p.172

p.259   On the entertainments organized for Ippolito's Entry into Lyon, see Saulnier; Tricou

p.261   The ambassador's report of Ippolito's reception at Fontainebleau is published in part, see Pacifici, p.63 n. 1

p.263   The ambassador's report of the visit to Madame d'Etampes is published in part, see Pacifici, p.63 n.1

Epilogue

p.264   On Henri II's reign, see Knecht 1996; Knecht 1998

p.265   Ippolito's letter to Henri II is quoted in Pacifici, p.104 n.3

Bibliography

Allerston   P. Allerston, 'Reconstructing the Second-Hand Clothes Trade in Sixteenth- and Seventeenth-Century Venice', *Costume*, vol. 33 (1999), pp.46–56

Ajmar   M. Ajmar (ed.), 'Approaches to Renaissance Consumption', special issue of *Journal of Design History*, vol. 15 (2002)

Anglo   S. Anglo, *The Martial Arts of Renaissance Europe*, New Haven CT, 2000

Babelon   J.-P. Babelon, *Châteaux de France au siècle de la Renaissance*, Paris, 1989

Baraldi   A. M. Baraldi, 'Gli apparamenti del banchetto', in J. Bentini *et al.* (eds.), *A tavola con il Principe* (exhibition catalogue.), Ferrara, 1989, pp.321–44

Bertolotti   A. Bertolotti, 'Spese segrete e pubbliche di Paolo III', *Atti e memorie delle RR. Deputazioni di storia patria per la provincie dell'Emilia*, vol. 3 (1878), pp.169–212

Bestor   J. F. Bestor, 'Titian's portrait of Laura Eustochia: The decorum of female beauty and the motif of the black page', *Renaissance Studies*, vol. 17 (2003), pp. 628–73

Blunt   A. Blunt, *Art and Architecture in France 1500–1700*, Harmondsworth, 1982

Bondt   Cees de Bondt, 'The Court of the Estes, Cradle of the Game of Tennis', *Schifanoia*, vol. 22/23 (2002), pp.81–102

Braudel   F. Braudel, *Civilization and Capitalism*, 2 vols., London, 1985

Brown   E. A. R. Brown, 'Sodomy, Honor, Treason and Exile: Four Documents concerning the Dinteville Affair (1538–1539)', in J. Fouilleron *et al.* (eds.), *Sociétés et Idéologies des Temps modernes*, Montpellier, 1996, pp.511–32

Bullard   M. Bullard, 'Grain Supply and Urban Unrest in Renaissance Rome: The Crisis of 1533–34', in P. A. Ramsey (ed.), *Rome in the Renaissance: The City and the Myth*, Binghamton NY, 1982, pp.279–92.

Cazzola   F. Cazzola, 'La città e il pane: produzioni agricole e consumi alimentari a Ferrara tra medioevo ed età moderna', in J. Bentini *et al.* (eds.), *A tavola con il Principe* (exhibition catalogue), Ferrara, 1989, pp.21–45

Cellini   Benvenuto Cellini, *Autobiography* (trans. G. Bull), Harmondsworth, 1956

Chambers 1966   D. Chambers, 'The Economic Predicament of Renaissance Cardinals', *Studies in Medieval and Renaissance History*, vol. 3 (1966), pp.287–313

Chambers 1992   —— *A Renaissance Cardinal and his Worldly Goods: the Will and Inventory of Francesco Gonzaga 1444–1483*, London, 1992

Chatenet   M. Chatenet, *La cour de France au XVIe siècle: vie sociale et architecture,* Paris, 2002

Chastel   A. Chastel, *The Sack of Rome, 1527*, Princeton NJ, 1983

Cipolla   C. Cipolla, *Studi di storia della moneta*, vol.1, *I movimenti dei cambi in Italia dal secolo xiii al xv*, Pavia, 1948

Coffin   D. Coffin, *The Villa in the Life of Renaissance Rome*, Princeton NJ, 1979

Cohn 1980   S. Cohn, *The Laboring Classes in Renaissance Florence*, New York, 1980

Cohn 1996   —— *Women in the Streets*, Baltimore MD, 1996

Cummins   J. Cummins, *The Hound and the Hawk*, London, 1988

Davis 1968   N. Z. Davis, 'Poor Relief, Humanism and Heresy: The Case of Lyon', in *Studies in Medieval and Renaissance History*, vol. 5 (1968), pp.217–75

Davis 2000   —— *The Gift in Sixteenth-Century France*, Oxford, 2000

Davis & Farge   N. Z. Davis & A. Farge (eds.), *A History of Women in the West. Vol. 3. Renaissance and Enlightenment Paradoxes*, Cambridge MA, 1993

Davis & Ravid   R. Davis & B. Ravid (eds.), *The Jews of Early Modern Venice*, Baltimore MD, 2001

Diario	*Diario Ferrarese*, in *Rerum Italicarum Scriptores*, vol.24
Dickens	A. G. Dickens, *The Counter-Reformation*, London, 1968
Dorez	L. Dorez, *La Cour du Pape Paul III d'après les régistres de la Trésorie Secrète*, Paris, 1932
Doyle	D. R. Doyle, 'The Sinews of Habsburg Governance in the Sixteenth Century: Mary of Hungary and Political Patronage', *Sixteenth-Century Journal*, vol. 31 (2000), pp.349–60
Erlanger	R. Erlanger, *Lucrezia Borgia*, London, 1978
Faccioli	E. Faccioli, *L'arte della cucina in Italia*, Turin, 1992
Fantoni *et al*	M. Fantoni, L. C. Matthew, S. F. Matthews-Grieco (eds.), *The Art Market in Italy*, Modena, 2003
Fenlon 1980	I. Fenlon, *Music and Patronage in Sixteenth-Century Mantua*, 2 vols., Cambridge, 1980–2.
Fenlon 1990	—— 'Gender and Generation: Patterns of Music Patronage among the Este, 1471–1539', in M. Pade *et al.* (eds.), *La corte di Ferrara e il suo mecenatismo 1441–1598*, Copenhagen, 1990, pp.213–32
Findlen	P. Findlen, 'Possessing the Past: The Material World of the Italian Renaissance', *American Historical Review*, vol. 103 (1998), pp.83–114
Folin	M. Folin, *Rinascimento estense. Politica, cultura, istituzioni di un antico stato italiano*, Bari, 2001
Franceschini	C. Franceschini, 'La corte di Renata di Francia (1528–1560)', in A. Chiappini (ed.), *Storia di Ferrara. Volume VI: Il Rinascimento. Situazioni e personaggi*, Ferrara, 2000, pp.186–214
Franzoni *et al*	C. Franzoni, G. Mancini, T. Previdi, M. Rossi (eds.), *Gli inventari dell'eredità del cardinale Rodolfo Pio da Carpi*, Pisa, 2002
C Frommel 1988	C. L. Frommel, 'Papal Policy: the Planning of Rome during the Renaissance', in R. Rotberg & T. Rabb (eds.), *Art and History*, Cambridge MA 1988, pp.39–65
C Frommel 1999	C. L. Frommel, 'La villa e i giardini del Quirinale nel Cinquecento', *Bollettino d'Arte del Ministero per i beni e le attività culturali*, special volume (1999), pp.15–62
S Frommel	S. Frommel, *Sebastiano Serlio*, Milan, 1999
Fussell	G. E. Fussell, *The Classical Tradition in Western European Farming*, Newton Abbot, 1972

Goering   J. Goering, 'The Invention of Transubstantiation', *Traditio*, vol. 46 (1991), pp.147–70

Goldthwaite 1980   R. Goldthwaite, *The Building of Renaissance Florence*, Baltimore MD, 1980

Goldthwaite 1987a   —— 'The Empire of Things: Consumer Demand in Renaissance Italy', in F. W. Kent & P. Simons (eds.), *Patronage, Art and Society in Renaissance Italy*, Oxford, 1987, pp.153–75

Goldthwaite 1987b   —— 'The Economy of Renaissance Italy: The Preconditions for Luxury Consumption', *I Tatti Studies*, vol. 2 (1987), pp.15–39

Goldthwaite 1993   —— *Wealth and the Demand for Art in Italy 1300–1600*, Baltimore MD, 1993

Goodgal   D. Goodgal, 'The Camerino of Alfonso d'Este', *Art History*, vol. 1 (1978), pp.162–90

Greengrass   M. Greengrass, 'Property and Politics in Sixteenth-Century France: the Landed Fortune of Constable Anne de Montmorency', *French History*, vol. 2 (1988), pp.371–98

Grieco 1991   A. Grieco, 'The Social Politics of Pre-Linnaean Botanical Classification', in *I Tatti Studies*, 4 (1991), pp.131–49

Grieco 1996   —— 'La gastronomia del XVI secolo: tra scienza e cultura', in *Et coquatur ponendo* (exhibition catalogue), Prato, 1996, pp.143–54.

Grieco 1999   —— 'Conviviality in a Renaissance Court: the *Ordine et officii* and the Court of Urbino', in S. Eiche (ed.), *Ordine et officii de casa de lo Illustrissimo Signor Duca de Urbino*, Urbino, 1999

Grierson *et al*   P. Grierson et al, *Medieval European Coinage*, 2 vols., Cambridge, 1986–98

Guerzoni 1995   G. Guerzoni, 'Playing Great Games: The *Giuoco* in Sixteenth-Century Italian Courts', *Italian History and Culture*, vol. 1 (1995), pp.43–63

Guerzoni 2000   —— *Le corti estense e la devoluzione di Ferrara del 1598*, Modena, 2000

Guerzoni 2001   —— 'L'oro bianco di Comacchio. Ovvero splendori e miserie delle saline estensi nella prima metà del Cinquecento', in M. Cattini & M. Romani (eds.), *Omaggio ad Aldo De Maddalena*, Rome, 2001, pp.103–36

Haar   J. Haar, 'Dalla Viola, Alfonso', in *The New Grove Dictionary of Music and Musicians*, vol. 6, p.862

Hale 1977   J. Hale, *Florence and the Medici*, London, 1977

Hale 1993   —— *The Civilization of Europe in the Renaissance*, London, 1993

Hale 1998   —— *War and Society in Renaissance Europe*, London, 1998

Hall   B. S. Hall, *Weapons and Warfare in Renaissance Europe: Gunpowder, Technology and Tactics*, Baltimore MD, 1997

Hollingsworth 1994 M. Hollingsworth, *Patronage in Renaissance Italy: from 1400 to the Early Sixteenth Century*, London, 1994.

Hollingsworth 1996 —— *Patronage in Sixteenth-Century Italy*, London, 1996

Hollingsworth 2000 —— 'Ippolito d'Este: A Cardinal and His Household in Rome and Ferrara in 1566', *The Court Historian*, vol. 5 (2000), pp.105–26.

Hollingsworth 2001 —— 'Materializing Power: Cardinal Ippolito d'Este in 1540', in L. Golden (ed.), *Raising the Eyebrow: John Onians and World Art Studies*, Oxford, 2001, pp.169–73.

Hollingsworth 2004 —— 'Coins, *Cavalli* and Candlesticks: The Economics of Extravagance', in E. Welch & M. O'Malley (eds.), *The Material Renaissance* (forthcoming)

Hope 1971   C. Hope, 'The Camerino d'Alabastro of Alfonso d'Este', *Burlington Magazine*, vol. 114 (1971), pp.641–50, 712–21

Hope 1983   —— 'Poesie and Painted Allegories', in J. Martineau & C. Hope (eds.), *The Genius of Venice 1500–1600* (exhibition catalogue), London, 1983, pp.35–7

Hurtubise   P. Hurtubise, 'La table d'un Cardinal de la Renaissance', *Mélanges de l'école française de Rome*, vol 92 (1980), pp.248–82

Jardine   L. Jardine, *Worldly Goods*, London, 1996

Jouanna *et al*   A. Jouanna et al, *La France de la Renaissance*, Paris, 2001

Kamen   H. Kamen, *European Society 1500–1700*, London, 1984

Knecht 1977   R. J. Knecht, ' Francis I: Prince and Patron of the Northern Renaissance', in A. G. Dickens (ed.), *The Courts of Europe: Politics, Patronage and Royalty 1400–1800*, London, 1977, pp.99–119

Knecht 1994   —— *Renaissance Warrior and Patron: The Reign of Francis I*, Cambridge, 1994

Knecht 1996   —— *The Rise and Fall of Renaissance France 1483–1610*, London, 1996

Knecht 1998   —— *Catherine de' Medici*, London, 1998

Knecht 1999 —— 'Francis I and Fontainebleau', *The Court Historian*, vol. 4 (1999), pp.93–118

Krautheimer R. Krautheimer, *Rome: Profile of a City 312–1308*, Princeton NJ, 1980

Lancerio S. Lancerio, *Della qualità dei vini*, in E. Faccioli (ed.), *L'arte della cucina in Italia*, Turin, 1992, pp.331–55

Lanciani R. Lanciani, *La Via del Corso dirizzata ed abbellita nel 1538 da Paolo III*, Rome, 1903

Lane & Mueller F. Lane & R. Mueller, *Money and Banking in Medieval and Renaissance Venice*, 2 vols., Baltimore MD, 1997

Lefevre R. Lefevre, *Madama Margarita d'Austria*, Rome, 1986

Leoni A. Leoni, 'Gli ebrei a Ferrara nel XVI secolo', in A. Chiappini (ed.), *Storia di Ferrara. Volume VI: Il Rinascimento. Situazioni e personaggi*, Ferrara, 2000, pp. 278–311

Lockwood L. Lockwood, *Music in Renaissance Ferrara 1400–1505*, Oxford, 1984

Lowe 1991 K. J. P. Lowe, 'A Florentine Prelate's Real Estate in Rome between 1480 and 1524', *Papers of the British School at Rome*, vol. 59 (1991), pp.259–82

Lowe 1993 —— *Church and Politics in Renaissance Italy*, Cambridge, 1993

MacCulloch D. MacCulloch, *Reformation*, London, 2003

McGrath A. McGrath, *The Intellectual Origins of the European Reformation*, Oxford, 1987

Mackenney 1987 R. Mackenney, *Tradesmen and Traders: the World of Guilds in Venice and Europe c.1250–1650*, London, 1987

Mackenney 1993 —— *Sixteenth-Century Europe*, London, 1993

Mantovano G. Mantovano, 'Il banchetto rinascimentale: arte, magnificenza, potere', in J. Bentini *et al.* (eds.), *A tavola con il Principe* (exhibition catalogue.), Ferrara 1989, pp.47–68

Mallett M. Mallett, *The Borgias*, London, 1969

Mariacher G. Mariacher, *Palma il Vecchio*, Milan, 1968

Martines 1979 L. Martines, *Power and Imagination*, London, 1979

Martines 1998 —— 'Review essay: The Renaissance and the Birth of Consumer Society', *Renaissance Quarterly*, vol. 51 (1998), pp.193–203

Mazzi M. S. Mazzi, 'La fame e la paura della fame', in J. Bentini *et al.* (eds.), *A tavola con il Principe* (exhibition catalogue.), Ferrara, 1989, pp.153–69

Messisbugo   C. da Messisbugo, *Banchetti, composizioni di vivande e apparecchio generale*, ed. F. Bandini, Venice, 1960

Molà *et al*   L. Molà, R. Mueller, C. Zanier (eds.), *La seta in Italia dal Medioevo al Seicento*, Venice, 2000

Newton   S. Newton, *The Dress of the Venetians 1495–1525*, Aldershot, 1988

Nigro   G. Nigro, 'I pasti nell'Albergo della Stella', in *Et coquatur ponendo* (exhibition catalogue), Prato, 1996, p.386.

Occhipinti   C. Occhipinti, *Carteggio d'arte degli ambasciatori estensi in Francia 1536–1553*, Pisa, 2001

Olivato   L. Olivato (ed.), *Il Palazzo di Renata di Francia*, Ferrara, 1997

Pacifici   V. Pacifici, *Ippolito d'Este, Cardinale di Ferrara*, Tivoli, 1920

Partner 1976   P. Partner, *Renaissance Rome 1500–59*, London, 1976

Partner 1990   —— *The Pope's Men: The Papal Civil Service in the Renaissance*, Oxford, 1990

Pastor   L. Pastor, *The History of the Popes from the Close of the Middle Ages*, 29 vols., London, 1894–1951

Peruzzi   P. Peruzzi, 'Lavorare a Corte: domestici, familiari, cortigiani e funzionari al servizio del Duca d'Urbino', in G. Chittolini *et al.* (eds.), *Federico di Montefeltro: lo Stato*, Rome 1986, pp.225–96

Pizetsky   R. L. Pizetsky, *Storia del costume in Itala*, Milan, 1966

Pope-Hennessy   J. Pope-Hennessy, *Cellini*, London, 1985

Porter & Rousseau   R. Porter & G. S. Rousseau, *Gout: The Patrician Malady*, New Haven CT, 1998

Prizer   W. Prizer, 'Isabella d'Este and Lucrezia Borgia as Patrons of Music', *Journal of the American Musicological Society*, vol. 38 (1985), pp.1–33

Prosperi   A. Prosperi, 'L'eresia in città e a corte', in M. Pade et al (eds.), *La corte di Ferrara e il suo mecenatismo 1441–1598*, Copenhagen, 1990, pp.267–81

Richardson   G. Richardson, *Renaissance Monarchy*, London, 2002

Rinaldi & Vicini   M. Rinaldi & M. Vicini, *Buon appetito, Your Holiness: The Secrets of the Papal Table*, London, 2000

Robertson   C. Robertson, *Il Gran Cardinale*, New Haven CT, 1992

Roover   R. de Roover, *The Rise and Decline of the Medici Bank*, Cambridge MA, 1966

Rosenberg   C. Rosenberg, 'Alfonso I d'Este, Michelangelo and the man who bought pigs', in G. Neher & R. Shepherd (eds.), *Revaluing Renaissance Art*, Aldershot, 2000, pp.89–99

Russell   J. G. Russell, *Peacemaking in the Renaissance*, London, 1986

Sarti   R. Sarti, *Europe at Home*, New Haven CT, 2002

Saulnier   V. Saulnier, 'M. Scève et la musique', in J. Jacquot (ed.), *Musique et poesie au XVIe siècle*, Paris, 1954, pp.89–103

Shankland   H. Shankland, *The Prettiest Love Letters in the World*, London, 1987

Shearman   J. Shearman, 'A Functional Interpretation of Villa Madama', *Römisches Jahrbuch für Kunstgeschichte*, vol. 20 (1983), pp.315–27.

Spufford   P. Spufford, *Handbook of Medieval Exchange*, London, 1986

Starkey   D. Starkey, *Six Wives: The Queens of Henry VIII,* London, 2003

Stinger   C. Stinger, *The Renaissance in Rome*, Bloomington IN, 1985

Strong   R. Strong, *Feast: A History of Grand Eating*, London, 2002

Syson & Thornton   L. Syson & D. Thornton, *Objects of Virtue: Art in Renaissance Italy*, London, 2001

Thieme-Becker   U. Thieme & F. Becker (eds.), *Allgemeines Lexikon der Bildenden Künstler*, Leipzig, 1907–50

Thornton   P. Thornton, *The Italian Renaissance Interior 1400–1600*, London 1991

Toselli   A. Toselli, 'Il palazzo attraverso i documenti', in L. Olivato (ed.), *Il Palazzo di Renata di Francia*, Ferrara 1997, pp.37–95, 281–301 (appendix)

Tricou   J. Tricou (ed.), *La Chronique Lyonnaise de Jean Guérard 1536–62*, Lyon, 1929

Tuohy   T. Tuohy, *Herculean Ferrara*, Cambridge, 1996

Vasari   G. Milanesi (ed.), *Le Opere di Giorgio Vasari*, 8 vols., Florence, 1906–10

Wilson-Chevalier   K. Wilson-Chevalier, 'Art Patronage and Women in the Orbit of Francis I', *Renaissance Studies*, vol. 16 (2002), pp.474–524

Zambotti   B. Zambotti, *Diario Ferrarese*, in *Rerum Italicarum Scriptores*, vol. 24

Zerbinato   G. M. Zerbinato, *Croniche di Ferrara*, Ferrara, 1989

Illustrations

Index